CW00321515

ALSO FROM MILLER HEIMAN ...

The New Strategic Selling
Stephen E. Heiman and Diane Sanchez with Tad Tuleja

The unique selling system proven successful by the world's best companies. The new edition of the highly acclaimed business classic confronts the rapidly changing world of business-to-business sales.

"The best book I have read on selling" *Scott De Gormo, Success Magazine.*

"Thousands of our sales people worldwide have been trained in strategic selling and its influence can be directly seen in the results they have attained" *John A. Young, President and CEO, Hewlett Packard*

0 7494 2833 3   318 pages Paperback

Successful Large Account Management
How to Hold on to Your Most Important Customers and Turn Them into Long-term Assets.
Robert B. Miller and Stephen E. Heiman with Tad Tuleja

The Miller-Heiman Large Account Management Programme (LAMP) is used successfully by some of the world's largest companies.

"LAMP" showed us how to further involve customer representatives with our sales team in setting an account strategy, and we're delighted with the outcome"
Larry Mead, Sales Vice President New Domestic Markets, AT&T Network Systems.

0 7494 1404 9   220 pages Paperback

Face-to-Face (Conceptual) Selling
Secrets of the Concept Sale
Robert B. Miller and Stephen E. Heiman with Tad Tuleja

"A must for anyone in the selling business"
Long Range Planning

0 7494 1404 9   318 pages Paperback

Available from all good book shops or directly from the publishers:
Kogan Page Ltd, 120 Pentonville Road, London, N1 9JN
Tel: 0171 278 0433 Fax: 0171 837 6348
or e-mail on kpinfo@kogan-page.co.uk

selling
machine

selling machine

How to focus **every** member of
your **company** on the
vital business of **selling**

Diane Sanchez and **Stephen E. Heiman**
(Miller Heiman, Inc.) and **Tad Tuleja**

KOGAN
PAGE

<u>YOURS TO HAVE AND TO HOLD</u>
BUT NOT TO COPY

First published in the US by Times Books, a division of Random House Inc., New York
First published in the UK by Kogan Page Ltd

Apart from any fair dealing for the purposes of research or private study, or criticism or review, as permitted under the Copyright, Designs and Patents Act 1988, this publication may only be reproduced, stored or transmitted, in any form or by any means, with the prior permission in writing of the publishers, or in the case of reprographic reproduction in accordance with the terms and licences issued by the CLA. Enquiries concerning reproduction outside these terms should be sent to the publishers at the undermentioned address:

Kogan Page Limited
120 Pentonville Road
London N1 9JN

© Miller Heiman, Inc., 1997, 1998

British Library Cataloguing in Publication Data

A CIP record for this book is available from the British Library.

ISBN 0 7494 2848 1

Typeset by Saxon Graphics Ltd., Derby
Printed and bound in Great Britain by Biddles Limited, Guildford and King's Lynn

F O R E W O R D

THERE IS AN INCREASING DEMAND THROUGHOUT the value chain for the world's best quality at the world's lowest price. At first, this seems like an impossible challenge, but it is achievable if suppliers and customers work in new, innovative ways that ensure their joint success. As a result, we are forming deeper, more intense customer relationships that are based on a well-defined selling process.

Our efforts began more than twelve years ago, when Dow adopted Miller Heiman's Strategic Selling process, and its teachings are even more relevant today. The chemicals, plastics, and related value-added services offered by Dow often represent a complex sale. Strategic Selling provides a repeatable method that allows our entire organization to understand what results must be delivered and to develop a tailored strategy that creates mutual value.

Today's business environment demands an even deeper understanding of customers, markets, challenges, and solutions. This led us to Miller Heiman's Conceptual Selling process. For many of our customers, our "molecule" is a small part of their buying decision; therefore, it's most important for Dow people to understand how to apply the right combination of Dow products, technology, information, and value-added services to support our customers' success.

Last of all, we apply Miller Heiman's Large Account Management Process (LAMP) to ensure that we deliver quantifiable value to major customers that buy millions of dollars' worth of products from many different Dow businesses. These mega-accounts are complex global companies, and LAMP provides a process for ensuring that our actions align with customers' strategies.

Strategic Selling, Conceptual Selling, and the Large Account Management Process together form important parts of our sales process. They constantly remind us that the customer is the ultimate judge in the marketplace. They also provide a proven, repeatable system of delivering value to

both Dow and our customers, and that is why we encourage our own suppliers to adopt the Miller Heiman processes in serving Dow. In short, the
processes work.

–William S. Stavropoulos,
President and Chief Executive Officer,
The Dow Chemical Company

A C K N O W L E D G M E N T S

IN PREPARING THIS BOOK, WE HAVE PROFITED greatly from the experiences of our corporate clients. Their successes have consistently and often dramatically demonstrated how the principles of the sales process can be turned into practical realities. We are particularly grateful to the following people for giving us an opportunity to draw on their insights and examples. (Asterisks indicate individuals who, since our interviews, have taken other positions.)

Sam Abia	*Marketing Analyst*	*SAS Institute*
Tina Aiken	*Sales Representative*	*Datex-Engstrom, Inc.*
Eliot Axelrod	*Account Executive*	*Apple Computer*
Al Bergonzi	*President, Enterprise Systems*	*HBO*
Ken Brandt*	*Healthcare Sales Specialist*	*Nemschoff Chair Company*
Kurt Bullard	*System Engineer*	*Documentum*
Robyn Crebs*	*Account Representative*	*Browning Ferris-BFI*
Lou Croce	*Environmental Waste Manager*	*Browning Ferris-BFI*
Tony Cueva	*Manager of National Accounts*	*Ceridian*
Bob Del Ciello*	*National Systems Sales Manager*	*Landis & Gyr Powers*
David Duff	*Major Account Executive*	*AEI Music*
John H. Erbland	*VP Strategic Global Accounts*	*Eastman Kodak*
Joel French	*VP Healthcare*	*Sentient Systems, Inc.*
Christine Jernigan	*Sales Manager*	*Browning Ferris-BFI*

Michael Johnson	VP Customer Alliances	Becton Dickinson Infusion Therapy
Dave Laabs	VP Sales and Business Development	MacFarland Office Products and Business Interiors
Robert F. Lee*	VP Sales and Marketing	Foxboro Canada
Leeanne Lehr	National Sales Training Executive	Hallmark Canada
Mike McCarver	VP Corporate Sales	KLA Instruments
Bob Mayes*	VP Sales	Las Campanas
Laura Nissen	Administrative Director of Sales	Mayo Medical Laboratories
Elizabeth Ngonzi*	Sales Executive	Micros Systems, Inc.
Charlie Parr*	VP Sales	VLSI Technology
Bob Pickens	Manufacturing Segment Director	Browning Ferris-BFI
Dan Salbego	Senior Territory Manager	Fort Howard Corporation
Margaret Shiver*	VP Marketing and Business Development	Sterling Healthcare
Jackie Smith	Area Manager	Air-Shields
Larry Smith	VP International Sales	Harris Corporation Communications Sector
Mark Starr	District Sales Manager	Browning Ferris-BFI
Bob Stewart	VP Sales	American Teleconferencing Services
Brad Teed	System Engineer	Documentum
Bruce Thomann	Technical Advisor	Powersoft Corporation
Bruce Thrush	Director, National Accounts	Kwikset
Robert Turfe	Management Consultant	Diamond Technologies
Mike Wyant	Pharmacy Manager	Syncor

We also owe a debt of thanks to several members of our company, Miller Heiman Inc. Holly Jenkins and Beth Rutherford not only arranged for dozens of interviews with clients but shared their experiences as the core of our client support team. Sally Glover wrote the original stories from which the examples in our company newsletter, *Best Few,* were drawn. Several members of our hardworking sales force shared insights from their years in the field: our thanks to Mike Joyce (Illinois), Sam Manfer (California), Vince McFarlane (Georgia), Robert L. Miller (Washington), Brian Polowniak (Missouri), Joseph T. White (Arizona and New York), and Sharon Williams (Texas). At corporate headquarters, Linda O'Neill supplied the graphics; Karen Brewer and Kelly Wentworth provided invaluable coordination; and Tom Martin, in addition to giving helpful feedback on issues of Funnel review and implementation, provided corroborative illustrations from the business press.

Among the published sources to which we refer in the text, the most useful were the following:

Mark Blessington and Bill O'Connell. *Sales Reengineering from the Outside In.* New York: McGraw-Hill, 1995.

Stephanie Anderson Forest. "Customers Must Be Pleased, Not Just Satisfied." *Business Week* (August 3, 1992).

Joe Girard with Stanley H. Brown. *How to Sell Anything to Anybody.* New York: Warner, 1977.

J. P. Guilford. *The Nature of Human Intelligence.* New York: McGraw-Hill, 1967.

Michael Hammer and James Champy. *Reengineering the Corporation.* New York: Harper Business, 1993.

Hewitt Associates. "Hot Topics in Sales Compensation." (Pamphlet.) Scottsdale, AZ: Management Compensation Services, 1996.

William Keenan Jr. "If I Had a Hammer." *Sales and Marketing Management* (December 1993).

Learning International. "Profiles in Customer Loyalty: An Industry-by-Industry Examination of Buyer-Seller Relationships." (Pamphlet.) Stamford, CT: A Target 2000 Publication, n.d.

Seth Lubove. "Don't Listen to the Boss, Listen to the Customer." *Forbes* (December 4, 1995).

Myron Magnet. "Let's Go for Growth." *Fortune* (March 7, 1994).

Christopher Power, Lisa Driscoll, and Earl Bohn. "Smart Selling: How Companies Are Winning Over Today's Tougher Customer." *Business Week* (August 3, 1992).

Catherine Romano. "Death of a Salesman." *Management Review* (September 1994).

"The Sales Manager's Challenge." *Sales and Marketing Management* (May 1994).

Fran Tarkenton with Tad Tuleja. *How to Motivate People: The Team Strategy for Success.* New York: Harper and Row, 1986.

Joe White. "The Emotional Side of Selling." *Best Few* (Spring 1992).

David Woodruff. "May We Help You Kick the Tires?" *Business Week* (August 3, 1992).

CONTENTS

PART ONE

THE SALES PROCESS:
ESSENTIAL REDEFINITIONS

PART TWO

SEVEN DEADLY SCENES: USING THE SALES PROCESS
TO SOLVE YOUR BUSINESS NIGHTMARES

PART THREE
THE SALES PROCESS AS AN OPERATING SYSTEM: THE THREE Rs OF IMPLEMENTATION

SELLING MACHINE

INTRODUCTION

BRINGING SELLING
IN OUT OF THE COLD

"It's the top line on any income statement. Without sales, there is no business."
—Bob Stewart
Vice-President, Sales
American Teleconferencing Services

S THE ECONOMY BOBS AND WEAVES ITS WAY INTO a new century, business professionals face a troubling question. Is it possible to reshape the way we do business so that we can meet the challenges and capitalize on the huge opportunities that have been raised by the information explosion and by worldwide competition?
tion explosion and by worldwide competition?

The answer to that question is a resounding *yes*–but a yes accompanied by two unavoidable conditions. First, in order to thrive in the twenty-first century, businesses will have to redefine themselves as *selling organizations*. Second, they will have to understand that selling itself is a complex process involving everyone in the organization; it can never again be considered just the job of the "sales force."

This is a book about how selling is undergoing a revolution. It charts the course of that revolution thus far, and it shows you how your company can come out among the winners. But because revolution by definition means difference and change, it is *not* a book about selling as that term is currently understood. In fact, *Selling Machine* isn't really about "selling" at all. It's about how to utilize a completely transformed sales process as the key to changing virtually everything about the way we do business.

"Everything" sounds like a tall order, but that's just what we mean. Right now, the vast majority of your company's people think of themselves as involved in something other than sales–they're in operations or order fulfillment, in R&D, or part of the clerical staff. That's the way it's always been, not just in your company, but everywhere. *The revolutionary agenda of this book is to change that mind-set.* If your business implements the principles that we outline here, everyone in your company will come to understand, as one of our corporate clients puts it nicely, "The entire company sells; the sales force orchestrates."

This is where business *must* move, if it is to survive a shrinking globe and a new millenium. But we're far from getting there yet, for a very simple reason. In the blizzard of makeover guides that have appeared in the past decade, corporate gurus have offered us everything from downsizing to diversification, from "theory Z" to reengineering, as the way to light a fire under the dinosaur's tail and make our companies more competitive in tough global markets. As timely and incisive as many of these guides have been, and for all their passion in uncovering and analyzing inefficiencies, they have all overlooked the one business process that keeps every business, large or small, in business. None of them has said a word about the engine of sales.

THE MISSING PIECE OF THE PUZZLE

The sales process is crucial, for a reason that ought to be obvious. Selling is the sole provider of every business's fuel–the revenue stream that pays for everything else. You can look at manufacturing, employee relations, marketing strategies–it doesn't matter where your business requires retooling or how much you hope that the retooling will reduce your costs. You still won't be able to pay for it without a revenue stream. And the revenue stream is the direct contribution of sales.

The best-engineered car in the world will not run on empty. That's why streamlining your business operations and ignoring the sales process is like having your Porsche tuned up but forgetting to buy gas.

This all seems so obvious that you'd think corporate executives would be discussing it all the time. You'd think they'd understand that every business depends on its fuel supply. You'd think that every book or article on remaking the corporation would have a hefty section on the process of sales.

You'd be wrong. In virtually all discussions of corporate renewal, the sales process is the missing piece of the puzzle. Whether you're looking at *Business Week* or an in-flight magazine or the latest report from the Harvard Business School, the world of sales and sellers is conspicuous by its absence. It's crowded out by prose poems to the power-tie honchos who are supposedly above such details as income generation because they're too busy running the company and taking bows.

It's strange but true. Even though every business would stop dead in its tracks without sales revenue, the sales process is never discussed in the same breath—or, for that matter, in the same room—as the "strategic" contributions of senior management.

In fact, most discussions of corporate renewal don't even recognize sales to be a process. Even Michael Hammer and James Champy, who wrote one of the best current makeover guides, *Reengineering the Corporation*, reveal the same blind spot as other business gurus when they claim, "Sales is not a process, but a department." In a recent interview for *Sales and Marketing Management* magazine, Hammer was asked by William Keenan Jr. why he and Champy had included in their book so "few examples of reengineered sales and marketing processes." Hammer's explanation? They "weren't available.... They weren't ready to be discussed when we wrote the book."

As specialists in the retooling of corporate sales processes, we can tell you from close experience that examples of these processes are available—and that the time when they should be discussed is long past due. Many of the processes are in place at corporations that are clients of our company, Miller Heiman. We record their successes, and their frustrations, in this book.

THE PARADOX OF THE ISOLATED SALES FORCE

The idea that sales is not a process but a department reflects a strangely common, and ultimately self-defeating, paradox.

On the one hand, anybody who has run anything from a corporate board meeting to a paper route understands the importance of sales revenue. Intellectually, everybody in business knows that if the revenue stream dries up, everything else comes to a grinding halt. Yet, in spite of this understanding, the people who generate the revenue are often treated like

Forrest Gumps. At best, their essential work is taken for granted. At worst, senior managers view it as a necessary evil.

As a result, the process that is most in need of reengineering almost never gets the attention that it deserves. Even though remaking the sales process nationwide could truly revitalize business, sales professionals remain the poor cousins of corporate management. Paradoxically, the very people who keep the business running are traditionally seen as being—and deserving to be—out in the cold.

Robert Atkins, a partner with Mercer Management Consulting, had it right in a recent article he wrote for *Business Week*. "I don't know a lot of CEOs," he said, "who are paying *any* attention to their sales channels." A recent report in the magazine *Training* underscored the same point, when it itemized the types of training available in selected American industries. Overall, the report found that of the businesses surveyed, 86 percent were trying to upgrade their managers' skills and 85 percent were providing training in communication skills—but only 55 percent thought that selling skills were worth equivalent attention.

As dangerously counterproductive as this situation is, there are logical, or at least traditional, reasons why it exists. One is the view of the sales rep as a slick-talking con artist—the kind of character who peddles refrigerators to Eskimos. Another is the image of the rep as somebody whose main ambition is to be "well-liked" and who is rightly seen as a loser. Underlying these stereotypes is a corporate peculiarity: the fact that, with a few notable exceptions (IBM's Tom Watson comes to mind), CEOs and other senior managers have never done any selling themselves. Their careers started in operations or finance, and they've never been educated about what sales-people do.

If you think that we're overstating the case, ask yourself how many CEOs you know who came up through the ranks of selling. We've been in business for a combined total of fifty years, and we can count the ones we know on the fingers of one hand.

The moral is all too clear. In the business literature, on the corporate organization chart, and in the traditional mind-set of most senior managers, sales and management are viewed as separate entities, and there's little question about which is more important. "Serious" decisions are made by senior management. The sales force might pump the gas, but it can't drive the car.

WHY THIS MATTERS TO YOUR COMPANY STRATEGY

The problem with keeping the sales force out in the cold isn't just that they "don't get no respect." It's much more serious than that. When the producers of your revenue are isolated, two things happen.

The first is *demotivation*. When they are treated as gas jockeys rather than fellow drivers, sales professionals are unable to see how their work connects to organizational goals. In fact, they are *prevented* from seeing it. As a result, many of them start to feel like mere hired guns, responsible only to themselves or, at best, to their quotas. Cut off from company strategy, they acquire tunnel vision, begin to lose sight of what they're selling for, and lose all sense of commitment to a common mission.

You can say that this doesn't matter, as long as the numbers are coming in. But sooner or later, if your salespeople aren't consciously committed to your organizational strategy–if they don't see how their contribution enhances the broader picture–those numbers won't be there. It's a scenario we've seen a thousand times: superstar reps who lose their spark and their loyalty because they've never been shown why their work is of value.

Many people in this situation jump ship, leaving the company and joining the competition. But even when it doesn't come to that, you can still count on one inevitable result: *The professional you put on the sidelines will not deliver.* Not for you, anyway. Isolating the sales force leads to a loss of motivation. And that leads, just as inevitably, to a loss of effectiveness.

The second result is *loss of strategic information.* This is less obvious, but just as important, because salespeople and their managers are uniquely positioned to acquire information that senior managers need. It's not the people in the boardroom or the CEO's office but the people in the field who have the inside track about customers' tastes, customers' personnel changes, and market conditions–the whole shifting scenario that can have an impact on buying decisions.

Senior managers need to be on top of such information in order to make sound strategic decisions, but they don't get that information when their sales force is isolated–or they get it too late to have it do any good. They're like the gentleman farmer who tunes in the weather report two days after a hailstorm has destroyed his crops.

One common result of this lack of information is that managers are forced to concoct revenue projections that bear little or no relation to market reality. You've seen the formula projections we mean: "We sold them

400 units last quarter, so we're going to sell them that plus 10 percent, or 440 units, this quarter." Numbers spit out by the great computer in the sky. It's unrealistic, yes–blatantly so. Yet without the information that only a sales staff can supply, this kind of pie-in-the-sky projecting is also inevitable.

Another result of lost information is a deadly lethargy about responding to changing tastes. One example was IBM's slowness, in the 1980s, to react to the growing fascination with personal computers. Customers were telling IBM field reps all the time about that historical shift, but the information didn't reach headquarters in Armonk (or the people there didn't listen) until the company lost millions of dollars preparing marketing plans that were obsolete even before the ink was dry–not to mention billions of dollars in sales. By the time Big Blue senior executives finally caught on, the PC battle was over, and IBM had lost ground it took years to regain.

WAKING THE DINOSAUR UP:
INTEGRATING SALES AND MANAGEMENT

The key to avoiding such deadly scenarios–and to breathing new life into the corporate dinosaur–is to integrate the work of sales and the work of management into a company strategy focused, totally and unambiguously, on account revenue. This is the type of management strategy we stress in this book. Unlike any other "corporate makeover" program you may have encountered, the Miller Heiman approach to the critical sales process recognizes revenue as the heartbeat of every business, and it focuses on renewing your business by building on that fact.

This means that we lean toward growth, not more belt-tightening. We're not knocking managers who have had to resort to cost-cutting. In a tough economy, you do what has to be done. But the downsizing trend, we contend, has natural limitations, and it's only one method of increasing overall profitability. Another method–an essential method, we say–is to expand your generating capacity and bring in more fuel.

There is evidence, moreover, that this "outside-in" approach to profitability is measurably more efficient than the old "trim the fat" method. A story in *Business Week* on "smart selling" certainly vindicates this thinking. Reporting on research from the consultants Bain & Company, Christopher Power writes that "boosting a company's customer-retention rate 2 percent has the same effect on profits as cutting costs by 10 percent."

Myron Magnet, in an article in *Fortune* entitled "Let's Go for

Growth," makes the point well. You can raise your profits, he says, by "shrinking the denominator of expenses," by "enlarging the numerator of revenue," or by some combination of the two. Under the influence of "denominator managers," the past decade has seen a tidal wave of shrinkage and force reductions. Reengineering gurus have looked at companies in trouble and said not "Your glass is half full" or "Your glass is half empty" but "Looks like you've got twice as much glass as you need."

Magnet suggests that the wind may be shifting. "Restructuring and reengineering work their wonders only up to a point," he observes. "Yes, they've pepped up profitability and toughened corporate America for global competition. But ... you can get only so far by cutting down and tightening up.... There comes a point when only growth is growth."

Hence the time may be due for a new look at "numerator enhancement," for strategic analysis that is proactive rather than reactive, that stresses the value of revenue regeneration. That's the type of analysis Miller Heiman has always recommended, and the type you will find applied to real cases in this book. Our vision is both revolutionary and immodest. We contend that the healthiest companies of the twenty-first century will be driven, from top to bottom, by a sales process that is both revitalized and fully integrated with company strategy—so integrated, in fact, that the organization functions like a "selling machine."

The word *machine* may require some clarification. In using it, we certainly *don't* mean to suggest that there is anything impersonal or mechanical about good selling. On the contrary: All the examples in this book prove exactly the opposite. The machine analogy is meant to highlight the fact that a good selling organization, like a good machine, demonstrates the *dynamic interaction of multiple components*, all working smoothly together to achieve a result.

The dynamic aspect is essential. When a machine is turned off, it can look to the casual observer like a mere assemblage of "parts." When it's turned on, though—when it's properly constructed, properly maintained, and properly supervised—you can begin to appreciate its interactive effectiveness. When a good machine is "humming" the way it was designed to, there are no "inessential" or "isolated" components. Everything meshes efficiently with everything else, the entire assemblage takes on a life of its own, and as a result the desired effect is achieved: The car moves forward, the daiquiris get blended, or—in the case of a selling machine—your profits go up.

It's because of our emphasis on profit and on company integration that we identify *Selling Machine* as more than a "selling" book. It speaks not

only to sales professionals and their managers but to every general executive, every financial manager, every CEO, who understands that the
lifeblood of business is sales revenue and who is committed to making the
changes that will keep it flowing.

It speaks to these leaders, moreover, no matter what their line of
business and no matter what the size of their companies. Although the
principles we explain in this book come out of our decades of experience
with large corporations, including many Fortune 500 clients, our experience with smaller firms has proven that these principles also yield solid,
bankable results for small and medium-sized businesses.

If you have responsibility for *any* company's revenue—from a monthly quota to an annual P&L statement—*Selling Machine* addresses your concerns. In correcting a type of management "dis-integration" that no one else
has even identified as a problem, it provides a revolutionary solution to today's
business crisis.

PART ONE

THE SALES PROCESS: ESSENTIAL REDEFINITIONS

1

REDEFINING SELLING: INVOLVING EVERYONE IN SECURING YOUR COMPANY'S REVENUE

"If you're in sales and you close an order, are you done? Not any more. Today it's a much more complex process. You've got to have standards, and you've got to show your people that the process is a living thing. Remember the old data dump–the old 'Show up and throw up' routine? Those days are gone."

–Larry Smith
Vice President, International Sales
Harris Corporation Communications Sector

"Something is happening. Call it the death of a certain kind of salesman."

–Christopher Power
Business Week

WHEN MOST PEOPLE TALK ABOUT "SELLING" OR "making a sale," they're thinking of something extremely narrow and precise. Webster's dictionary, that venerable guide to popular usage, gives a definition that is close to the given wisdom. According to Webster, a sale, or an "act of selling," is "the transfer of property from one person to another for a price." Not much to argue with here, but it's a definition that only a lexicographer—or a lawyer—could love.

The problem is that this bare-bones description is often supplemented with connotations about selling that make it sound not only narrow but negative. Take Webster's again. Look up "sell" and you'll find nuggets like these: "To persuade or influence to a course of action." "To influence or induce to make a purchase." Worst of all: "To deceive, to impose on, to cheat."

The implications are unpleasantly clear. According to everyday usage, people engaged in selling are either dim-witted order takers who deliver goods in exchange for money; or they're con artists who will lie and scheme to get their way; or they're some unsavory combination of the two. Moreover, the sole purpose of selling is defined as "making a sale"—securing a "transfer of property" and pocketing the price—even if you have to "impose" on the customer to do so.

Notice that in none of these definitions do you hear anything about customers' actually needing the property that is transferred or about the benefits—to customers and sellers—of doing business together. Nor is there anything about the vast array of pre-sale preparation and post-sale support which, in today's cutthroat environment, are critical to keeping customers on your side. The impression is that selling means "closing business," period. It's a numbers-driven, generally merciless enterprise that is handled exclusively by a cadre of oily specialists: those glib and shady characters known as salespeople.

If that definition was ever on target—a debatable point, which we seriously doubt—it's certainly not on target today. The company we run, Miller Heiman Inc., does sales consulting for many of the nation's leading corporations. Not one of our extremely successful clients would be in business today if its approach to sales dovetailed with this definition. And all good people know this. They know that the "old strategies for sales success" have long been defunct—and they know it even before they come to us to learn and implement strategies for the twenty-first century. The idea of selling as simply the transfer of property–what our fellow consultants Mark Blessington and Bill O'Connell call the "transactional" model–doesn't relate to how winning companies do business.

Many of the most successful, most aggressively customer-oriented companies have known this for decades. A few examples:

Procter & Gamble. At this Cincinnati-based consumer products giant, company literature refers constantly to "P&G's partner, the consumer." This indicates a "beyond the transaction" philosophy, and it suggests the long-established focus of the home products leader. Procter & Gamble has been taking customer satisfaction seriously for so long that it pioneered market research back in the 1920s.

JC Penney. When James Cash Penney founded his company in 1913, he formulated a credo called the "Penney idea" that stressed not just "fair remuneration" but such modern-sounding values as "complete satisfaction," employee participation, and the "human factor." Even today, JC Penney's company brochures call the founder's credo "the cornerstone upon which the success of our Company is based."

John Deere. In 1850, the partners John Deere and Robert Tate had a celebrated disagreement over improvements to their legendary "plow that broke the plains." With the plow selling phenomenally, Tate favored sitting tight on the design, suggesting that customers "have got to take what we make." "Oh, no," responded Deere. "They haven't got to take what we make, and if someone else improves on our plow, we shall lose our trade." This successful rebuttal, which became company legend, also established the infant manufacturer's reputation for quality.

THE SALES REVOLUTION: PROSPECT AND PARADOX

Until recently, such stories were largely anomalous–shining exceptions in a world of "caveat emptor." Today, however, we are in the middle of a sales revolution, one that will be as momentous for the way we practice business as the industrial, credit, communications, and marketing revolutions. We say that not as observers, but as insiders, because at Miller Heiman we have been sales revolutionaries from the beginning, and our corporate programs have been partly responsible for what *Business Week* calls the advent of "smart selling."

Smart selling, according to *Business Week*, means "focusing the entire company on its customers"–a process that requires "changes in everything from how salespeople are hired, trained, and paid to how the CEO does his or her job." It means taking nothing for granted, least of all the customer. It means chucking the old rules overboard and following new prerogatives. Specifically, says *Business Week*, in "smart selling" companies these four things happen:

- **Top management** *gets involved in the sales function. The CEO, ideally, becomes "salesman in chief."*
- *Slam-dunking is out;* **relationships** *are in. In the words of one GE executive, "Customers demand a new intimacy."*
- *Salespeople don't take orders;* **they solve customers' problems—** *even (or especially) problems that are not sales-related.*
- *Most important, perhaps, the company* **refocuses**. *"The entire organization, from manufacturing to finance," sets its sights on sales and customer service.*

Business Week made these recommendations in the summer of 1992. By that time we had already been making the same recommendations to our clients for fourteen years, since the first Miller Heiman program in 1978. We say this not to open a fruitless argument about who got to the barricades first. What's interesting to us is not just that more and more companies are utilizing the "smart selling" principles we recommend. It's that these principles have been *independently* discovered by researchers from very different industries and with very different agendas. We've all sniffed the same change in the wind, and we've all pointed to where it's moving.

In doing so, moreover, all of us—journalists, consultants, and professors—keep applauding the same leading companies for doing it right. Perhaps it's not surprising to learn that several of the firms Peters and Waterman rated as leaders in staying "close to the customer," including Hewlett-Packard and Marriot, have been our clients. Or that, of the ten firms identified by *Business Week* as "leading the way," over half are either our clients or our clients' customers.

Yet—and here's the paradox of the current revolution—these leaders in selling represent a very small percentage of the total number of firms that make up the American economy. While their successes may be impressive predictors of the future, that future is recognizable only by these occasional glimmers. Most American companies are doing business as usual, and even the ones who are frantically rethinking everything from production to shipping have left the sales function pretty much where it's always been. One result of that omission, as we pointed out in the Introduction, is an increasingly isolated sales force. Another is that the selling function itself is lagging behind.

The term "lagging behind" is used by two consultants, Mark Blessington and Bill O'Connell, whose stimulating book *Sales Reengineering from the Outside In* gives a good overview of the current sales situation and its paradoxes. Identifying selling as traditionally a "transaction-oriented" operation, Blessington and O'Connell suggest that, until recently, it has been unable to adapt to the demands of a "procurement-driven" playing field.

> Although mass-manufacturing operations no longer drive the U.S. economy, mass-distribution thinking still rules in the marketing and sales arms of most firms. Flexible marketing and sales and service processes, able to anticipate and adjust to the increasingly complex and rapidly changing demands of customer procurement processes, still do not exist in most firms.

The important phrase, tellingly repeated, is "most firms." Like us, Blessington and O'Connell are writing about a sales revolution that is still imperfectly realized in most firms and staunchly, vociferously resisted in many others.

If what is happening can be seen as a kind of revolution, then this division of opinion will not surprise any student of history. All revolutions have their vanguards, their middle-of-the-roaders, and their opponents. In the American Revolution, the spectrum ran from the Sons of Liberty to the Tories. In the Russian Revolution (today we should probably call it the First Russian Revolution), there were Bolsheviks, Mensheviks, and White Guards. Even the Industrial Revolution had its naysayers: the Luddites who tried to stop the future by smashing machinery. There are parallel divisions today. "Smart selling" may be the inevitable wave of the future, but there are plenty of businesses who haven't yet gotten that message. The sales revolution is still waiting for its *Common Sense.*

We're not Thomas Paine, but when it comes to selling, long experience has taught us what is common sense and what is not. This book is designed, above all, to clarify the distinction. It lays out, in practical detail, what our clients and other successful companies already know. And it shows how the sales revolution can transform your business practice, even if you work for a company where "sales rep" still means "Lone Ranger," or where there's tension and resentment between the sales force and everybody else.

We showed in the Introduction how timeworn stereotypes about selling contribute to the isolation of sales professionals, not only in society at large but in their own organizations. Because this isolation hurts both these professionals and their companies, we say that the first step in charting the sales revolution is to throw out the ancient assumptions and redefine our terms.

The first term that needs redefining is *selling* itself:

> *In managing the sales process, we redefine selling to mean all corporate activities that contribute, directly or indirectly, to the integrity, growth, and profitability of your company's revenue stream. Anything that helps secure the necessary "fuel" must be considered an essential part of the sales function.*

REDEFINING SELLING MEANS RESHAPING THE CULTURE

If you want to keep your competitive edge in today's heated environment, accepting this redefinition of selling is imperative. But accepting it is only "square one," for the redefinition has precise and practical implications.

Companies that understand the imperative will also understand the need to radically reshape the way "sales" is positioned within their corporate organization. Specifically, they will be prepared to make the following fundamental changes.

First, individual sales—individual "transfers of property"—come and go, but the work of *securing revenue* must go on. This work must be seen as continuous, so that it encompasses and transcends individual transactions. Understanding that, the most competitive companies will treat selling as a *process*. They will abandon the idea of the sale as an isolated event or even as a series of events that a sales force has to "nail down."

Second, recognizing the importance of process, they will necessarily give up the fragmented sense of accountability that makes the closing of business a job performed only by the sales department. Managing the sales process will be seen as a *company* effort, with the targeting of accounts as the responsibility of account *teams*. Members of teams drawn from various departments, not just sales and marketing, will share a common focus: securing an unbroken stream of revenue from customers.

Third, these teams will *integrate* the sales process into corporate strategy. Bridging the ancient gap between the boardroom and the field, managers will treat sales and planning as mutually supportive. Realizing that information from the field is critical in drafting forecasts and marketing plans, they will involve their sales force in setting company strategies; at the same time, they will include senior management in the sales process itself. Selling teams that target major revenue will work jointly with managers at the highest levels. The goal will be to create a seamless interface between all levels of the selling organization, so that valued customers are aware that the vendor's commitment to them runs unimpeded from the shipping dock to the boardroom.

Fourth, the revitalized sales process will be constantly *reinforced* by managers who buy into its practicality and who understand that even the world's best performers still require coaching. In Part III of this book, we describe various reinforcement techniques that our clients use effectively in keeping people committed to the revenue stream. We present techniques like "assessing rather than evaluating," checking your reality with that of the person you're coaching, and concentrating on a single behavior at a time. Here we make the overall point about reinforcement: Revitalizing the sales process is *itself* a process. It implies continual reassessment and management of change.

All of this starts with a sales process that is well understood and properly implemented, but it goes far beyond that. The ultimate goal should be the establishment of a "sales operating system," where sales and operations are two sides of the same coin. One of our clients, Dave Laabs, a vice president at McFarland Office Products and Business Interiors, says that "business development is part of the job description of every sales representative in this organization." Christopher Power of *Business Week*, writing about Dell Computer, speaks about the creation of a "customer focused selling culture" where the CEO acts as "salesman in chief." In an article in *Forbes* on the West Coast retailer Nordstrom, Inc., Seth Lubove recalls "Mr. Jim" Nordstrom telling his store managers, "Don't listen to us in Seattle. Listen to your customer. We give you permission to take care of your customer."

Different voices and different terms, but the same message. What we're announcing, in our version of "common sense," is an emerging revolution not just in sales but in corporate *culture*–in the values and attitudes that determine companies' missions and set the guidelines for *how* they carry on their business.

"CHAMBERS": THE CASE OF THE TEETERING GIANT

There's nothing warm or fuzzy about this concept. When we talk about company culture, we mean something that is eminently *practical* because it directly affects how a company secures–or fails to secure–its revenue stream. We were reminded of this on a recent trip to the Northeast, when we visited the headquarters of a major industrial manufacturer.

This company had once been the undisputed leader in its field. We'll preserve its privacy here by calling it the Chambers Company, and just say that its products carry a brand name that's in the same league as Band-Aid and Kleenex. Up until about ten years ago, nobody in the country—nobody in the world—ran even a close second to "Chambers" in market share.

About that time, however, this front-runner was threatened by a combination of technological changes and foreign competition. In a frenzied reaction, it turned first to a series of costly restructurings and then to a virtual mania for diversification. It started gulping down other companies like a Pac-Man run amok, betting its future on buying everything that wasn't tied down. For almost a decade, Chambers merged with a vengeance, hoping to nurse its ailing business back to health with income from what it saw as fresh new fields.

On paper a nice idea—in reality, a bomb. In fact, as the scope of the company's operations widened, its market share, even in its core business, continued to slump. The very changes that were designed to expand its revenue base had led, by the 1990s, to a P&L disaster.

At that point, Chambers called us in for some on-site consulting.

During our visit to the teetering giant, our first job was to uncover the reasons behind the fiasco. It didn't take long. After just one afternoon in the Chambers headquarters, it became apparent to us that the company's nosedive was a *predictable* result, not just of reckless diversification but of the particular style in which their executives managed—or rather failed to manage—the revenue stream. That style was part and parcel of a company culture in which selling and management weren't considered even distant cousins.

An Account Philosophy That Wasn't: "If It Moves, Go for It"

We got our first hint that this was the problem when we asked one of the company's senior executives—let's call her Chris—where the bulk of Chambers's revenues came from. Who were the key accounts, the customers whose business was most critical to the bottom line?

"It's hard to answer that question," Chris said, "because we don't really target key accounts as such. We've always tried to reach as many customers as we could, to go after as many dollars as possible. We have overall sales figures for our divisions and territories, but we don't follow individual accounts that closely. I guess you could say our philosophy is 'If it moves, go for it!' "

"What about *relative* volume?" we asked. "If you had to name one customer who consistently brings you good business, year after year, who would that be?"

After thinking a minute, she named a large retail chain that her company had been selling to for twenty-five years.

"Who calls on that account?"

"It depends," Chris said, "on which division you're talking about." On an organization chart, she indicated that Chambers now had eight separate divisions, each with its own management hierarchy and its own sales force. The retail account in question was handled by reps from at least half of them, each one accountable to a different divisional management.

In addition, as the chart showed, the recent acquisitions had created some interdivisional overlap of product lines, and as a result some Chambers reps were actually selling not only in competition with their own distributors but in competition with each other. In this crazy-quilt world of the "new and bigger" Chambers, not only was no unified face presented to customers, but the many faces the customers saw often seemed to be on opposing teams!

"Is there anybody in charge of handling the account as a whole?" we asked. "Who's responsible for the ongoing customer relationship?"

The "Disintegrated" Manager

What we had in mind when we asked that question was an account manager or a senior sales executive whose personal responsibility was to steady that account. In response, Chris introduced us to a junior executive whom we'll call John. His responsibility, she said, was the personal supervision of certain large accounts. That sounded hopeful, but when we talked to him, it turned out that John had a very different, and very jaded, view of things.

"I don't know what I'm supposed to be doing in this job," he said. "The position was created to handle customer relationships—to keep our key accounts happy over the long run. I wasn't supposed to be doing any selling. But as it turns out, I'm like an extra member of the sales department. All they want me to do is to help close business."

We've never seen a more vivid example of the traditional divorce between sales and general management—or of the fragmentation this leads to. Here was a bright young up-and-comer who obviously thought of himself as executive timber, as someone who specialized in long-term nurturing of the business, and he was resentful and confused at being asked to sell. In his mind, evidently, the lofty business of management was worlds away from the everyday, dirty-hands business of bringing in revenue. And it was supposed to stay there. John saw his "selling" position as almost a demotion.

The real kicker here was that John wasn't alone. He wasn't a freak or a complainer but a perfect embodiment of the internal chaos that Chambers had planned itself into. Maintaining a gulf between selling and managing wasn't his quirky preference. As Chris's lack of a handle on account revenue also clearly indicated, the entire company culture underwrote that gulf.

If Chambers had been focused clearly on the revenue stream, both Chris and John would have seen themselves–enthusiastically–as part of the overall selling effort. That wasn't happening here. The whole thrust of the Chambers culture, however unintentional it may have been, was to keep the spheres of sales and management "*dis*integrated."

There was only one reason that Chambers had gotten away with this traditional attitude for so long: lack of competition. For decades, nobody had even been close to Chambers in name recognition, price, or quality. As a result, the company hadn't really needed a revenue strategy. When you're the only game in town, your products sell themselves.

In the middle of the go-go 1980s, that abruptly changed, as a foreign supplier scampered onto the playing field with a highly competitive product and a hungry eye. Within a matter of years, the Chambers edge dulled, as the new player ate up more and more of its "old reliable" accounts. By the end of the decade, with its market share down fifteen points, Chambers found itself selling off many of its newly acquired properties, and thinking seriously, for perhaps the first time in its history, how to recapture the hordes of core customers who had gotten away.

This is not a unique story. Today, you can't turn around without bumping into newcomers who are eyeing your customer base, and most of them are as technologically astute as they are hungry. There's no room for business as usual in today's global shoot-outs. That's why, before you even think about going up against the latest crop of cyber-savvy young guns, you've got to dedicate your resources fully to targeted accounts and put general management and sales on the same page. Because Chambers failed to do that, it paid the price.

DOING IT RIGHT: EXAMPLES FROM OUR CLIENTS

What could Chambers have done differently?

The simple answer is, "Everything." A better answer, though, would be that Chambers could have adopted our redefinition of selling. It could have discarded the "everything that moves" philosophy and adopted an attitude that stressed the three elements we have highlighted: (1) the sales *process*; (2) *team* selling; and (3) the coordination of the sales force and *senior* management into an *integrated* strategy for securing revenue from major accounts.

Obviously, this kind of mental change can't happen overnight. We've confirmed that ourselves over the past year, as we've worked with Chambers executives to transform their culture. A lot of progress has been made, as managers begin to realize how damaging a "disintegrated" structure can be, and as they take the first steps toward integration, by identifying all the people who can have an impact on the revenue from specific large accounts, and then holding team meetings to clarify their opportunities in those accounts.

There's also been some resistance—both from middle managers who naturally resist everything that's "not invented here" and from senior managers who don't see the need to be involved in something as "low-level" as sales. That hasn't surprised us, because we're far from being believers in anybody's quick fix. Nobody says that changing a culture is easy.

But change can and does happen, often with remarkable results. In fact, what is just getting off the ground at Chambers has been up and running at many of our other client companies for years. These innovative companies have long accepted the fact that the redefinitions we're proposing are essential, and they have been devoting constant effort to renewing their cultures by implementing the principles we outline here.

Here's how some of these innovative companies are doing it right.

"Living" the Selling Process at Harris Corporation. The fact that selling can be—indeed, must be—considered a process rather than an event has major implications for how it is managed internally. Harris Corporation's vice president for international sales, Larry Smith, alludes to one such implication in the chapter epigraph, when he calls the selling process a living thing.

Living things need nurturing in order to thrive. The nurturers, Larry understands, must be sales and senior managers. "We don't believe," he says, "that we can make the process work just by saying 'Here it is—God bless you.' Management has got to be constantly on top of its implementation. At Harris, we do that aggressively. When you spend money putting a new process in place, it's dumb not to. We audit our people every six months on how they're managing it, and there isn't a meeting that goes by where somebody doesn't ask 'How are you doing with this?'"

In other words, the selling process must be constantly reinforced, or–to pick up Larry's metaphor–it will die on the vine. We'll return to this critical point in Chapter 12, on reinforcement.

Team Selling at Foxboro, Documentum, and HBO. Foxboro sells a wide range of electronic and quality control systems. Over the past several years, the company has adopted two separate Miller Heiman processes, Strategic Selling and Conceptual Selling. But even though these processes target sales, they are not designed for salespeople alone. In our early meetings with Foxboro management, we emphasized the value of having account teams manage the sales process. Foxboro's people translated that lesson into a very practical decision: they asked us to deliver our programs not just to their sales force but to representatives from all of their departments.

We do mean *all.* When the Foxboro "sales force" came to our programs, it included not just the obvious salespeople and their managers, but people from engineering, accounting, distribution, and human resources. Selling was redefined as a shared responsibility, and one that could be met only by interdepartmental cooperation–by everyone working together to secure account revenue.

Even before this team system started to have an impact on Foxboro's balance sheets, there was an increase in the company's internal efficiency. If a customer was unclear about technical capacity, for example, there was no need to route the question to the engineering department: engineers were already part of the selling team. If a system needed fine-tuning after installation, scheduling service calls wasn't a "post-sale problem": it had been built in to the sales process from the beginning.

With everyone working as a team to target key business, Foxboro virtually eliminated two of the nightmares that give "disintegrated" managers insomnia: duplication of effort and interdepartmental turf battles. The resulting savings instantly improved the bottom line. In acknowledging this, one manager explained, "We got an immediate payoff because everybody who could affect the account was on the same page."

A second illustration of team selling comes from Documentum, a nationwide software supplier. Kurt Bullard, the company's Central Region Technical Manager, notes that the complexity of its sales efforts practically require it to adopt a team approach. "We deal with pharmaceutical firms, for example, who need us to help prepare 500,000-page documents for FDA certification; and with General Motors, which might need design materials for a new line that requires 15,000 or 20,000 drawings. Our sales are so technical that we have to involve the expertise of our technical people.

On a lot of our business, we use people we call technical coaches to watch the development of the sale on a day-to-day basis. They're very much a part of the selling function. In addition, part of our system engineers' pay is based on sales."

Brad Teed, one of the system engineers that Kurt is referring to, describes himself as "the technical half of the sales team. When I go out on calls, it's with a sales rep who is the commercial half. But I'm still obviously part of the sales effort, and at times my selling input goes way beyond the technical.

"For example, recently the rep I had been working with left the company. Between his leaving and the hiring of a replacement, somebody had to keep on top of the accounts—ask customers about their needs, scout for opportunities, maintain Documentum's presence. I was the logical choice, and I would have done it whether or not a manager said I had to. If I saw myself narrowly as the technical 'answer man,' our accounts would have been neglected and we would have lost business. To avoid a crisis, somebody had to put his finger in the dike. So I put on my sales representative cap and became the little Dutch boy." The result? The solid maintenance of accounts that might otherwise have eroded.

A team approach also brought great benefits at HBO & Company, whose Amherst Products Group sells information systems to the health care industry. In a recent major competition, HBO was third on one customer's potential vendor list until it drafted a targeted account plan that utilized the input of everybody from account representatives to product managers and R&D staff. "It was the biggest deal we've ever had," Vice President and General Manager Al Bergonzi told our newsletter writer Sally Glover. "With the account plan and the team selling approach, people know who's who, and it helps focus everyone involved with the account." The result was a multimillion-dollar contract.

And that was only the lion's share of a broader success. In 1991, before we coached the Amherst Products Group, its annual sales revenue was $5 million; four years later, it was $27 million. "I'm not saying it was all because of Strategic Selling," said Al. "But it was the same number of people who did that business. They all work with an account plan. It's not just the Lone Ranger—we don't send one person out to talk to everyone. The team approach has definitely made us more productive."

Integrating Management at Landis & Gyr Powers. Another Miller Heiman client, Landis & Gyr Powers, is a leading manufacturer of building controls. A couple of years ago, its national systems sales manager, Bob Del Ciello, decided to introduce his people to our processes; the first meeting was attended by the top one-third of the national sales force, along with their branch managers. One thing that became apparent in that opening session was that account planning couldn't be separated from corporate direction strategy. As a result, if an effective sales process were to become a reality at L&GP, senior managers would have to become involved.

Realizing this, Bob and his fellow participants shot straight for the top. At the next meeting, participants included not only the rest of the national sales force–a total of 230 people–but also the president of Landis & Gyr Powers and several vice presidents. "We knew that getting the initial commitment from the top," Bob said, "was going to be essential to the success of the program."

And to the success, it turned out, of the bottom line. Strategic Selling is now in place, and running effectively, at L&GP branch locations worldwide. Virtually all of them are showing increased account penetration. That success would have been impossible without top-down commitment. It's this commitment that makes the sales process everybody's priority–up and down the business chart, and at all locations.

"FULL ORGANIZATIONAL COMMITMENT TO THE OVERALL SALES JOB"

It is impossible to exaggerate the importance of this last point. The companies that are most successful today, and that will continue to be successful into the next century, reflect what a client associate of ours once called "full organizational commitment to the overall sales job." In the best-run companies–like those we've mentioned here–the three elements of redefined selling operate in coordination with each other, from the top to the bottom of the organization.

To a certain degree, technology makes this easier. "Instantaneous information should be used to improve a company's communications processes," writes Catherine Romano, "since strong internal communications are a must." At General Electric, she points out, a formalized integration process called "quick market intelligence" enables sales and manufacturing to work swiftly together via conference calls to resolve issues that the old bureaucratic loop might have stalled. The system has already led to a significant success:

> When the opportunity arose to get a contract for washing machines from a large builder, General Electric didn't debate over whether or

not they could make the needed modifications. Instead, they were able to make the decision to take the order in one day, instead of the usual one or two weeks.

The hero here was something as simple as a conference call, but similar tales might be told of other technological catalysts.

The laptop computer, for example, has dramatically opened up communications between salepeople in the field and their factory supply lines. As William Keenan Jr. reports from his interview with Michael Hammer, "instead of guessing or lying" about delivery dates, the salesperson can now "use the laptop to check inventory, availability, and production schedules, and either commit existing inventory or make a reservation in a plant production schedule to guarantee when the goods arrive." You could make the same point about "strong internal communications" with regard to E-mail, which is providing electronic integration for so many companies today—including ours.

Integration, however, is ultimately less a matter of technology than of human actors who are dedicated to opening up the lines. A telling example is provided by our client Dave Laabs, who is vice president for sales and business development at McFarland Office Products and Business Interiors, an office supply and furniture dealer near Chicago. Dave had worked previously with the office furniture giant Herman Miller, where he had been exposed to our processes, and McFarland had hired him to improve its furniture sales. Once he was on board, however, he quickly discovered that a more structural revamping of the company was in order. As with the "disintegrated" manufacturing firm we described earlier, McFarland's approach to its customers was frequently unfocused, principally because it sold out of two separate divisions whose sales representatives behaved more like rivals than allies.

"Many firms in our industry," Dave explains, "are 'pure' furniture dealerships. They primarily represent one manufacturer, and they sell its desks, its cubicles, and so on, but no staples or calendars or copy paper. We're an exception. In addition to representing Haworth Corporation's furniture lines, we also deliver a full range of office supplies. We're like Herman Miller or Steelcase *plus* Office Depot. That gives us, potentially, a lot of flexibility. But for years it also created a communications problem.

"You had two divisions, and the way they were set up, it made you see the connection between 'division' and 'divisive.' Furniture reps dealt in furniture, period, and supply reps dealt in supplies. You'd have reps from each division calling on the same account but not comparing notes, not working together—almost going out of their way not to cooperate. Commissions were based entirely on personal closes, so there wasn't really an incentive for them to work together. In fact, they saw themselves, realistically, as competing with each other, for the bigger slices of their 'shared' customers' pies.

"We've started to turn that around with a unified strategy, one whose ultimate goal is long-term relationships. Soon after I got here, we started having joint sales meetings with salespeople from the two divisions. We started sending furniture people and supply people out together, working as a team on a single call. And we changed the compensation to reflect the team idea. Now everybody who contributes to the sales revenue from a given account is rewarded for his or her role in the common effort.

"What our people are starting to see," Dave concludes, "is that their personal interests are tied to McFarland's growth, not just to the success stories of their own division. It used to be 'You're over there and I'm over here and never the twain shall meet.' We're a more integrated, and therefore more productive, company now, because we're exploring multiple opportunities in each account. The lesson we learned from this reengineering is clear. It's reflected in my own responsibility for sales *and* business development. The two are tied together. They've got to be. Business development is part of the job description of every sales representative in this organization."

Every sales representative—and everybody else. If the engine of sales is going to drive revenue effectively, everybody on board must be committed to treating it like the engine. And that all-levels commitment must start at the top, because that's where company cultures are made or broken. We totally agree with another of our client associates, who says that in reshaping the sales process, "The worst thing you can do is to teach it to your salespeople and not your executives."

Commitment has to be visible, not just verbal. More and more in strategically integrated companies—especially in companies that have learned this lesson from us—senior managers are dealing with customers directly. Out of necessity they're on the phone to their clients, working closely with their key account managers—even going to call on customers themselves. Gone are the days when senior executives could give the marching orders and then sit back and let the selling troops do the grunt work.

In an article in *Business Week* on Dell Computer, Stephanie Forest notes that, at this Texas company, the founder, Michael Dell, is often on the line himself. At a company that "makes every employee focus on selling," this shouldn't be surprising, but it does surprise Dell's customers, with excellent results. When a network manager for a software company met Michael Dell recently, he recalled with delight that Dell "asked me what I'd like to see. He actually took notes."

One of our oldest clients, Hewlett Packard, sets the same example—the CEO himself often goes on calls. This was true under John Young, who was running the company when H-P first became a Miller Heiman client, and it's true under John's successor, Lewis Platt. It's H-P policy that at least once a month—more frequently, if necessary—the CEO calls on a major account.

This is not a personal idiosyncracy. The tradition of executive sales calls is bred into the H-P culture; *all* its senior managers regularly call on customers. It's not window dressing or a PR gimmick either. Hewlett Packard managers understand that this tradition sends a signal up and down the organization that the development of key account relationships at all levels of both organizations is what helps to secure key account revenue—and that this is priority number one.

The immediate and obvious benefit of full commitment is that it provides focus and efficiency to your account activity. It saves time and effort by keeping everybody on the same page.

But there's a less obvious benefit that is just as important. Full organizational commitment sends your customers the one message that you most want them to hear. It tells them that your company strategy is not to push the product but to help customers improve their strategy and their bottom line. It lets them know that what you are about as a selling organization is addressing their business issues and helping them to solve their problems.

In doing that, you are selling to customer need. That's the second concept that has to be redefined.

2

REDEFINING CUSTOMER NEED: ZEROING IN ON "SOLUTION IMAGE"

"Customers buy so you will make their problems go away. Every great salesperson is a discrepancy eliminator."
–Joe White
Sales Consultant
Miller Heiman

"How did he know that's what you wanted?"
"He asked."
–PaineWebber advertisement

THE LIFEBLOOD OF YOUR BUSINESS IS THE revenue stream. The source of the revenue stream is sales to your customers. But since every sale is the result of a buying decision, the better you understand your customers' decision-making process, the more security you bring to the revenue stream. In this book we provide a unique perspective on buying, one that reveals the logic of your customers' decisions (even when they seem entirely illogical) and that shows you how to use this logic to your mutual advantage.

We say "use," not "manipulate," and "mutual advantage," not "your advantage." That's no accident. This is not a game plan for spinning your customers' weaknesses into gold or playing with their heads so that they don't know they've been sold. What we introduce here–and what we define in greater detail in later chapters–is a field-tested, time-tested blueprint for *why people buy*. Understanding that "why" is critically important in determining what you can, and cannot, sell them. We show you how to do this so that everybody wins.

WHY PEOPLE BUY: THE ONE REASON

In the workshops we run for our corporate clients, we begin our discussion of buying by asking the participants to identify the reasons that their customers have bought in the past. Here are the kinds of answers we usually get:

> *"We had the most advanced product on the market."*
>
> *"It was the best presentation I've ever done."*
>
> *"The competition couldn't touch our service guarantee."*
>
> *"We just happened to be in the right place at the right time."*

Four different responses with one thing in common. They all focus on something that the seller did rather than what went through the buyer's mind.

That's predictable. Those of us who sell for a living are used to thinking of ourselves as initiators. Star sellers are supposed to be in charge of the sale, aggressively and heroically making it happen. Naturally, we think of a sale as something that flows, irresistibly, from us to them.

But that's not the way it happens. Never has been. When it comes to the close, it's your customers' thinking that counts; it's their reason for buying that actually makes things happen. Certainly, you can positively affect your customer's decisions by having state-of-the-art products, great presentations, competitive service packages, and good timing. But such seller-driven elements of the buy-sell situation are *not* the reason that your customers buy.

The reason that customers buy is almost painfully simple—so simple that, to our peril, we often overlook it. It is only indirectly related to the superiority of your product, and even more tangentially related to the sizzle of your spiel. Here's the plain truth:

> People decide to buy on the basis of **expectation.**
> They buy what they believe your product
> or service will do for them.

THE CUSTOMER'S CONCEPT: DEFINITIONS

In our *Conceptual Selling* programs, we refer to "what they believe" as the customer's *Concept.* We don't mean your concept, or your company's. As we use the term, *Concept* has nothing to do with the production design that brings tears to the eyes of the technogeeks in your R&D unit. Nor is it the same as the concept behind your latest ad campaign. The customer's Concept is inside his or her head. It's a mental picture of what he or she expects to accomplish. It may have a lot, a little, or nothing to do with your product.

We've been running Conceptual Selling programs for fifteen years. During that time, our colleagues and customers have offered numerous refinements to the basic Miller Heiman idea of the customer's Concept. Here are two that we've found to be especially helpful:

- **Concept as the "elimination of discrepancy."** *This spin on the idea comes to us from Joe White, who sells for Miller Heiman out of New York City and Scottsdale, Arizona. "Customers buy," he says, "to make problems go away. They see a discrepancy between where they are and where they want to be. If they think you can eliminate the discrepancy, they'll think about buying. If not, forget it. Every great seller is a discrepancy eliminator."*

- **Concept as "solution image."** *If you spend more than two minutes a day reading the business press, you know that it's fashionable today to offer the customer "solutions." Unlike many fashions, this one* *actually has a point, and in fact at Miller Heiman we've been practicing "solution selling" for years.*

But we do it with a twist that puts the spotlight, again, on the customer. Most "solution sellers" fall all over themselves trying to convince the customer that their solutions are inherently better than those of the competition. We don't believe that any product or service has inherent value. It's fine to have what you think is the perfect solution for a customer's problem, but if the customer doesn't see it that way–if it's not his or her mental picture–then the ideal answer you're supplying will fall on deaf ears.

We talk more about this common problem in Chapter 5, when we discuss customers who, out of "pickiness" or dimness, just "don't get" why they should buy your product. And we'll return to Joe's idea of discrepancy in Chapter 6, when we discuss the four Buyer Response Modes. For now, the main point of both these definitions is this: As a sales professional, you're not just selling your solution. You're selling what your customers see your solution as achieving for *them*.

WHAT ABOUT THE PRODUCT?

None of this would be any more useful than the average biz-school buzz talk if you couldn't also deliver products or services to your customers, and bank on the resulting revenue and commissions. To do that, you have to take a second step. Once you fully understand *what* the prospective buyer wants to get done, you still have to make it clear to him or her exactly *how* your product or service would accomplish that. That's what we call making a Product Sale.

There's nothing mysterious about this. Sellers are perfectly used to making Product Sales. The problem is that they often try to make a sale too early, before they have a clear understanding of the customer's *solution image*. That leads inevitably to miscommunication, to force-feeding the customer with *your* mental picture, and in the worst cases to closing doors.

Yes, you have to demonstrate the excellence of your product. But no product is excellent in itself. It's excellent only if it fulfills a customer's need, and it does that only by satisfying a solution image. That's why every successful sales scenario is composed of *two* separate steps.

1. *In understanding the* Concept, *you develop as clear a picture as possible of the customer's solution image.*

2. *In making the* Product Sale, *you demonstrate how your company can provide something that fits this image.*

"Developing a clear picture" doesn't sound very much like "selling." True enough, according to the old definition of selling. But recall that in Chapter 1, we greatly expanded the old definition, so that selling entails everything you and your company do to keep your revenue flowing. These days, understanding what your customers want to accomplish is an essential element of this overall picture—so essential, in fact, that it's a prerequisite to doing anything else.

In other words, there's a logical sequence to the two steps we've mentioned. Not one customer in a hundred will agree to buy a product or service without *first* believing that it's going to accomplish something for him or her. So, if you're selling smart, understand the Concept first.

Here's a personal example of what can happen if you don't.

DOING IT WRONG: THE "CHEAP JEEP" SCENARIO

A while ago we decided that we would like to buy a Jeep. We went to a local dealer and were approached by a friendly lot salesman who thought he knew, before either of us had said a word, exactly what we wanted: a tough, bottom-of-the-line workhorse.

"The great thing about Jeeps," he told us, "is that they're the sturdiest little animals on the market. There's really no comparison. Look at all that storage space. Great for camping, hauling, any off-road work you might have. You couldn't kill this baby with a hammer. . . ."

We let him ramble on for a minute or so before breaking in. "What about features?" we asked him. "A/C, a good stereo system. Isn't there something called a Limited Edition, something with power windows?" We had done enough homework to know that Jeep made such a model, and these relatively luxurious features were important to us. What the salesman didn't know—because he didn't ask—was that we wanted the vehicle as an exotic but comfortable runabout, not for cruising the hills or hauling scrap iron.

If the salesman had bothered to ask, he might have steered us, and himself, toward a sale. But he didn't listen. He was so intent on painting his own picture of the Jeep that he missed the point: our picture was completely different. "The Limited Edition? Yeah," he commented drily. "But another great thing about the Jeep is that it's such a bargain. It's an off-the-road experience. Why would anybody in his right mind spend $34,000 for a Jeep?"

We refrained from pointing out to him that an off-the-road experience was not even the last item on our wish list. Instead, we thanked him for his time and left the lot. Across town, at another dealership, we found a salesperson who was smart enough to let us define our own Concept. That was the person who pocketed a great commission.

That's the common outcome of pushing the product: no sale. Admittedly, very rarely, you do make a sale. There are those one-in-a-hundred situations where you get "lucky" with a customer whose Concept is ill defined and who takes your product on the glimmer of a hope that it will work for him. But if you and your company are smart, you don't want that business. Nine times out of ten, it comes back to haunt you in the form of Buyer's Remorse and Buyer's Revenge. We'll return to these common problems in Chapter 5.

We've all heard the phrase "nailing down business." Selling products or services without understanding Concept is like swinging a hammer merrily away in the dark. Pretty risky—for your fingers and for whatever you're nailing into. The old-fashioned wisdom on this point is: "Every nail is a good nail. Just keep pounding." We say: "Turn on the light and look. *Then* swing the hammer."

WHO NEEDS A SWIMMING POOL?

Here's an example of doing it right, from one of our clients. Sterling Healthcare manages hospitals and behavioral counseling centers in states ranging from the Great Lakes to the Northwest. At many of their facilities, upper management, clinicians, and support personnel have all been introduced to our processes, and the outcome has been a dramatic improvement in "referral communication."

Margaret Shiver, the company's vice president for marketing and business development, explains that potential clients with adjustment or dependency problems are referred to Sterling by physicians, teachers, and guidance counselors, and that it is to these specialists that the company "sells" its services. "What we're doing isn't selling per se," says Shiver. "It's referral communication, where the goal is first to determine what each referral source is trying to accomplish, and then offer a solution that fits his or her needs."

Shiver stresses that the order of operations here is crucial. First, determine the source's solution image. Second, highlight the advantages of a Sterling solution. "Following the traditional path—the old talk-talk-talk method of shoving benefits down the customer's throat—just won't get you anywhere in our business, because until you ask the referral source what he or she needs, you have no idea which benefit you should be describing. Trotting out features at random is just a waste of time.

"For example, many of our facilities are equipped with indoor swimming pools. *We* like that feature. We think it's one of the things that sets us apart from our competition. But our experience has shown us that it's not a key point for our referral sources. They appreciate it as a value-added item, but it seldom relates directly to what they're trying to accomplish. Finding out what that is, on a case-by-case basis, has got to be the first step in providing a solution."

On a case-by-case basis—that's the key. Sterling's experience consistently confirms the individuality—and the attendant subjectivity—of the customer's solution image.

"We work frequently with guidance counselors, for example," Shiver explains. "Suppose that on a given day one of our staff sits down to speak with three counselors. The first one may have just been assigned twenty additional kids; with that added workload, what he's looking for is constant, ready access to our clinicians. The second counselor may be experiencing personal problems that impinge on her normal nine-to-five schedule; she wants to know if she can reach us at two in the morning. The third one is professionally committed to home-based care; she wants to hear about noninstitutional options we can suggest.

"Each of these three people has a different, personal reason for being interested in Sterling's services. That means three different, personally customized solutions. We'd get nowhere pitching the swimming pool to any of these folks. That would obscure the flexibility of our services—and insult their intelligence."

Why don't more salespeople follow this eminently logical pattern? The answer has to do with the way we are trained, and with the emphasis placed on what Shiver calls the "talk-talk-talk" method of pushing benefits.

BEYOND "TALK-TALK-TALK"

That "method" is deeply embedded in the selling tradition. According to countless images in popular culture and (bizarrely enough) according to many salespeople themselves, the super sales rep is a perambulating gab machine, mouth going a mile a minute and ears stuffed with wax.

Consider the clichés. "He could sell snow to the Eskimos." "She could talk the hair off your head." "You're not a great salesman until you can sell something to someone who doesn't want it." "Don't take no for an answer." "The selling doesn't start until the customer says no." All of these phrases—which are part of our profession's occupational folklore—define selling as telling: telling customers what they want, what they need, and where to sign. The "compleat salesperson," according to the conventional wisdom, bears no relation to the careful listener of the PaineWebber ad quoted at the beginning of this chapter. The conventional picture is smilin' Sammy, the arm-pumping used car salesman—or his female counterpart—whose philosophy is "Tell 'em whatever you have to. Just make the sale."

We won't suggest that this ancient philosophy is still chugging along very smoothly outside of used car lots. The increased savviness of customers, the information explosion, the rise in competition (and therefore in available options), the spread of "close to the customer" corporate strategies—all of these developments combine to create a selling environment where smilin' Sammy and other quick-buck types are rapidly becoming as obsolete as their patter. This is especially true in the high-stakes blue-chip arena. From a practical as well as an ethical standpoint, you can't survive by yakking your customers into signing. Everybody worth a six-figure commission already knows this.

But you don't have to be smilin' Sammy to fall victim now and again to his disease. Even the best and most ethical of sales professionals sometimes practice "talking cures" which can be almost as deadly to your revenue as smilin' Sammy's scams. The most common examples are variations of "product push," in which the seller is mesmerized by the product or service itself, rather than trying to identify a Concept or need.

Variation 1: "Take This—You Need It"

In one variation, sellers confuse what the customer needs with what their company needs to sell—that is, the marketing requirements of the organization they work for. In other words, the seller mistakes the company's solution for the customer's solution image.

Although this approach is closely related to smilin' Sammy's hand-pumping style, there's not necessarily anything underhanded or treacherous about it. In all but the most sophisticated of selling organizations, salespeople confuse customers' needs with their own companies' marketing needs because the relationship between salesperson and customer is only one factor that influences what a company produces and markets. When you're face to face with a customer, you're not there alone. Behind you is your entire corporate organization, filled with fellow professionals whose day-to-day concerns may have less to do with providing solutions than with manufacturing issues, inventory costs, sales forecasts, or profit margins. Those concerns affect what you believe you need to sell, which in turn affects your perception of the customer's need.

A colleague of ours once worked for a furniture manufacturer. In the early 1970s, this company came out with a line called "the Toledo," which the design department and the company president were convinced would replace American Colonial as the look of the decade. The sales force was therefore instructed to "push the Toledo," while the assembly line worked overtime on Spanish-style grillwork.

The field staff followed directions, only to discover, six months down the line, that the Mediterranean vogue that was supposed to drive sales skyward was a figment of the design department's imagination. Results? A record number of returns, irritated retailers everywhere from Tallahassee to Tacoma, a revenue nosedive—and the sales staff, caught in the middle, taking the hit for a misconceived marketing policy. The policy makers had never asked retailers, or homeowners, what they wanted in the first place.

Our colleague still refers grimly to the "wholly Toledo disaster." It was a classic case of trying to invent "customer preference," or of letting a product create a need, rather than vice versa. It was also, of course, an example of corporate disintegration, where design and marketing and sales weren't talking to each other.

Variation 2: "Whatever You Need, We Have It"

In a second variation, sellers make a perfunctory attempt to determine the customer's need but then revert to type, assuming that whatever the customer needs, their company can supply it. Maybe the customer isn't interested in marketing's latest run-out, or the old man's pet project. No matter. With our volume and variety, they've got to be interested in something.

This error in judgment is most common in large corporations which have enjoyed a major market share for a long time and whose product lines (they feel) are infinitely adaptable. If you're big enough, and the menu of your products or services is diverse enough, it's very tempting to assume, in the words of the old hash-house joke, "If you don't see it on the menu, you don't really want it."

Here is a bitterly humorous example. A major manufacturer of office machines—let's call it Pix, Inc.—recently closed a deal with a medium-size accounting firm to replace their outmoded copiers with a new, hotshot system. The Pix representative insisted that the system was perfect for the customer's needs. Was it a great system? No question. Its speed, capacity, and flexibility made it the most advanced design on the market, well worth the premium price that Pix was getting for it. There was only one glitch. When the installers arrived to put the new units in place, they didn't fit. Literally.

The accounting firm was housed in a genteel old building with narrow hallways, and–short of knocking down walls–there was no way to wheel in the new units. So the hotshot new copiers had to be trucked back to Pix, the sale fell through, and the accountants, amazed that so elementary a spec had been overlooked, decided to give their business to another supplier. Even though Pix had smaller units that *would* fit, it was too late to rescue a deal that had been so mismanaged.

Ostensibly, the problem here was space limitations. But that wasn't the real deal-killer. What really did Pix in was its own failure to understand the customer's mental picture of the solution. That picture included, as a kind of baseline given, the physical presence of the machines inside the offices. There was no alternative picture of the copiers out on the curb, with the installers scratching their heads and a light snow falling.

We tell this story not to laugh at a dumb mistake, the sales equivalent of painting yourself into a corner. We use it because it highlights the importance of "fit," not just in the obvious physical sense, but in the sense of a match between the seller's and the buyer's expectations. By focusing on product first, you can forget that fact, and shoot the foot that you've just got in the door.

One last point. Notice that, even though the accountants could have renegotiated with Pix for copiers that did fit, they chose not to. Why? Because Pix, in allowing its enthusiasm for the product to control the sale, had sent this customer a deadly message: not just "One size fits all," but "Everybody wants our product, and you're no different." The customer was different, though. Every customer is different. Recognizing that is the beginning of selling solutions–and of the long-term stability that only such selling guarantees.

Variation 3: "Give the Customers What They Want"

In this third variation of pushing a product, sellers deliver a product or service package that they know, for one reason or another, isn't right for a customer, justifying the sale with the excuse that it's "what the customer asked for." This seems to absolve the seller of responsibility for the sale, but in fact it sets up both buyer and seller for a fall.

If the oldest cliché in business is "caveat emptor," then the second oldest is probably "The customer is always right." It's a generous-sounding idea, but it often has dire consequences, because the plain fact is that the customer isn't always right. Sometimes, in making buying decisions, the customer is a 24-karat idiot. Because this is so, it's wise to think "caveat vendor" before you "generously" give a customer what he or she wants. If you allow customers to dictate, rather than explain their Concept, you're little more than a sophisticated order-taker. And you can end up paying dearly for your generosity. We'll let a couple of our clients make the point.

The Fast-Food Slowdown. The first client, Micros Systems, Inc., sells hospitality management systems and cash registers to a variety of food service operations, including chains, hotels, stadiums, and independent restaurants. Sales executive Elizabeth Ngonzi works out of their Massachusetts offices.

"One of our more advanced products," Elizabeth recalled recently, "is a handheld mobile ordering device. We've had great success with it in large-capacity stadiums, where an order-taker can move up and down the aisles, taking customers' orders. About a year ago, we were working with the owner of a European-style fast-food chain in the Boston area. The guy knew next to nothing about high-tech and would never be caught touching a computer himself. But for some reason he felt he needed the industry's most cutting-edge technology, and that meant installing our handheld capability.

"We were so happy at his interest that we never looked closely enough at whether it was *in* his interest to have this particular product. It was a classic case of making the Product Sale first. The result was a disaster.

"The restaurant where he wanted to test the device was incredibly crowded at lunchtime, with customers waiting ten deep in line for two order-takers. The owner's idea was to speed the process up by having a third order-taker work the lines, taking some pressure off the two at the counter. That turned out to be an incredibly bad calculation. As soon as the mobile orders started coming in, the kitchen staff went crazy. They'd *already* been overworked, and the owner's so-called solution only made matters worse. After a few insane noon hours, it was obvious that the last thing he needed was faster ordering. What he really needed, I guess, was more kitchen staff. We're not in the kitchen staff business, so we didn't see that."

The result? Well, the immediate result was that Micros lost the sale after it had been made. Since the handhelds were clogging the system, they had to be removed—and Micros's relationship with that client was almost destroyed.

"We did manage to salvage it," Elizabeth explained, "but only by going back to before square one, and digging out, bit by bit, what the owner's problem was. Eventually we helped him work his way to a real solution. But it had nothing to do with what he first 'had' to have."

Interior Desecration. Dave Laabs of McFarland Office Products and Business Interiors, whose eloquent comments on integration we cited in Chapter 1, agrees with Elizabeth's assessment.

"You can't just give a customer what he says he wants, no questions asked. Doing that is asking for major headaches down the line. We see this all the time in the office design business. Customers think they know exactly what they want. But they only know what they know, not what they don't know. It's our job as responsible vendors to fill them in, to help develop their Concept with them.

"We worked with a law firm recently where one of the partners had very vocal opinions about office design. 'I need this kind of desk here and that panel has to be this color and it has to go here. . . .' Listening to him reminded me of that crack about some famous writer: 'I wish I were as cocksure about anything as he is about everything.' But the partner didn't have a clue about workable design. There are interior decorators, and then there are interior desecrators, and he was definitely not in the first category. We could have just gone along—and wrecked the place. Instead, we told him that he was paying *us* for design. Made some suggestions, gave him choices—and the design came together. Helping him to develop a viable Concept—that was what worked.

"A lot of customers," Dave says, "go just for cosmetics. 'This filing cabinet will look fantastic in that corner.' They often forget the long-term logistical considerations that a supplier's questions can help them identify. When someone tells us she wants a certain desk, we don't just deliver it. We ask, 'Will this desk be holding a computer? What size? What about keyboard location? Would an adjustable desktop give you more flexibility?' And so on. We're not in the hardware delivery business. Our goal is to provide solutions for customers' problems. The hardware is just a means to that end, and we know how the means work better than they do.

"This doesn't mean just pushing the higher-priced hardware, either," Dave says. "That's a mistake novice salespeople make, confusing 'better' with 'more expensive' or 'higher commission.' Say that one of our customers is considering an individual cubicle design, and we discover, after looking at the work flow and level of interaction, that an open, bullpen design would be more appropriate. We'll recommend it even though the immediate return for McFarland is a lot less. The customer will get a better system than she thought she wanted, and that will be a long-term plus for us both."

DOING IT RIGHT: SWEEPING UP AFTER HANSEL AND GRETEL

One of our clients, Dan Salbego, is a senior territory manager for Fort Howard Corporation. His division sells recycled paper products–paper towels, toilet tissue, and cleanup wipes–to industrial accounts, hospitals, hotels, restaurants, and office buildings, including many of the skyscrapers in Chicago's downtown Loop. During a recent call on the head of maintenance for one of these landmark buildings, Dan employed the principle of understanding the Concept first to dislodge a long-entrenched competitive supplier.

"What most salespeople do," Dan told us, "is to say, 'Shift your business to us because our price is better.' Of course everybody wants to save money, and you *can* sell to price. But you can't assume that that's what the customer wants to hear. You've got to ask, and sometimes the answer will surprise you.

"Talking to the maintenance chief, I started out the way I always do now, by asking, 'What don't you like about your current system?' He didn't hesitate for a second: 'The mess,' he said. 'Every time you pull the paper towel out of the dispenser, it chews off little bits of paper and spits them on the floor. People come in, it gets on their shoes, and they track it into the hallways. It's like the bread crumbs that Hansel and Gretel trail behind them, only it's not bread but little chunks of towel. Half the day I follow people around with a vacuum or a broom.'

"What the guy was describing," Dan continued, "was what people in our industry call tabbing. It happens when the folded towels are too tight inside the dispenser, so that they bind and tear when they're pulled out. Of course it's a pain in the neck, but it's easy to fix. You insert an adapter to relieve the pressure, and in about thirty seconds your problem is solved.

"You should have seen the guy's face when I told him that. It was like *he* was Hansel and Gretel and I was leading him out of the woods. We got their business without even having to ask for it–and without having to play lowball with the competition. The solution he wanted was getting rid of the tabbing. Once I showed him how we could do that, price was not an issue."

BEYOND THE BIDDING GAME: MORE BENEFITS OF
UNDERSTANDING THE CONCEPT

Dan's observation about price is typical of our clients, and that's one of the great hidden benefits of understanding the Concept. If you solve a problem that's giving your customers heartburn, they'll very frequently be willing to pay top dollar. In fact, it's the sellers who have few solutions to offer–what Dan amusingly calls "quoting reps"–who are constantly butting heads over the issue of price. You sell yourself cheap either (1) when you have no choice or (2) when it's the only way you can distinguish yourself from the competition. The selling process that we outline in this book makes such desperate measures unnecessary. It may seem ironic, but it's true: Letting the customer's solution "control" the sale is a revenue enhancer.

A second advantage of understanding the Concept is that it establishes personal trust between you and your customers, and this trust is the basis of all reliable, long-term business alliances. Sterling Healthcare's Margaret Shiver speaks of a "respectful" process that honors the intelligence of all parties. Bob Mayes, Vice President of Sales for the Santa Fe development company Las Campanas, uses the same term: "What we aim for is respect between buyer and seller." A third client calls it a "process for adults." All of these comments point to the same truth: When you see your job as making your customers' problems go away, you and the customer meet as equals, logically committed to nurturing the ongoing relationship, and each other's business.

Third, understanding the customer's Concept helps you focus on corporate results–the concrete, bottom-line results that every business needs and that in most cases are intimately related to buyers' solution images. Whatever business issues your customer's company is wrestling with–from inventory control to more effective marketing strategies, from reducing downtime to improving automation–a focus on Concept will enable you to understand them better. This is critical because delivering results for customers is what brings in your revenue.

Finally, selling to Concept is actually *easier* than the ancient, Sisyphean task of pushing the product. In "product pushing," you're fighting for a foothold every minute, hoping desperately that you can persuade each customer to buy. In Conceptual Selling, that kind of pressure is off, as you investigate the customer's problems, ask questions, and explore the options. In a client-driven, mutually supportive atmosphere, Margaret Shiver says, you don't have to knock yourself out searching for a fit. Often the solution "bubbles naturally to the surface."

SELLING AS THE ART OF CONVERSATION

Not always, of course. And even when it happens, it never "just happens." It happens as a result of a conscious effort to listen—to hear what the customer is saying, not what you want to hear, and to do this even when the customer isn't being very helpful.

The sad truth is this. Some of the time customers aren't clear themselves what they're trying to accomplish, so they have difficulty articulating a Concept right from the start. In addition, there are language barriers between buyers and sellers. The salesperson's working vocabulary, especially in today's increasingly high-tech world, often turns on product-related, technical terms with which prospective buyers may or may not be familiar. Customers too may express themselves in specialized, industry-specific jargon that can baffle everybody but fellow specialists. Getting at the Concept, then, involves translation.

Sam Abia is a marketing analyst for our client SAS Institute, which deals in information systems software. "Ninety percent of the time," Sam says, "the customer knows what his problem is and what he wants to do, but he's using a different terminology than we are accustomed to, so we have to spend some time comparing terms, spelling our capabilities out for him in language he can relate to.

"Our software enables customers to access information quickly and more efficiently than they've been used to. They don't necessarily want to know the details about how our products do that, but they do want to know details about the results. You hear them say it all the time. 'If only I could have a report that comes out looking like this, with the volume figures here at the bottom and the credit history in a column over here...' They'd like you to snap your fingers and say 'zap,' so the paper jumps out on their desk like in the Wizard of Oz.

"When that happens," says Sam, "you have to translate, to talk them through it. This is what we can do, this is what we can't. What about this alternative? Have you considered these other formats? Correlating their Concept with our software is always a process of adjustment and revision. It doesn't just fall in your lap. You have to develop it. Which means a lot of give and take." In other words, conversation.

Even when customers do know right away what they want, they might be reluctant to let you in on the secret. Misperceptions about your company, loyalty to your competition, internal politics—for these and a hundred other reasons, customers might not want to share with you just what problem it is that's giving them ulcers. So you end up in the default mode of "talking up the product" because there doesn't seem to be anything else to talk about.

In addition, as Margaret Shiver's story indicates, the customer's Concept is highly subjective. It's driven not just by the business results the customer expects to achieve, but also by what we call personal *Wins*. Not only are these Wins–as our clients never tire of telling us–notoriously difficult to ferret out and identify. In addition, different decision makers in a complicated sale always have different personal Wins, and therefore different solution images. Getting into one person's head is hard enough. When you're trying to sell to three or four different Concepts at once, it might feel as though you're selling to a multiple personality.

We acknowledge the difficulty. Like you, we've been there. That's why, to show how your sales organization can, and must, get a hold on your customer's buying decision process, we return frequently in this book to Concept and Wins, and why we emphasize the importance of questioning in pinning them down.

We can illustrate that importance with a client's success story.

"YOU DON'T KNOW WHAT YOU'RE SELLING UNTIL YOU ASK"

David Duff is a major account executive for AEI Music, which sells customized music programs to restaurants and retail outlets, including such market leaders as the Olive Garden, the Gap, and Banana Republic. Recently he told us about his company's experience with a major toy retailer that had been using a competitor's service for almost twenty years.

"They had been in there since the Carter administration, when I was in grade school. The customer had gotten used to things as they were, and on the surface it seemed that everything was going fine, until we started asking questions. This is standard procedure for us, because what we sell, really, isn't taped music. We sell atmosphere, background, feelings. The official term is 'ambience,' but that's just another way of saying surroundings–emotional surroundings. So we've got to talk to our customers about what surroundings they want. Inevitably, that also means asking about their current service. It's partly, 'What kind of atmosphere do you want your music to create?' and partly 'How well do you feel your current system is doing that?'

"With the toy people, when we started asking questions like that, we discovered one area where they were very dissatisfied–and it didn't have anything to do directly with the ambience issue. It turned out that their current vendor had an incredibly complicated fee structure, and billing formulas to match. As a result, the toy company got four different bills every month. It was driving their accountants crazy, and it had been for years.

"It was bad all over, but especially when it came to service calls. Some cost $45, others cost $65, and to the customer's accountants it seemed the vendor had made the distinction by rolling dice. When we came out with a set service fee of $55 a call, they couldn't believe it. A problem that had irritated them for years had suddenly gone away.

"And it was a problem, ironically, that we were totally unaware of before we made that first call and opened up the questioning. The lesson is pretty clear: You don't know what you're selling until you ask. Pay attention to the customer's problems—that makes the difference.

"We went in thinking we would try to offer this customer a background sound that made shopping for toys a great, enjoyable experience. It turned out that wasn't what he was looking for at all. He figured he already had that. What he didn't have was billing that he understood. We were able to meet that Concept, so we got the sale."

With a "talk-talk-talk" approach, that Concept would never have emerged, and Dave's company might never have replaced the incumbent. The fundamental message is untraditional but clear. In selling real solutions rather than prefabricated ones, you have to fight your natural inclinations and let the customer do the bulk of the talking.

Here's a practical tip for making that advice a reality. In our Conceptual Selling programs, we introduce a simple but powerful technique—*Golden Silence*—that we recommend you try on your next sales call. In practicing Golden Silence, you simply *pause* for three or four seconds at two different points in the call: after every question that you pose to the customer, and again after every response that you get back.

The first pause, which we call Golden Silence I, allows the customer to think through a relevant reply, without being hustled toward the close—or getting a feeling of being hustled. The second pause, Golden Silence II, gives you, the seller, an equal opportunity for thoughtful reflection. The result of these two pauses is a better conversational flow—something that the "talk-talk-talk" style invariably destroys.

Good listening also implies letting the customer set the conversational agenda. That's something that traditional sellers are reluctant to do, because they think it risks letting the call get "out of control." But the most accomplished sellers know it's central to success. There are hard data on this point. In a recent study of top sales professionals, a consulting firm found that high achievers were almost twice as likely as average achievers to adapt their selling to a customer's "change of agenda." Thus your job as a professional seller is twofold:

1. *First, ask questions designed to help the customer articulate a solution image.*
2. *Second,* shut up and listen.

We realize that this is pretty general advice. If you've been exposed to sales training that stresses "being a good listener" so that you can identify your customers' "hot buttons" and overcome their objections, it may even sound like familiar advice. It's not. In Chapter 5, when we discuss your customers' decision-making process, we'll return to the importance of questioning and active listening. There you'll see again that we take a uniquely client-driven approach to the "sales conversation"–one that allows the customer to take the initiative, because that's the only way you'll find out "what you're selling."

You'll see there why we agree with the sales manager who once told us, "Asking pertinent questions always gets the answers you're looking for. They may not be what you want to hear, but that's why you're asking." You'll see, too, why we think Dan Salbego has it right when he says, "It's the person who talks the least who usually wins."

PART TWO

SEVEN DEADLY SCENES:
USING
THE SALES PROCESS
TO SOLVE
YOUR BUSINESS
NIGHTMARES

3

PROLOGUE:
REAL PROBLEMS,
REAL SOLUTIONS

"Your business card might say that you're in sales, but your work has got to show that you're in problem-solving."
–Dan Salbego
Senior Territory Manager
Fort Howard Corporation

SELLING IS A PROBLEM-SOLVING PROFESSION. Its entire focus is, or ought to be, on eliminating whatever is giving customers headaches by providing solutions that make their business run more smoothly. But that noble end is often frustrated. Solving customers' problems is a difficult process, one that entails countless migraines of its own. Hence the combative, tension-laden metaphors of sales conversations. We go "out in the trenches" to "fight for the order." We "battle" the competition and recount "war stories."

Well, nobody ever said selling was a stroll in the park. If it were, only strollers would do it. In fact the sales profession attracts just the opposite kind of person. Its ranks are filled with people who are stimulated by challenges and who welcome the excitement of meeting and overcoming obstacles. Maybe it's predictable that so many sales professionals play golf—the game one cheerless critic called "a good walk spoiled." If you've caught the golfing bug yourself, you know better. The excitement of golf is the opportunity to unspoil the course, to weave through the traps successfully to that eighteenth "close."

Of course you can do that better if you know what's coming—if you've got a map of the course or have played it before. That's what we provide in this part of the book.

The seven deadly scenes we describe here are the revenue obstacles that come up again and again, like recurrent nightmares, in the daily work of every sales organization. We focus on them precisely because they're so common. Whatever your business and no matter how complex your sales, it is virtually guaranteed that you'll run into these seven problems, not occasionally but over and over in your career.

How do we know this? First, because in our years as sales professionals and corporate consultants, these are the scenes that have most often given us headaches. Second, because they're the headaches that our clients always bring up when they come to our programs and say "Make this one go away."

Why only seven? If selling is such a difficult and complicated profession, isn't it simplistic to reduce its problems to this handful?

Not at all. We're focusing on recurrent patterns, not freak horror stories. As you read about these seven major problem areas, we don't promise that you'll gasp in recognition and shriek, "That's exactly what happened to us in the Robbins fiasco!" We do promise this: Most of the problems you routinely encounter in your organization can be identified as variations of these seven scenes. You'll find, too, that the organizational process that we present for making them go away will work just as effectively for you as for us and our clients.

"Organizational" is the key word here. In Chapter 1, we stressed the value of a team approach–of getting *everybody*, salespeople and non-salespeople alike, onto the same page–in bringing coherence to the management of account revenue. You may recall Brad Teed, the Documentum system engineer who spoke of "putting on his sales representative's cap" when bringing his technical expertise to a customer's problem. That's an example of "full organizational commitment." It can happen only when the culture says "Sales is the driver." To resolve these seven deadly scenes, it *must* happen.

THE SEVEN DEADLY SCENES: AN OVERVIEW

In presenting these nightmare scenarios, we follow roughly the sequence of a typical selling cycle. We begin with problems usually encountered in the early stages of contact with a customer, move to those that hinder the smooth evolution of the buy-sell relationship, and finish with those that arise near the close, or even after the sale. But the sequence is neither prescriptive nor definitive. It's presented not as a "step-by-step diagram to success" but as a fresh perspective on all-too-familiar sand traps. Here they are, in the order that we'll be addressing them.

First Scene: "Who's in Charge Here?"

For decades, sales literature has talked about the importance of getting to the "decision maker"–presumably a single person in the buying organization whose attitude can make or break your chance of making a sale. This person is relatively easy to identify if you're a door-to-door drummer and the buying organization is Mr. and Mrs. Jones. But when the customer is a multidivision corporation with fifty vice presidents, getting to the decision maker is like walking a maze: you can't get to that person if you don't know who, or where, he or she is.

In Chapter 4, we point a way through the maze, but we begin by rejecting the fiction of a single decision maker. In large account sales, there just isn't any such animal. We define the three separate decision-making functions, or *Buying Influence* roles, that exist in every sales scenario, and we explain why getting to the people playing these roles often requires the development of a fourth Buying Influence that we call a *Coach*. We show how salespeople who focus on roles, rather than titles, dramatically improve their chances of surviving in the labyrinth. And we show you how our corporate clients, in scenes set from Utah to the former Yugoslavia, have utilized our Buying Influence process to make sense of even the most Byzantine corporate structures.

Second Scene: "What Do They Want, Anyway?"

What do you do when customers just don't get it–when they don't see the value of your perfect solution, or when they seem congenitally committed to raising objections? We've all encountered customers who, faced with a seemingly ideal fit between our products or services and their needs, remain unconvinced and adamantly unwilling to sign.

In Chapter 5, we show you how these customers are driven not by some mysterious mule gene, but by a perception that their personal interests will not be served by agreeing to the perfect solution you're offering their company. We revisit the principle of the customer's *Concept* that we introduced in Chapter 2, expanding it to focus on the logical decision-making process that customers need to follow to get to that Concept. Then we explain why customers' unstated, personal Wins are every bit as crucial to their satisfaction as the business results that they acknowledge they're looking for. Chapter 5 shows how managing every sale toward a Win-Win outcome is the only way to ensure long-term revenue stability.

Third Scene: "Can't You Come Back Tomorrow?"

In principle we endorse the old chestnut "The customer is always right." But let's face it. Some customers don't deserve that kind of generosity. They're cantankerous, demanding, unresponsive, and so cocky about being in the driver's seat that they play you like a puppet on a string. In Chapter 6, we show you how to identify these "problem children" at the beginning, not the middle of a sales cycle, and how to make judicious, pragmatic decisions about the value of their business to your business. It takes more than selling to make a sale. It takes the investment of numerous company resources. You need a process that can measure this investment against the return individual customers give you.

Following the process explained in Chapter 6, you'll be able to measure your customers against an *Ideal Customer profile*, so that you can tell in advance which prospects you can actually move to Win-Win and which ones get a secret thrill out of seeing you lose. We show how important it is to get incremental *commitment* from each Buying Influence as the sales process evolves, and how to identify the signs that it's time to pull out.

Above all, we show you how to avoid Pyrrhic victories–those dubious achievements that leave you muttering to yourself, "One more victory like this and we're out of business."

Fourth Scene: "Is This Really Your Rock-Bottom Price?"

As competition increases and customers become more savvy about products, they also become more demanding and more price-conscious. If your company isn't clearly differentiated from your toughest competition, you can easily end up playing the no-win game of lowball, jockeying desperately to underbid indistinguishable rivals for the privilege of parading your products before a lukewarm public.

In Chapter 7, we provide a path out of this mess. By focusing on improving your position in the *Buy-Sell Hierarchy*, you will see how value-added selling reduces the importance of price and enables you to deal with your customers as an equal, not as a beggar, because you give them what the competiton does not: help with their business. With the emergence of "consultative selling," the business world is hungry for a practical guide for replacing the shackles of price with the freedom of partnering. In Chapter 7, we provide that practical guide, and we show how making it work involves, once again, the commitment of your entire organization.

Fifth Scene: "Why Didn't We See That Coming?"

In Chapter 8, we encounter one of the most painful scenes in all of selling: the loss of a major piece of business that you thought was in your pocket. Losing business in this way is "snatching defeat from the jaws of victory." We show you how the common explanations for why it happens–whether they focus on price or on internal sabotage–never get to the real reason that the business was lost. That reason, we show, always has to do with missing information.

To secure the essential information you need to keep both the customers that are "in your pocket" and your more tenuous customers, we provide a detailed *Situation Analysis* format. And we show you how Situation Analysis gives you 360-degree vision, so you will never again be blindsided by missing information.

Sixth Scene: "How Did We Let Them Get Away?"

Chapter 9 focuses on the *follow-up snafu*, when your company drops the ball after the touchdown, by failing to provide the client with adequate support and service. Here we revisit the concepts of "full organizational commitment" and the Buy-Sell Hierarchy, showing how anything less than white-hot attention to supporting clients results, inevitably, in the erosion of even rock-solid accounts. We stress that you can lose millions in a sale even after the ink is dry; and we explain, with examples from Miller Heiman's own experience with client support, how regular follow-through is an essential part of the sales process.

Seventh Scene:
"Does Anybody Have a Twenty-Five-Hour Day?"

How do you manage your most precious resource, selling time, so that no customer gets shortchanged and you don't go crazy? Chapter 10 confronts an issue that is as old as selling itself, and that only the best organizations have been able to get a handle on: setting priorities among the various types of selling work that have to be done to keep your revenue flowing—and to do this in the rough-and-tumble world of key accounts and huge territories.

After describing the four types of work that always have to be done—prospecting, qualifying, covering the bases, and closing—we provide a nontraditional answer about what to do when, which brings the security of process into territory management while eliminating the thrills and chills of boom-and-bust cycles.

MANAGING THE SALES TEAM

In identifying support and service as essential to the sales process, we are reaffirming the value of teamwork as a key to selling success. Here's where we bid good-bye to the analogy with golf. Even in the Ryder Cup, golf remains a fundamentally individual sport. In the old days of drummers and snake oil, maybe selling was too. Not anymore. To avoid the revenue sand traps of the twenty-first century, your entire staff must contribute to the sales effort. As numerous articles in the business press have been pointing out, the best companies are in the early stages of a "customer-driven selling culture," where all corporate efforts, from the boardroom to the stockroom, are focused unambiguously on securing account revenue.

In Part III of this book, we give examples of how this new selling culture operates at Miller Heiman and at our client companies—and how it has begun to spell revenue success around the nation. Here we want to emphasize only one feature of team selling: the central role that must be played by management—both line sales management and senior management—in ensuring the ongoing success of a revitalized sales process. To that end, in each discussion of the seven deadly scenes, we include a series of guidelines that hands-on managers can use in applying our principles to their own team selling. We provide, for each scenario, questions that can facilitate the uncovering of "Red Flag" danger spots—and that can prepare you to turn those threats into sales opportunities.

That's the organizational logic behind what follows. Let's move now to the first of our seven deadly scenes.

4

WHO'S
IN CHARGE
HERE?

"You can't tell the players without a program."
—Traditional American saying

"You think you can keep track of everything in your head, but it doesn't work that way. Writing it down helps you see how many players are really involved. It showed me that my so-called final authority wasn't playing that role at all."
—Robyn Crebs
Account Representative
Browning Ferris-BFI

WHEN ACCOUNT REPRESENTATIVE ROBYN CREBS agreed to be interviewed for this book, she had just made BFI's prestigious President's Club, which recognizes excellence in marketing and sales during the course of a year. Her success story illustrates how following a systematic sales process can help you overcome perhaps the single most common problem in corporate selling today–the inability to identify, and get to, the relevant players.

Robyn joined the Utah branch of the waste-handling firm in 1993, after a decade and a half of secretarial work and then a brief stint selling paper products. One of the first and most challenging accounts that she got at BFI was a huge regional food warehousing complex. When she first went on site, she found the warehouser's current system a shambles. "They had over thirty separate Dumpsters inside the warehouse," she recalled, "which were emptied every morning into a truck. With that many pickup points, the system was constantly clogged, inefficient–and dirty. They were paying for an incredible amount of man hours, and getting constant spillage."

"What we suggested as a replacement was two large compacters, one at each end of the complex. Each one would be run by one person, and the two would be serviced by BFI once a week. It was a proposal that would clean up the mess *and* cut costs."

In spite of being able to offer this seemingly ideal solution, however, Robyn soon encountered problems of her own. The principal problem was that the warehouser's head of maintenance claimed to be content with the current system and refused to consider funding such a major switch. "I worked for two years on this guy and just got nowhere," Robyn says. "I was about to give it up as a loss when I took Strategic Selling."

Strategic Selling is Miller Heiman's flagship sales consulting program, a two-day workshop in which participants set strategies for problem sales. The account Robyn brought to the program was, not surprisingly, the "stuck" warehouse account, and during the two-day program–it ran in the spring of 1995–she learned an entirely new process for analyzing the components of the account, including a method for targeting all the key players, not just the maintenance head who was giving her grief.

Here's what she learned that helped her make the sale.

First, the head of maintenance wasn't in charge of the decision. He was important, yes, but he didn't have final say over whether or not his company would shift to BFI. The person who had that say was a senior buyer—a person whom Robyn had never met, and whose existence our process of analysis helped her to discover.

Second, the maintenance head was opposed to the project for a simple reason: he thought that the purchase of a new system would demonstrate a history of his own incompetence. "Why," he was afraid his boss would ask, "didn't you fix this before?"

Third, although the maintenance head was obviously not crazy about having Robyn talk to his superior, there was another person—someone Robyn knew from her days selling paper—who knew the senior buyer well and was willing to put Robyn into contact with him.

Working with those three new pieces of information, Robyn went back to the field with a refined strategy. Once the process had helped her identify who really had the authority to approve the sale, she contacted the senior buyer and replayed the proposal. Since lower costs and a cleaner house were exactly what he had been looking for, he was eager to make the change. Within three months, a deal that had been stalled for two years went through, and Robyn got credit for securing a customer that is now the Utah branch's single largest account.

Robyn's success was impressive but not unique. One of her senior colleagues, Environmental Waste Manager Lou Croce, tells a similar success story about BFI's recent securing of a mammoth contract to clean up a contaminated area along the Ohio River. On the surface, the complexity of the playing field was truly bewildering. "Following a referendum," Lou explains, "plans were laid for a riverboat casino complex to be put on a park site where the level of contamination was unknown. Since environmental management is our area of expertise, the technical parts of the project were relatively easy. Testing the soil, arranging to cart away 8,000 yards of it, finding a suitable landfill—a big project, but a straightforward one."

What wasn't so straightforward was the kaleidoscope of players that Lou and his BFI team had to contend with. "Apart from the voters," Lou says, "there were people from all levels of government—from municipalities to the feds—to be dealt with. There was the construction firm hired to build the site, the casino owner who had hired it, the owners of the riverboat that was going to be the centerpiece of the complex, an environmental management corporation—and a whole range of local interest groups that, for one reason or another, opposed the whole idea. Handling all of those variables was incredibly complicated, but it was also absolutely essential if we wanted the contract."

Lou's handling of all these pieces paid off handsomely, not just in the soil-removal contract, which was worth several hundred thousand dollars, but also—as is often the case—in further business down the line. Among the "extras" that BFI realized as a result of its diligence were waste- and trash-removal contracts for the casino itself, for the accompanying riverboat, and for a nearby hotel.

Or consider the example of Air-Shields's Jackie Smith. Air-Shields supplies hospitals and clinics with perinatal technology, including incubators, monitors, and transport isolettes. Jackie has been either first or second in sales volume for three of the past four years, and much of his success, like that of Robyn Crebs and Lou Croce, is attributable to his skill in sorting out the field.

"Some of our equipment," he says, "can be $12,000 to $15,000 a unit, so our sales run from $15,000 to $500,000. At all levels, there are always a lot of players involved. On a typical sale, there's going to be a clinical administrator who's probably, although not certainly, going to give final approval. There will be a clinical nurse specialist, a nurse manager, and a couple of doctors, all functioning as 'user buyers.' Then there will be the various 'technical buyers'—anybody from a biomedical manager to an information systems specialist. All of these people have to be covered, and all of them sold. On sales where we've won against stiff competition, we've done that well. On the sales we've lost, it's frequently because we haven't covered all the bases."

ONE IS NEVER ENOUGH

Jackie has it exactly right. The decisive word in covering the bases is "all." If there's one error that does in more sales than any other, it's probably the tendency to talk to only one person, and to assume that if this person is sold, everything else will fall into place. That works only when the single person is a hermit, and the last time we looked, there weren't any hermits in corporate life. Typically, in every business-to-business transaction, there are many individuals whose input, in one way or another, can affect the outcome. Covering all those bases is critical to success.

Salespeople routinely ignore this fact, for two reasons.

The first reason is a type of inertia that's allied to our comfort level. We tend to contact people we've contacted before. We concentrate on selling the players we already know: those to whom we've already been introduced, who we know (or who we think) like us, or who have bought from us before. That was Robyn's error before she attended the Strategic Selling program. She kept talking to the head of maintenance because she already had a relationship with him. It was a bad relationship, yes, but at least she knew the guy.

The second reason that we don't cover all the players is the conventional wisdom about the lone "decision maker"–the person in charge who can make or break a given deal. For years salespeople have been told that one key to success is getting through to this ultimate mover and shaker.

This proverbial wisdom isn't totally wrong, because every sales transaction does require a final approval, and it's essential to connect with the person whose authority can release it; that, of course, is how Robyn won her contract. But the "decision maker" concept is so comfortingly simplistic that it obscures essential complexities of selling today, and this often gives the seller a false sense of security. The problem is that locating the final authority is a necessary but insufficient criterion for a sale. Even if you've gotten to Mr. or Ms. Big, that's still just one person–and that's not enough when you need three or four approvals to pass "Go."

SACKING THE QUARTERBACK

We can clarify this problem with a sports analogy.

On a football team, the quarterback is in charge of the plays. He's the player to whom the ball is snapped. He's the one who runs with it, hands it off to another runner, or passes it downfield. He's the operational leader of the offensive side, and because of that he's the chief target of the defending line. Their collective goal, every time he gets the ball, is to get to him as quickly as possible and tackle, or "sack," him. Sacking the quarterback is a defensive lineman's dream. If he does that consistently, it defines him as a success.

Because of the hoopla that now surrounds quarterback-sacking–including many sackers' preening little victory dances–a novice spectator might be forgiven for supposing that the only thing important in football is what happens to the quarterback. That's the attitude many fans bring to the game, and it's the reason that quarterbacks may earn double the salaries of their teammates.

But the quarterback, as important as he is, is not the team. In order for this star performer to perform effectively, ten other people wearing the same jerseys have to perform their tasks just as professionally. He may direct the plays, but he does not–he cannot–implement them by himself. A successful offensive play is the result of multiple performances, and those performances are the result of multiple decisions.

The same is true of a successful defense. When a defensive team throws the Dallas Cowboys' quarterback Troy Aikman for a loss, it's not because everybody on that team has focused on the sack. It's because eleven professionals have performed their separate functions so effectively that the synergistic result is more than the sum of its parts. In fact, if the Cowboys' opponents had tunnel vision—if they focused only on "getting Aikman"—by definition they would be ignoring their other responsibilities, and the Cowboys would win the Super Bowl every year.

We've gone on at some length with this football analogy partly because, as you already know, we believe that teamwork is a critical element of good selling. But we are also making a point about key decision makers, and about the dangers of assuming that any single person is "in charge." Targeting only the "quarterback" of a buying organization (or a person you erroneously think is the quarterback) is a recipe not for focus but for missed opportunities, because in corporate sales today, two things are clear:

- *Successful sales happen at **multiple** sites. Every close is the outcome of multiple decisions, and these decisions are rarely made by the same key person.*
- *The people making these decisions are **moving targets**. Their decision-making functions change from sale to sale, and sometimes even within a given sales cycle. There's no such thing as someone who is always the "quarterback." That role, and its attendant authority, is constantly shifting.*

If you're involved in corporate selling, this isn't news. You already know that the typical buying organization sometimes resembles a maze or a hall of mirrors. You've probably had the thrill of presenting a major proposal to a room containing everybody but the manager with signatory authority. Perhaps you've spent weeks or months calling on an account's "key" player, only to discover that somebody else signs the checks. You're probably familiar with corporate versions of the backfield fake, where you exhaust yourself, and your company's resources, scrambling after somebody who doesn't have the ball.

If any of these scenarios sound familiar to you, you would probably benefit from a selling version of a program: a framework that would help you to identify the key players, to understand their individual roles in the sale, and perhaps most important, to keep track of decision-making authority when a player *shifts roles*—when the approval authority "drifts" up or down the organization.

That's the program we presented to Robyn, and it's the same program that we present to you in this chapter. By taking a uniquely dynamic look at the concept "decision maker," it shows how to avoid being suckered by organizational razzle-dazzle, and how to identify, consistently, the yeses that count.

THE THREE BUYING FUNCTIONS

In every sale, there are always *three* of these yeses–three distinct approvals that must always happen before any sales transaction becomes a reality. The yeses come from three distinct decisions, and each of those decisions plays a different role in the sale.

Notice that we are *not* saying "There are three decision makers in every sale." You know as well as we do that, in complex sales, there may be five, or ten, or twenty distinct individuals whose decisions may in some way affect the outcome. We're saying that, in every sale, there are three decision-making *functions* that must be performed, and that each of those functions must lead to a separate yes before that million-dollar contract can be signed. Those functions are *funding, performance assessment,* and *screening.*

Funding

Someone has to approve the budgetary expense that acceptance of your proposal will cost the company. In our programs, we call the person who performs this function for a given sales objective the *Economic Buying Influence,* or *Economic Buyer.*

Let's anticipate one misconception right away. When we use the short form *Buyer* rather than the more precise term Buying Influence, we do so merely for ease of expression. In Miller Heiman terminology, Buyer and Buying Influence are used interchangeably to reflect key people's ability to influence buying decisions. We're not referring to "store buyers," "purchasing agents," or any other individuals commonly associated with the procurement function. A store buyer might indeed be a Buying Influence. But it's rare that he or she would play the role of Economic Buyer.

Performance Assessment

We're speaking here of the buying company's assessment of how your product or service will perform. Since this is logically the concern of the person who will be using the product or service in his or her own work situation, we refer to "performance assessors" as *User Buying Influences,* or *User Buyers.*

Screening

The third function is the checking–and often the checking out–of potential vendors on the basis of how well, or how poorly, they meet specifications. The people who perform this often negative function base their decisions on various technicalities. Technicalities must be met in technical or technological areas; in the areas of delivery, pricing, and legal issues; and in many other areas. In Strategic Selling, we call all the people who screen for technicalities *Technical Buying Influences*, or *Technical Buyers*.

It's important to make one clarification up front. No company has an Economic or User Buyer per se. It has people who perform those functions–or, as we commonly say, *play those roles*–for individual sales and individual buying decisions. Identifying the Economic Buyer for a given sale means finding the person who releases the funds *for that sale*. There's no such thing as the Random Company's Economic Buyer, because the person who screens out vendors on one sale might have final approval authority on another. That's why zeroing in on titles (purchasing agent, vice president) can actually lead you off in the wrong direction–like chasing a quarterback who has long ago handed off the ball. As one of Robyn Crebs's colleagues at BFI, Environment Waste Manager Lou Croce, puts it bluntly: "Titles mean nothing."

In this book, as in our corporate programs, we help you to find the people playing certain roles. There are always three of these roles, and they are always "filled." In every sale, no matter how big or how small, someone funds it, someone (or more than one person) uses it, and someone (or more than one person) screens.

And every one of those people has to be covered.

THE UNCOVERED BASE: INVITATION TO A LOSE

In baseball, an uncovered base is an invitation for a runner on the opposing team to advance around the diamond–to steal a base or possibly to score a run. You give a similar invitation to your competition when you fail to "cover a base" with a Buying Influence: that is, when you fail to identify, contact, and win over every single person who is (or who might be) playing a Buying Influence role. Whether there are three or thirty of these players, you're taking a risk by leaving any one of them up to chance. When you leave a base uncovered, one of three things happens:

Loss of the Sale

This is the most obvious outcome, although in the long run it may not be the most painful one. In the most common variant, the salesperson misidentifies or fails to contact the Economic Buyer, believing wrongly that a lower-level player has final approval. Sales can also be lost, however, by ignoring other Buying Influences, in the fanciful hope that *only* the Economic Buyer counts.

Sabotage

You make the sale, but the solution you put in doesn't work, because you've failed to get buy-in from the people who have to make it operational. Typically, these are the customer's User Buying Influences, people who could make it work if they wanted to—and if you'd asked them.

Buyer's Revenge

You make the sale but live to regret it down the line, because the Buyers you've ignored kill your chances for solid future business. We'll explain this a little more fully in Chapter 5. The basic point is that Buyer's Revenge, like sabotage, is the reward you get for leaving a Buying Influence uncovered. The lesson of both variants is the same: *Unsold Buyers undo sales.*

THE ECONOMIC BUYER: THE FINAL WORD

Now let's profile the people who usually fill the three roles.

When salespeople talk about getting to the "key" decision maker, it's usually an Economic Buyer they have in mind. The people performing this function are typically highly placed in their organizations, and they focus on the organization's growth and stability. They are experts (or are believed to be experts) in risk management and risk avoidance, and they therefore strive to be judicious in the disbursement of funds. This doesn't mean that they are nervous Nellies or penny-pinchers—only that they focus on the company's bottom line. Their decisions necessarily reflect that concern.

An Economic Buyer's function is to give final approval. But people playing this role can also say no, and in the cases where this occurs, there is no appeal. The Economic Buyer by definition has the last word. That word can be "Sign the papers" or "Proposal denied."

People playing the role of Economic Buyer base their approval or denial not on products per se, but on what impact those products can have on the firm's bottom line. This goes back to what we said in Chapter 2 about people buying the *expectation of results*. The results that interest the person in charge of the funds are, logically and inevitably, related to *return on investment*. So when you sell to a person playing the role of Economic Buyer, you must help him or her to answer the question, "If I agree to invest in your proposal, what return will we get?"

Two wrinkles. First, although the Economic Buyer is defined as the single individual who has both approval and veto power over your proposal, sometimes this function is handled by a group or committee. In cases like that we speak of the group as the Economic Buyer, and we point to the necessity of getting its collective approval. Yet even here, we have found that there's usually one member who has a little more say within the group than the other members—a committee chair, for example, if you're selling to the government. Such an unofficial leader may be, to paraphrase George Orwell, "a little more equal" than the others. In that case you have to sell both to the group and to this principal.

The second wrinkle: Economic Buyers are protected. Because of their typically high placement in their organizations, their calls and meetings are screened, and they're usually hard to get to. Often, as Robyn's story showed, a Technical Buyer will act as a wall between the Economic Buyer and your proposal. Or the Economic Buyer just "won't see sales reps." It's an irritating problem, we admit, but it does have solutions, and we'll address them directly in Chapter 7, on price competiton.

USER BUYERS: ON THE JOB

The main question that User Buyers ask is, "How will this work?" Unlike the person acting as Economic Buyer, they are very concerned with the day-to-day operation of your product or service. The reason is simple. If you deliver as promised, their jobs are smoother. If your proposed solution backfires, it's the User Buyer, personally, who is left facing the negative consequences.

A friend of ours recently went shopping for a snowblower. Looking at one floor model, he was approached by a young clerk who threw him a blizzard of numbers—horsepower, compression ratios, and the like—which our friend imagined were supposed to dazzle him into buying. "Son," he said politely, "you can save your breath. Just tell me if this machine can remove two feet of snow from a driveway that's thirty feet long and ten feet wide."

It was a classic User Buyer's question—and it covered all that he really wanted to know. When the young man answered, "Sure," our friend said, "Deliver it."

The interest of the User Buyer is the job to be done. In corporate sales, however, there may be many jobs that are affected, positively or negatively, by a given proposal. This means that more than one person may have an interest in performance, and that all of them may function as User Buyers. In fact, that's typical in business-to-business selling. Your role as a salesperson is to identify *all* those people whose personal performance could be affected by your company's proposal–and to be sure that you can deliver what each of them needs.

TECHNICAL BUYERS: GUARDING THE DOOR

Nobody we know is crazy about Technical Buyers. Their job is to screen potential vendors–as in "screen out"–and to most professional sellers, they're like the six-foot-five doorman who lives for the joy of keeping you out in the cold. As our friend Ross Mitchell, who hosts the morning news on a Reno radio station, puts it, the Technical Buyer's job is to "come up with the short list."

These guardians at the gate may come dressed in various uniforms. Some Technical Buyers are technology wizards, devoted to numbers and cutting-edge, high-tech spec sheets. These folks actually understand compression ratios, and they perform their role by calibrating you out of the running. Others, however, are experts in finance or law, in service requirements or price or government regulations. Anyone who can recommend you, or show you the door, on the basis of product or service specifications is performing the function of a Technical Buyer. Hence, even more than User Buyers, Technical Buyers tend to come in droves.

Dealing with Technical Buyers is never a cakewalk, but it's something a salesperson cannot avoid. Your best preparation for handling these sticklers for detail is to become intimately familiar with the details of your product. It's the product itself that the Technical Buyer is judging. The better you know it, the better you can anticipate objections.

READING THE PROGRAM: A CLIENT EXAMPLE

How do these three buying functions play out on the ground? And how valuable is it to be able to identify them?

One answer comes from a client based in Louisville, Kentucky. Mike Wyant, a registered pharmacist, is employed as a pharmacy manager by Syncor International, a distribution group working in alliance with Du Pont to supply hospitals and cardiology clinics with radioactive drugs or, as they're often called, "nuclear" pharmaceuticals. When you hear him explain how Syncor approaches its clients, you understand the growing complexity of the medical market as well as the usefulness of the process we've just outlined in understanding the functions of individual players.

"We're basically a nuclear pharmacy," explains Mike, "like a Walgreen's that stocks only items with an extremely short shelf life. Because the products we deliver are so technical and so specialized, we deal with sophisticated players and a *very* specific market.

"The people we talk to most often are nuclear medicine technologists. They're the ones who administer the diagnostic tests–dynamic lung scans, for example–that utilize the Du Pont line of radioactive tracers. For years they were practically the only people we dealt with. We would seldom see the physicians who had ordered the tests, or the purchasing people who had signed the budget allotments. We didn't have to. Until recently, nobody questioned such purchases. So we dealt with technologists who served in a dual role, as Technical Buyers and User Buyers.

"With the current diversification of health services and the increased competition for patients, that's all changed. More and more, people at the administrative level are becoming involved in technical decisions. When your census is down, Medicare and HMOs are breathing down your neck, and you're trying to run at a profit, you have no choice. For us this means that the playing field is getting crowded. There are people suddenly emerging from the hospital woodwork who a decade ago you barely knew existed. They're having an impact, day to day, on our business.

"The same test that Dr. Smith ordered without comment ten years ago now has to be approved at a much higher level. And sometimes Dr. Smith doesn't get her way. If the director of radiology wants a cheaper test, or if the vice president of purchasing wonders why *any* test is needed, Syncor's sales are in peril even though our traditional contacts are still hot for our products. More and more we've got to contact the Economic Buyers– on our own behalf as well as that of the physicians–to show them that the testing costs are warranted."

Three lessons may be drawn from Mike's example.

1. *First, the example underscores our point about the presence of three separate functions in every complex sale. Every time one of Syncor's medical clients buys a radioactive tracer, somebody pays for it, somebody checks it (and Syncor) against specifications, and somebody uses it.*

2. *Second, the people performing those functions have different reasons for doing business with Syncor. Those different reasons must be separately addressed. You can't sell an Economic Buyer on a User Buyer's reason.*

3. *Third, the funding function, and consequently the visibility of Economic Buyers, intensifies in times of budgetary constraint or perceived risk. In such situations, the role of Economic Buyer may "float" upward. In Mike's case, it can float upward to the vice presidential level.*

In a case that another client reported to us, the role of Economic Buyer actually floated, as it were, out the door. Mark Starr, a BFI district sales manager, confirmed something that our experience has proved time and again: identifying Buying Influences, even in solid, existing accounts, can be especially problematic—and especially valuable—at contract renewal time. "When you're on a two- or three-year contract cycle," Mark says, "you can never assume that the original players haven't changed. We have a contract coming up for review this year, and we just found out that the guy who was company president when we wrote the original contract has retired. The new president wants to put the whole thing up for bid.

"In cases like this—and there are plenty of them—we have to start all over, to reintroduce ourselves. We have to deal with a whole new slate of players, or at least a slate of old players with very different responsibilities. We use the concept of Buying Influence to remap the field. It helps us to find out who's there, who's gone, and who we have to deal with *now* to keep the business."

The "floating" of Economic Buyers is just one factor in the inherent variability of business-to-business selling, and it indicates the need to redetermine for each new selling objective which people are playing the critical decision-making roles. One of the commonest mistakes in selling to corporations is forgetting that rosters change not just year by year, but sometimes even within a given selling cycle. In these days of downsizing and reengineering, even if that million-dollar contract is not up for review, it can be fatal to assume that Tim, who bought from you last month, still has the authority (and the interest) to do so today. You determine that by remapping the field, and that process starts with roles.

Some of the players, we admit, may not give you much help here. Technical Buyers, for example, are notorious for attempting to convince the salesperson that only they can give final approval for a sale (Robyn's head of maintenance was one example), and the players who *can* give that approval don't wear name tags that say "Economic Buyer."

That's why you need a fourth "buyer."

THE FOURTH "BUYER": YOUR COACH

The three decision-making functions we've just described are always present. In every sale, you will find them already at work. The primary tasks of the seller are to identify each person who is performing these functions, and then to tailor the presentation or proposal so it answers that person's needs. We'll give recommendations for going about this in Chapter 5, when we discuss the importance of individual Win-Results.

First, though, we want to introduce a fourth Buying Influence—a vitally important individual we call a *Coach*.

Like the other Buying Influences, a Coach plays a precise role. That role is to provide data that will improve your company's selling position, for one reason and one reason only—*to help you make the sale.*

The definition of the Coach's function points to one very significant difference between this Buying Influence and the others. User Buyers, Technical Buyers, and Economic Buyers may be well disposed, antagonistic, or neutral to your sales proposal; your strategic goal is to get them on your side. But by definition a Coach is already on your side. For whatever reason, he or she wants you and your company to close the deal.

That is not the only difference, however, between the Coach and the other key players. Two other differences must be kept in mind.

First, while the other players are inherent to the sale—that is, they're already part of the decision-making process—the person who provides Coaching must be located and developed. There's always an Economic Buyer, for example, for every sale. But Coaches will emerge only if you seek them out, and if you ask them directly for the information you need to succeed. Coaches are therefore, in a sense, your creation.

Second, while the other Buying Influences in general exist within the buying organization, Coaches are not confined to that location. You may begin by asking for Coaching from the other Buying Influences, and in fact the ideal situation is to turn an Economic Buyer into a Coach. But our clients also find Coaches elsewhere, especially within their own organizations.

When we introduce the concept of Coaching in our programs, people often ask us for clarification. They want to know specifically *where* they should be looking for Coaches and *how* to develop relationships with Coaches once they're located. There's no standard, gimmicky answer to those questions, like "Look in accounting or marketing, and send people Super Bowl tickets." But there are some guidelines for identifying good Coaches, and a couple of tips we can share on how to develop them.

One guideline is to look for Coaches among people who have had profitable relationships with you in the past–people, in other words, with whom you have already established Win-Win relationships. No matter how well-placed Tina Jones may be in the Turbo account, she's not a good candidate for a Coach if the two of you have never met–or, worse, if your previous involvement with her turned out to be a Lose. This guideline applies wherever you're looking "geographically," that is, whether you're looking in the buying organization, in your own organization, or somewhere else.

A second guideline follows logically from the definition of a Coach. Look for people who would want you to make the sale because your solution provides a personal Win for them. Maybe Tina is a User Buyer whose job headaches will be eliminated by your solution. Maybe she's your own boss and is looking for a Win in the increased business you're developing. Or maybe she works for another one of the buying organization's suppliers and sees your solution as a prerequisite to some solution of her own. In all of these cases, the Coach sees a personal Win in the successful completion of your sale. If a "Coach candidate" doesn't see such a Win, you're looking in the wrong place.

One final guideline. When you're looking for Coaching within the buying organization, seek out potential Coaches as *high up* in the organization as you can. Since the Coach's role is to provide you with information about how to get your solution accepted, you want Coaching from people who are privy to that information, and who won't see giving it to you as a threat to their own power or reputation. At middle organizational levels, you sometimes encounter the perception that someone who gives a salesperson information is a traitor. It's not a logical perception, but it exists, and it can certainly impede your ability to understand the buying process. You're less likely to find it at upper levels, where managers are usually willing to make it easier for you to provide solutions that will make things easier for them.

Once you've found a possible Coach, how do you develop that person? Here we'll provide two related tips. The first is simple: Ask for *Coaching*. We mean that literally. Don't ask the potential Coach to do your selling for you or to "get you in." Use the word *Coaching*. It's a positive word in our culture, and it is a signal to the person hearing it that you need some information to do your own job more effectively. If the potential Coach has the information, that's the quickest way to find out if he or she is willing to share it.

A second tip is to ask open-ended questions designed to elicit the information you need. In addition to confirming or modifying information

you already have, good Coaches can be invaluable in providing new information–but they'll do that only if you give them the opportunity to talk.
Coaches are like anybody else: they don't know what you don't know.
You'll be most successful in developing good Coaching quickly if you ask
general questions about how the buying organization works–how it is
structured, who has what authority, and how this purchasing decision is
likely to be made.

The specific location where you find a Coach, then, is not ultimately of the greatest significance. What's important is that individual's
ability and willingness to serve as a source of information that can improve
your likelihood of delivering your proposed solution.

In order to perform this function effectively, a Coach has to be
more than simply a friend, an "introducer," or a source of information–
three types of individuals with whom Coaches are often confused. It's fine
to obtain information from people who like you personally or who can
usher you into an office that once seemed closed to you. But a Coach has
to meet certain criteria that such individuals may or may not be able to fulfill. Those criteria relate to an element of the selling process that is indispensable to the building of long-term relationships: *credibility*.

In macro business relationships, such as the ones you work to establish between your company and your customers, credibility is an operational "superglue." If the trust between you isn't mutual, things fall apart. On
a micro level, a similar "glue" is essential between you and your Coach–and
between the two of you and the buying organization. In a solid Coaching
relationship, there is a network of support that is composed of two inter-
woven lines of credibility.

First is the credibility that *you* need to have with the Coach. A
Coach has to trust you and your organization enough to put his or her own
reputation on the line by helping you. We've said that the Coach's function
is to help you win. But Coaches, like everybody else, will do that only if
they feel that your winning will lead to a Win for them too. No matter how
much your golf buddy Jim likes you, he's not going to give you good
Coaching unless he believes that your firm can deliver as promised to the
buying organization–and that his personal self-interest will be served by
the way you perform. If he likes you personally, fine, but that's not enough.
The Coach must want your proposed solution.

Second is the credibility that the *Coach* must have with the buying
organization. This is common sense. No matter how seemingly well-con-
nected an individual is to the key players in your customer's company, the
information that person gives you will be suspect, if not worthless, if the

company doesn't have a history of trust with him or her. That type of trust, of course, is typically established by the Coach's having been involved in previous transactions that turned out to be profitable for the buying organization.

One key to finding good Coaches, then, is respect that is based on the expectation of mutual *reward.* In developing a Coach, you as the seller need to ask not just "How can this person's expertise benefit me?" but also "How will my making this sale benefit the Coach?" Credibility leading to mutual advantage: it's the same process that you want to establish in growing any type of long-term relationship.

OPENING THE ROAD

Let's summarize what we've been saying with an example.

We've been improving people's sales process for nearly twenty years. In that time we've received our share of fan mail from clients who have used our principles to sort out key players and then target them individually on the basis of their roles. We've never had a thank-you that was more gratifying than the one we received recently from Robert Turfe. Rob is currently a management consultant with Diamond Technology Partners, Inc., a Chicago-based strategy and information technology consulting firm. When we first heard from him, however, he was a captain in the U.S. Army, stationed in the former Yugoslavia under the auspices of the United Nations.

As a logistics officer with the Corps of Engineers, Rob recognized soon after his assignment to the UN mission that a certain stretch of road along the Serbian border was extremely hazardous for soldiers escorting refugees. In rain and snow, especially, the surface became so slippery that the passage of emergency vehicles was seriously impeded, exposing them for prolonged periods to potential mortar fire. The road could be fixed, but it would take mission money, and attempts to sell this idea to United Nations headquarters had consistently met with budgetary disapproval.

Fortuitously, just before going to Yugoslavia, Rob had read *Strategic Selling,* which outlines much the same Buyer identification process that we describe in this chapter. "We can use this," the young officer said to himself—and he proceeded to target key "Buyers" on the basis of its principles.

"It wasn't too hard to identify the Economic Buyer," he told us. "The repair allocation we needed would run over $3 million, and money like that had to be okayed from the top. Approval had to come from the Fund Certifying Officer at UN headquarters—a guy who had vetoed the idea several times before. The odds were against me, I knew that. But I had to try."

Rob's try started with the identification of the other decision makers who, he knew, would also have to give their approval. "There were so many Buying Influences with personal agendas," he said, "that I felt I really had to get things down on paper. I set up these charts to outline the decision-making process, and I used the players who shared my views about safety to get through to the ones who were more resistant."

Among the players who didn't have to be sold were the military personnel who used the road every day. These User Buyers were directly concerned with performance: it was the people they were responsible for—soldiers and civilians—who were being put in jeopardy by the impassable road. Another User Buyer was the region's surgeon general. He liked the idea, Rob admitted wryly, both for professional and for personal reasons. "Opening the road meant that medical supplies would reach sick locals more readily. But it would also be a boost to his individual reputation—and, coincidentally, to his chances for reelection."

The Technical Buyers were harder to deal with, as these screening, gatekeeping Buyers often tend to be.

"There were two major blocks that we had to contend with," Rob recalled. "One was the person responsible for recommending all military projects to UN headquarters. He had identified our sector as the lowest of priorities—a view that the Economic Buyer had unfortunately bought into. The other was a Corps of Engineers planning officer. She resisted the project because her people hadn't thought of it. It was an obvious example of the 'not invented here' syndrome."

One factor in turning these negative influences around was Rob's skill in bringing the planning officer on board by suggesting that they add her name to the project report; that move gave her the recognition that she had been seeking, and it turned her from an impediment into a sponsor. Rob also developed a sophisticated Coaching network to help him demonstrate to the fiscally conservative Economic Buyer how an improved road system would vindicate the outlay of UN money. That network began with Rob's own chief of staff at the regional headquarters, who arranged an introduction to the fund-certifying officer. It included the surgeon general, a natural sponsor, and the troubled region's hands-on minister of defense, who was impressed by Rob's commitment to use local contractors to infuse money into the troubled economy, and who used his influence with those contractors to keep the price fair.

The result was that the long-resisted project got funded—and 90 percent completed before the arrival of the devastating Serbian winter.

The reason that Rob succeeded where others had failed had virtually nothing to do with the value of his "product." The improvement project had always been a good idea; what had repeatedly killed it were road blocks in the decision-making process. What Rob had done was to survey the complicated field, isolate the many separate players who had to get to *yes*, and use Coaching to "open the road" to final approval.

COVERING ALL THE PLAYERS

He couldn't do that alone. You never can in complicated sales; there are just too many players and too many variables for a single seller to handle everything directly. That's why Rob did what every successful seller is forced to do today: he put together a *team* of results-oriented professionals to help him cover the field of moving targets.

The surgeon general, the minister of defense, the company commanders whose men were in danger on the muddy road–all of these Coaches became members of Rob's selling team, and each of them was "assigned" to cover one or more individuals whom Rob, as orchestrator of the sale, could not handle personally. That "recommender" who served as a Technical Buyer, for example? It was the chief of staff who handled that piece of the puzzle, who was in charge of bringing this negative Buying Influence around.

Although his sales occur in a narrower and relatively less complex arena, Mike Wyant also relies routinely on teamwork to help him make the case for Syncor solutions. "You're never exactly sure what questions you'll be asked," says Mike. "So when I go in to a client with a testing proposal, I'm not alone. Typically, three of us approach the prospect together: me, a Syncor sales rep, and a representative from the manufacturer, Du Pont. It's all part of the team approach we call alliance selling."

That's perhaps the primary lesson of both Rob's and Mike's stories. To identify and cover all the players in a complex buying organization, you need to develop a team that is just as complex–just as varied, well-focused, and finely tuned–as the people whose solution images you are trying to fulfill.

A second lesson is one that reinforces the first.

HEAD PROGRAMS AND PAPER PROGRAMS

Virtually everyone who has ever been through a Miller Heiman workshop thanks us for the plethora of visual aids–charts, diagrams, worksheets–that we make available to program participants. That's the second lesson. As Robyn Crebs expresses it in the quotation at the beginning of this chapter, in order to track all those moving targets effectively, you've got to get it on paper. *Write it down.*

There are two related benefits to this approach. The obvious one is that it provides you with a visible record of the players you have to cover, and who should do it–a record that you and your team can use as a benchmark for strategy.

The less obvious plus has to do with the learning process. Psychologists know that the process of writing something down energizes the memory; writing inscribes the information internally, creating a mental correlate to the physical record. Writing something down helps you keep it in your head, while trying to keep it in your head alone almost ensures that you'll forget it.

In our programs, we encourage participants to record their information on printed Situation Analysis sheets, which give participants a space to summarize all their information about Buying Influences, including

SITUATION ANALYSIS:
A Basic Snapshot

Name	Title	Pos/Neg/Neutral	Covered by
Economic Buyer			
User Buyers			
Technical Buyers			
Coach(es)			

the players who are performing each decision-making role and the member of the selling team who should cover each one. It's a rare participant who isn't enthusiastic about these sheets. Your company may feel more comfortable with a different approach to situation analysis. But we strongly encourage you to use some standardized record to assess the positions of the players on your shifting fields. At the minimum, we recommend that you write down the information in the chart on page 81 as a first, early snapshot of your situation.

MANAGERS' CHECKLIST 1: BUYING INFLUENCES

A common tendency in working with such informational charts is to use them not as guides to creative thinking but as a series of empty boxes to be "filled in." You can avoid this error by focusing on the decision-making roles first, then determining which of your players is fulfilling each one. Team leaders can help here by asking a few tough questions, and suggesting a few appropriate actions, regarding key players.

1. *For the person that we've identified as the Economic Buyer, how do we know that he or she actually has the authority to release the funds for this sale? At what level in our own organization would an equivalent budgetary decision be made? In the customer's organization, is there anybody above this individual who can "disrecommend" us or even veto our proposal? Let's get Coaching on this if we aren't positive.*

2. *For our User Buyers, how will the acceptance of our proposal directly affect their job performance? Have we covered everyone in the buying organization who will be using our product or service on the job? Does every one of these individuals know how his or her performance will be improved by this sale?*

3. *Are we sure that we have located all Technical Buyers, both within and outside of the buying organization? Our proposal must comply with specifications in the following areas: finance, legal issues, government regulations, pricing, quality control, technical specs, delivery and service schedules. Have all these potential hurdles been addressed by somebody on our team? If there's a hurdle we haven't overcome, let's get Coaching.*

4. *Do we have at least one reliable Coach? How do we know he or she is reliable? What's the history of our credibility with the Coach and his or her credibility with the customer? Is the Coach more than just our buddy? Why does each Coach want us in there for this sale?*

Depending on the answers to these questions, your selling team may want to stick with the current program, or regroup on the basis of emerging information. We've said it once, but it bears repeating: Identifying and covering the key decision makers isn't a matter of filling out forms or fixing labels. Your goal is to understand the role that each person plays–and to address each one's particular focus in the sale.

One secret to doing this effectively is to uncover not only each person's desired results, but the personal Wins that those results will generate. Often, that's no easier than identifying key players, yet failure to do it is the cause of countless lost sales. We address this difficulty in Chapter 5.

5

WHAT DO THEY WANT, ANYWAY?

"We don't believe we close. We co-create a communication process that assists our clients in their decision-making process."
–Bob Mayes
Vice President of Sales
Las Campanas

"It's seldom an in-and-out situation. To get to the close, you've got to motivate the customer. And it's pretty hard to motivate somebody who doesn't have a Win."
–Ken Brandt
Healthcare Sales Specialist
Nemschoff Chair Company

WE'VE ALL HAD THEM. THE CUSTOMERS WHO seem committed to watching you fail. The tough, recalcitrant ones who just won't budge, no matter how brilliant your presentation or how perfect the fit. The "dim bulb" prospects who just don't get what you're saying, who cannot see how they would possibly benefit from your proposal, even though the evidence is staring them right in the face. Or the "picky" ones who rummage delightedly through their bag of trick questions until they find one, finally, that you are unable to answer. All those perfect matches who won't see reason—who would rather shoot themselves in the foot, grinning while you squirm.

The conventional way of handling such difficult characters is to suppose that they are just that—ornery "characters"—and to take a defensive posture against their endless objections. The old-time selling guides all tell you that. "There is no objection that cannot be overcome." "Anything they can dish out, you can respond to." "Here are sixteen surefire ways to get them back on track." And a host of similar routines for turning no into yes.

The image that comes to our mind when we think of this advice is that of the salesperson as a reasonably competent club player who is being run ragged trying to defend himself against André Agassi. Somehow he's managed to return the superstar's serve, and to get a modest rally going, but Agassi is bearing down, and the poor club player is racing from side to side of the tennis court, desperately managing to pat back Agassi's lightning bolts, knowing that it's only a matter of time before one gets through.

The conventional wisdom says that this is what selling is about. It's a rapid-fire, high-stress game—definitely not for the fainthearted—and its principal activity is striving to bat down objections, to neutralize an opponent so that you'll beat him at the game. Many common metaphors for the close are in line with this mind-set. Think of the phrases: "You want the customers where you can *put a close* on them." "You've *hooked* him. Now all you have to do is reel him in." Or this gem, from a popular memoir by a "supersalesman": "Let the customer reveal himself, while you watch and listen, and he'll *lay himself open* for the close." Language like that makes customers seem like small-time boxers, dropping their guard so that you can drop *them*.

THE PERILS OF COMBAT

All of these phrases, like the emphasis on "overcoming objections," reveal an attitude toward the customer that may generously be called combative. Not antagonistic, exactly, but certainly not friendly—and hardly focused on fulfilling the customer's real need.

There are two dangers in this lamentably common attitude. The first, ironically, is that it sometimes works. If you're skilled enough, glib enough, and persistent enough, you can talk some reluctant customers into buying. It happens all the time, and not just on used car lots. But it works only in the short term. Eventually the customers whose "foolish" objections you have neutralized will remember why they had reservations in the first place, and when that happens, unless you've been rigorous about meeting their needs as well as your own, your success in keeping Agassi at bay will come back to haunt you.

We're not telling you to accept every customer objection as an ace against you and to fold your tent at the first murmur of doubt. Some customers, it's true, are ornery; some objections are frivolous. But in most cases that's not true. Most objections arise because customers have some honest confusion about what you (or they) are trying to accomplish, and they need clarification of those issues before they're willing to proceed. If you make the sale without clarifying those issues, the person you've "beaten" is not the only one who will be facing trouble.

Pushing through a sale over a customer's valid objections sets up *Buyer's Remorse*–buyers' uncomfortable feeling that they've been had, specifically, that they've been suckered into making a decision they knew all along was not to their own or their company's best advantage. "Remorse" comes from the Latin word for "biting again," and the remorseful buyer feels bitten, again and again, by self-reproach; that's why we speak of remorse as a "gnawing" feeling.

That's not the worst of it, though, from your perspective. The worst of it is that remorse, routinely, leads to revenge. And *Buyer's Revenge* is a real and very deadly danger.

Some years ago, the federal government's Office of Consumer Affairs conducted a study on buyers' post-sale behavior. It found that customers who felt they had been treated well by the salesperson typically talked about their experience to three other people—for the seller, these would be three prospective new customers. Customers who felt that they had been treated badly, however—who felt that the salesperson had lied or cheated them—typically complained to an average of *eleven* other people.

Naming names, of course. That's a lot of bad press for a seller to have to contend with—a lot of potential new business written off at the start.

Joe Girard, whom the *Guinness Book of Records* calls "the world's greatest salesman," thinks it's worse than that. Judging from the average attendance at weddings and funerals, Girard estimates that everybody has about 250 friends and acquaintances—every one of them a potential new prospect who could be positively, or negatively, influenced by the way he treats a customer. This leads to what he calls his "rule of 250":

> If I see fifty people in a week, and only two of them are unhappy with the way I treat them, at the end of the year there will be about 5,000 people influenced by just those two a week. I've been selling cars for fourteen years. So if I turned off just two people a week out of all that I see, there would be 70,000 people, a whole stadium full, who know one thing for sure: Don't buy a car from Joe Girard!

The math here is a little shaky: at two times 250 people a week, in a year Joe would actually alienate 26,000 people. But his point is well taken. The initial problem in "countering" customers' objections is that it kills your rate of repeat business and positive referrals.

The second problem is more subtle but just as severe. It's that "selling" buyers who have unresolved issues about your proposed solution violates the *natural order* of their decision-making process. It forces them to turn their logic and their thinking upside down. The *least* of your problems, when you do this, is that they won't buy.

THE LOGIC OF CONVERGENCE: LESSONS FROM UCLA

When we speak of "upside-down thinking," we are referring to pioneering work on human intelligence that was done in the 1960s at UCLA. Distilling a vast literature on how people think, the psychologist J. P. Guilford and his colleagues suggested that, in making rational decisions, people used several different types of thinking, among the most important being *cognition*, *divergence*, and *convergence*. Rational decision making always puts these three types of thinking in the same logical order: first cognition, then divergence, and finally convergence.

> 1. In *cognitive thinking, people seek to **understand** a situation. Cognitive thinking provides an overview: it gives people the information they need to know where they are and what kind of problem they are facing. Cognitive thinking doesn't seek solutions and doesn't project what things*

will look like when the problem goes away. It merely provides a fix on what things are like now.

2. *In divergent thinking, people* **consider alternatives.** *Divergent thinking enables a person to survey the various solutions that may be available. When work teams or task forces "brainstorm" a problem, they are engaging in divergent thinking. The point is to explore the possibilities.*

3. *In convergent thinking, people* **make the decision.** *Having surveyed the entire scene and considered the alternative ways of solving the problem, they converge on the solution they believe to be best. Convergence is the final step in the decision-making process, the step that most of us have in mind when we say, "I decided." It's the logical, final outcome of narrowing down your options.*

The diagram that appears on the following page illustrates how the three steps work—or at least how they are supposed to work—in practice. Notice three things in particular.

First, the three steps occur in a definite *sequence.* They are numbered 1, 2, 3 to indicate that there is a natural direction from cognition to divergence to convergence. You can't generate options to solve a problem until you visualize the problem clearly, and you can't make a sensible final selection until you've seen those options.

Second, the three types of thinking *interlock.* Despite the natural sequence of the thinking process, they occur not as distinct, punctuated episodes but as parts of a "flow." You might think of them as three sequential stretches of a river: the first broad and calm, the second turbulent, the third a waterfall. The transitions between these stretches might be marked on the shore by flags, but the water would not dutifully obey these markers. The turbulent stretch might have calm patches within it, and you could not mark with any precision where the waterfall began.

In addition, as the rotating arrows indicate, a certain degree of "backflow" is involved. Just as eddies move river water momentarily upstream, decision making sometimes requires double-checking—backtracking to check the big picture again, or to reconsider an option you had prematurely discarded. You can no more eliminate these "reversals" than you can eliminate a river eddy. They are a necessary feature of the flow from cognition to convergence.

Third, the circles get *smaller* as you approach the decision. We have drawn them this way for two related reasons. As you move from cognition to convergence, the volume of *information* that you have to process gets smaller, and so does the *time* needed to process it well. In a logical de-

RATIONAL DECISION MAKING:
The Three Steps

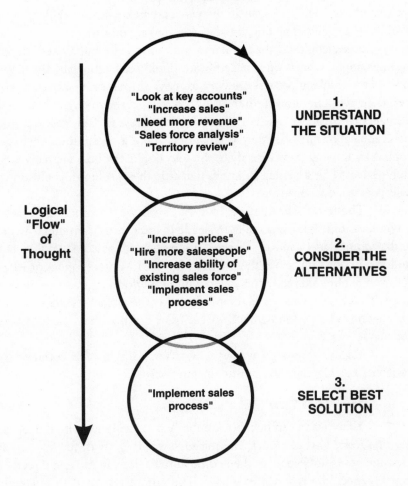

Logical
"Flow"
of
Thought

"Look at key accounts"
"Increase sales"
"Need more revenue"
"Sales force analysis"
"Territory review"

1.
UNDERSTAND
THE SITUATION

"Increase prices"
"Hire more salespeople"
"Increase ability of
existing sales force"
"Implement sales
process"

2.
CONSIDER THE
ALTERNATIVES

"Implement sales
process"

3.
SELECT BEST
SOLUTION

cision-making process, you spend the most time at the outset, assessing the problem, and the least time at the end, actually "making" the decision. In fact, the more time you spend analyzing the situation and comparing options, the less time you need to spend on selecting the best: In the words of Sterling healthcare executive Margaret Shiver, when you've thought the front stuff out clearly, the solution usually "bubbles to the surface."

"SLAM-DUNK" SELLING: TAKING THE LONG CUT

That's the ideal. It's the way the decision process is supposed to work. Unfortunately, in too many cases, the process doesn't work that way. This happens not because the customer is reluctant to "go the course," but because, ironically, the sales professional–the one whose job is to make the customer's decision easy–gets in the way and makes it more difficult by ignoring, or actually impeding, the decision-making process.

Salespeople do this, sometimes in good faith and sometimes not, by engaging in what is often called "slam-dunk" selling. Bucking the natural flow of the thinking process, they try to move the customer *directly* to convergence, without allowing him or her to work through cognition and divergence. Instead of working toward Bob Mayes's "co-creation" of a communication process, they prematurely force a decision on their customers by moving them directly to the selection of the best alternative. You don't have to be a genius to know that this "best" solution is always the salesperson's own proposal.

The term "slam-dunking" for this "rush the customer" approach is a common one, but it's actually misleading, because a "slam dunk" in basketball comes *after* a player has sized up the field, dribbled down the court, and finally gone up under the boards. Not even Michael Jordan or Magic Johnson could go directly to a layup without performing these preliminary steps. That makes you see all the more clearly the illogic of rushing the decision–and why customers tend to get "picky" when they encounter this technique.

Various things go wrong when you resort to this common approach. Let's highlight the most damaging ones.

You Waste Time

There was a self-help book published in the 1960s with the intriguing title *Don't Push the River.* The message was to go with the flow–to accept the course of events as they come in their time. In moving directly to convergence, you ignore this advice. The rationale is that it's quicker to "move directly to Go," to circumvent the whirlpools of explanation and indecision by taking a shortcut through the woods that heads directly for the falls. The problematic reality? *The shortcut is always longer.* By pushing the river–or rushing around the river–you set yourself up for getting lost in the communications woods, creating major problems with the customer later down the line. Fixing those problems always takes more time than you've "saved."

You Ignore the Customer's Concept

In forcing a customer to converge on your solution before he or she has a clear understanding of the situation, you are engaging in a variant of *product push,* whose dire consequences we explained in Chapter 2. There's a correlation, in fact, between *cognition* and Concept, and at the far end of the decision process between *convergence* and product. When you ask customers to "pick me" before they fully understand what else is available, you're committing the cardinal sin of selling product first. We've seen how that can backfire in the "cheap Jeep" story and other scenarios. People don't buy products; they buy expectations. So, by short-circuiting a customer's Concept, you shortchange yourself.

You Deprive the Customer of Choice

Finally, rushing to convergence cheats customers of their choice. To the illogic of forcing them into upside-down thinking, it adds the insult of giving them the impression that you know best. In a culture where consumers feel deprived if they have fewer than 300 brands of breakfast cereal to choose from, giving that impression can be a deadly mistake.

Think of a police lineup with only one suspect, a grocery store that sold nothing but red potatoes, or a multiple-choice question where the only answer was A. Such scenarios are nonsensical. By preempting choice, they violate the very basis of decision making, which is that a rational being gets to select among alternatives. When you force your customer's thinking toward your proposal, you create a scenario that is equally illogical, further complicating a process that is already complicated. This makes it not more but less likely that the customer will choose your solution.

There are two possible outcomes to slam-dunk selling. One of them, Buyer's Remorse, we've already mentioned. It's what happens when you get the sale anyway, even though it's a Lose for your customer. We've seen how that leads, statistically, to Buyer's Revenge, and to Joe Girard's deadly "rule of 250."

The other outcome is that you don't get the sale. This happens more often than not because, although customers love to buy, they hate to feel that they've been sold. Forcing them into convergence makes them feel just that, and they easily become confused, angry, and resistant. In probably the majority of cases, this is the reason that those "picky" characters just don't get it. And when they don't get it, you don't get the sale. Hence the paradox: Perfect fit but no commission.

DOING IT RIGHT:
DEVELOPMENT FACILITATORS AT LAS CAMPANAS

That's the conventional, and wrong, way to go about it. For an example of the right way, we'll point to a Miller Heiman client associate, Bob Mayes, vice president of the Santa Fe area real estate development firm Las Campanas. In a business whose professional etiquette is often as manipulative and high-pressure as that in the used-car business, Las Campanas follows our Conceptual Selling principles to nurture what Bob calls "respectful partnerships between buyers and our representatives."

In a recent interview with Sally Glover, who writes feature articles for our company newsletter, *Best Few*, Bob made it clear that, at Las Campanas, there's no jumping the gun to convergence, no product pushing, and no fretful, whizbang overcoming of objections. There doesn't have to be, because the entire point of a Las Campanas sales interview is to "co-create a communication process that helps someone decide." "Most buyers," says Bob, "have been through so much of the 'Come on in and commit ninety minutes, pay your dues and then find out if the development is for you.' We allow them to come in and tell us what they want to achieve, and then we honor their request. They're stunned. They know right off the bat that something is different here."

What's different is that this Miller Heiman–trained sales force focuses on Concept first ("what they want to achieve"), and avoids "inundating the buyer with product." What's different is the value placed on questioning: "We're switching the percentage from what we talk about to letting the client talk 80 percent of the time." What's different, finally, is that the company's method, and its goal, is to let prospects follow the natural order of their thinking. As Bob explained it to Sally:

> We help them process information, show them alternatives and provide them with a better way to verbalize what they're seeking but may have only been internalizing. If it turns out that it's not Las Campanas, then we've still helped them determine what they want. It's really a personal real estate decision, and the sales representative acts as the facilitator of that decision—whatever that decision may be.

One immediate effect of this approach is to take the pressure off. Off the buyer, to be sure: "I have had zero complaints," Bob says, "about hard-selling salespeople." But off the seller too. Bob's field people are unanimous in their appreciation of that benefit. One of them expressed his delight in not needing to have all the answers: "Conceptual Selling helped me to improve my credibility, create trust, and make the sales interview a conversation rather than a hard sales pitch." Another one reflected on the relief she felt at "not being in a contest with the customer.... I was not putting pressure on myself to sell, sell, sell at any cost! Conceptual Selling helped me understand that if a customer walked away, we both still won."

The best news, though, is that customers don't walk away. Rarely do customers who are encouraged to walk through their natural decision-making process balk at the end and take their business elsewhere. The proof of that is in the close-rate figures. Through a combination of highly selective marketing and a dedication to "coexploring the best solution," Bob and his team have kept theirs unbelievably high.

In the real estate development business nationwide, for lots priced at $100,000, the close-to-prospect ratio is 8 percent; before they took our program, the Santa Fe sales force had achieved a marginally healthier ratio of 10 percent–for lots whose average price was three times that. Now, by attending to Concept and by "facilitating" the decision-making process, Las Campanas salespeople are closing 30 to 40 percent of their prospects, on parcels priced 30 percent higher than the local competition's. In the last two years they have realized over $100 million in sales revenues. As for creating satisfied customers: an astonishing one-quarter of their new business comes from referrals.

WINNING REVISITED

At Miller Heiman we began talking about the importance of winning almost twenty years ago. At that time, the concept was relatively novel, and we were one of the companies responsible for putting the Win-Win ideal at the center of customer relationships. Today, the concept may be losing some of its impact, as it's bandied about by firms where it's more fashionable than functional. Like many other good ideas, the Win-Win ideal can be watered down by overuse. Today, in some quarters it has been stretched so thin that, as Woody Guthrie once joked, "even one of these politicians could see through it."

It's still an important business concept, though, and as competition heats up and customers become smarter and more demanding. it's becoming more important every day. As much as ever customers need to Win, and more than ever they know that this is their right. As Ken Brandt puts it succinctly in the second epigraph at the beginning of this chapter, you can't get people to buy if they don't see a Win. In fact, after upside-down selling, failure to see a Win is the second major reason that your customers turn "picky." That's why we revisit this benchmark concept here.

People Win when they perceive that their *personal self-interest* has been well served. This is a psychological necessity. Hence, fulfilling the need leads to feelings of satisfaction and well-being, and being prevented from winning causes frustration and anger.

This definition may seem fairly straightforward, but the phrasing hides three subtleties that are often overlooked, yet are critical in delivering Wins in a business context. First is a subtlety of omission: the absence of "victory" as even a shadowy element in the definition. Second is the importance of mutual benefit: the fact that you must Win as well as your customer. Third is a subtlety of emphasis: the importance of the "personal."

Winning Does Not Equal Victory

We've observed how common images of combat are in selling. From being "out in the trenches" to telling "war stories" to improving "kill ratios," sales professionals have thought of themselves as warriors. Many of them still refer to "winning a sale" as a boxer or soldier might speak of "winning a fight."

That's fine if all you mean is "achieving success." But if achieving success means victory over somebody else, your concept of winning is inappropriate for the modern sales arena. This is true even when the party you "defeat" is your competition. It's even more true, and more damaging, when you beat out your buyers by making your Wins their Loses. For long-term business, that is the kiss of death.

The ancient Greeks knew the hazards of "victory in itself." One of their popular legends concerned King Pyrrhus, whose penchant for costly "wins" gave us the term "Pyrrhic victory." After his defeat of a Roman army in 279 B.C. he is said to have been so appalled at his own troops' casualties that he muttered to an aide, "One more victory like this and I am lost." A word to the wise—including the wise sales professional. The leading sellers today are "no-fault" players. If you live to make others lose, you should take up Monopoly.

From Win to Win-Win

Throughout our programs, we stress the necessity of managing each sale toward a *Win-Win*, or mutually beneficial, outcome. It's just as important for you, the seller, to Win as it is for you to deliver Wins to your customers. Playing Lose-Win, where you "give away the store" in the hope of future business, is just as much a mistake as playing Win-Lose. It's just as certain to spin you, your customer, and the sale itself out of control, so that the ultimate outcome is mutual disadvantage, or Lose-Lose. We'll speak more about this concept in Chapter 6, where we explain the customer's obligation to serve *your* self-interest.

Wins are Personal

We may speak of managing a sale so that "the customer" Wins. But in business-to-business selling, there are always several people who make up the corporate entity known as "the customer." In Chapter 4, we called them Buying Influences. It's those Buying Influences to whom you're actually selling. It's their personal self-interests that you have to satisfy. It's these people, not their companies, who actually Win. What their companies get, in a solid sale, is business Results.

The distinction between Wins and Results is crucial. We consider it so important that we put it in the form of an axiom:

Companies get Results.
Only people Win.

This concept is among the trickiest in all of our programs. But the participants who "get it" invariably tell us that it's central—that distinguishing between business Results and personal Wins is one of the most useful skills that they have ever acquired. In managing "picky" customers, it's indispensable.

But if Wins and Results are distinct, they are also related, and learning to understand their linkage is a crucial part of strategy. In our programs, to clarify that linkage, we introduce our own novel term: *Win-Results*. And we provide participants with the following essential definitions:

- **Result**—*The impact that your product or service has on one or more of your customer's business processes. Results are objective, tangible, measurable—and corporate. That is, they affect many people in an organization at the same time, although they may affect no two people in exactly the same way.*

- **Win**—*The fulfillment of a promise made to oneself to serve one's own perceived self-interest. Wins are subjective, intangible, difficult to measure—and highly personal. Even when two Buying Influences get the same Result, they don't win in exactly the same way.*

- **Win-Result**—*An objective business result that brings one or more of your Buying Influences a personal win. For the successful salesperson, these are the only results worth delivering.*

WHY BOTHER WITH WINS?

Usually, when we introduce these terms, we get two questions. The first is "Why?" Why do I need to identify Wins in the first place? Why concern myself with something that subjective? Isn't it enough for my customers that by buying my product or service they get great Results?

The answer to this one is implicit in the concept of Buying Influences—those individuals whose approval can make or break your sales. It is those individuals, not their "company," whose needs you've got to satisfy, and you can only do that by attending to them all as individuals. The reason that delivering a Result is never enough is that a single Result generally has multiple impacts, some of which could be perceived as negative by a Buyer. If you don't pay attention to Wins, you'll risk selling "Lose Results" without even knowing it—delivering a dynamite product that makes someone your enemy.

BFI's Robyn Crebs experienced this situation in her sale to the food warehouser. Recall that one of her key players, a picky Technical Buyer, wanted no part of the compacting system she was proposing, and in fact threw blocks in her way to prevent its approval. The Result that the new system would bring the corporate customer—cleaner, more efficient waste removal—was objective and, to an unbiased observer, indisputably worthwhile. But the new system threatened the authority of this one Buyer, who rightfully feared that it would make him, personally, look incompetent. For him, the Result was, just as indisputably, a personal Lose.

Robyn's attempted solution was to try to bring him into the sale—to make him see that, if he brought her to the Economic Buyer, he would be able to share the kudos for introducing the new system, and thus turn his potential Lose into a Win. That solution fell through. Robyn got the sale anyway, by going around the blocker. But she reflected on it later with a certain misgiving. "You hate to close a sale where anybody Loses," she told us. "You never know if it will come back to haunt you down the line." Our experience shows that such wariness is often justified. Leaving any of your Buying Influences without a personal Win is always risky. As we put it in Chapter 4, "Unsold Buyers undo sales."

Another BFI employee, sales manager Mark Starr, confirms the importance of covering all the Buying Influence bases—and doing it in a way that recognizes individual needs:

> In a complicated sale, you're dealing with a lot of different people. You can't relate to all of them in the same way. You have to mean something different to every person. Part of the difference is function—User Buyers have different needs from Economic Buyers. But a lot of it is beyond that; it's very personal. You have to step inside individual personalities to find out what matters to them, and you can't predict what that is by looking at their roles. Whatever role people play, they still want to Win.

Or consider the example of AEI Music's David Duff. Dave is the account executive whose comments on questioning illustrated the Concept principle in Chapter 2. What he said there is equally relevant to Win-Results. The AEI Music sales team was able to dislodge the toy company's entrenched supplier precisely because they queried *all* the Buying Influences about what they liked, and didn't like, about their current system. Although in general that system was seen as a worthwhile Result, one aspect of it—the billing jumble—was creating a Lose for every Buying Influence in the accounting section. It was by addressing their personal concerns that AEI Music won.

The bottom line, perhaps, is that selling to "a company" is a fiction. You sell to the Buying Influences inside a company. To make a sale, you've got to get a decision from each one. That means motivating each one to make the decision. And that, as our client Nemschoff's Ken Brandt says, means focusing on their Wins. Ken spelled this out more fully in a recent conversation:

> Looking for Wins gives the salesperson a distinction that really differentiates you quickly from the competition. It's common to think of selling as an in-and-out deal. In fact you're dealing with a range of outside and inside influences and personalities, so you've got to approach things from a suitably complex perspective. Get beyond your own paradigm and read the situation from inside your customers' heads. Even over the telephone, you can learn to pick up cues. A lot of selling is learning how to read why people Win.

But how do you learn to read that? If you're not a psychic, just how do you determine how your individual Buyers win? That's the second question our corporate clients often ask us.

HOW NOT TO READ WINS

"Real Wins," says BFI sales manager Mark Starr, "aren't easily spoken. Somebody might say something with regard to price, as if that's all that he and his company are interested in. But the way he relates, his signals, are saying something else. They're saying, 'We want better service, better representation. You're not treating us the way we want.' When you hear that, you've got to zero in on the personal."

In our experience, there are three ways that you can do this—and two ways that, although they are common, never work. Let's eliminate these negatives first.

Equating a Win with a Result

Since Results are corporate and Wins are personal, the illogic of this equation ought to be obvious. In identifying Wins, you can start with a Result; but it's confused, and often dangerous, to stop there. Results are preconditions to Wins, not equivalents. And it's perfectly possible to deliver an objectively great Result that translates, to one or more Buying Influences, as a Lose.

Suppose I'm trying to sell a department head a computer system that will reduce his personnel costs by 15 percent. That objectively great Result would certainly be seen as a Win by the CEO, who is vitally concerned with cost issues. But the department head himself may see it as a Lose—a shrinking of his bailiwick—unless I point out that the cost saving can increase his prestige by advertising his increased productivity to senior management. At the same time, to a department employee whose overtime the new system will reduce, the same Result will translate only as a Lose. No Result, in short, is an automatic Win.

Projecting Your Win onto the Buying Influence

This error follows naturally from the common tendency to put yourself in the customer's mind by saying "If I were in her place. . . ." You're *not* in her place. The feeling of power that you get from driving a Jaguar may tell you little or nothing about why your neighbor wants to buy one. Your neighbor may be attracted by its power, like you, or by its prestige, its resale value, or its leather upholstery. Never assume that a Result will bring Alice or Joe the same Win that it would bring you. If everybody Won alike, we could sell with our eyes closed.

READING WINS: THE RIGHT WAYS

How do you determine a Buyer's Wins? There are three methods. You can infer. You can ask a Coach. Or you can ask the Buyer directly.

Inferring the Win

"Inference" means the drawing of a reasonable conclusion based on data which are necessarily limited. Since Wins are related to Results, and since different types of Buying Influences typically want different Results, you can begin by inferring the Win from the desired Result. The danger here is in equating the two. The advantage is that it keeps you focused on those concrete business successes which typically generate Wins for categories of buyers.

Economic Buying Influences, for example, typically want bottom-line Results: a better return on investment, increased sales, reduced costs, increased efficiency or productivity, a smoother cash flow. If you can deliver a Result that enhances the overall profitability of the buying firm, the chances are good that the Buying Influence will Win.

User Buying Influences judge the impact of your proposal on their own jobs. The Results they want are to be found in such performance-related areas as ease of operation, versatility, efficiency, reliability, training, and service. If your Result has a positive impact in these areas, you might be able to infer that a User Buyer will Win.

For *Technical Buying Influences*, the focus areas are product or service specifications. Examples of a Technical Buyer's Results might therefore include delivery schedules, discounts, product specs, credit, and legal requirements. If you deliver the Result that a given Technical Buyer is looking for, you increase the chances that he or she will Win.

Coaches, unlike the others, only have Wins. Since the Result they want, by definition, is to have your solution accepted, they Win when that occurs.

Since Wins are always highly personal, you should check your inference from Results against surrounding data. What does Alice's office look like? Is it plastered with pictures of her children, or with her diplomas? What is her small talk? Is she enthusiastic about golf, about politics, about food? What can that tell you about her attitudes, her interests, her achievements? What kind of company has Alice chosen to work for? How flexible and open, or how repressive, is the corporate culture? What does that say about her day-to-day values, her motivation?

Buyers' Wins are reflections of their values and attitudes. When you are trying to read how an individual might serve his or her self-interest, examine the atmosphere in which that individual operates. The more you know about how Alice feels and thinks about her life, the better you will be able to predict what serves her self-interest.

Asking a Coach

We've said that the role of a Coach is to help you make the sale, and that to do so this critical Buying Influence must fulfill certain criteria. Most relevant here is the third criterion: credibility with the other Buyers. If a Coach is trusted by them, he or she can serve—perhaps already has served—as a confidant. This means that the Coach might be able to clarify those "not easily spoken" values and attitudes which, in delivering Wins, you're attempting to speak to.

Asking the Buyer Directly

The most untraditional of the three methods is also the simplest one: ask Buyers to spell out how they will Win if you succeed in delivering a given Result to their companies.

We say "untraditional." We might just as easily have said "radical" or "unthinkable." The fact is that, as useful as it is to know how your Buyers will Win, it is still considered intrusive, if not actually rude, to ask customers directly what's in it for them. Salespeople are reluctant to do so for two related reasons. First, it violates the comfortable fiction that Buyers don't have personal interests, that they may be safely treated as passionless agents of the corporate machine. Second, it embarrasses people by introducing an allegedly nonprofessional, "touchy-feely" element into the buyer-seller exchange. We've been told countless times by a client that he or she "couldn't possibly" ask Buyers how they feel; it "wouldn't be appropriate," and besides, "There's no way on earth they would answer such a question."

Wrong on both counts. Not only is it perfectly appropriate to sell from emotion–sales professionals have been doing it for centuries–but the answers you can get from asking questions about Buyers' attitudes will often be as useful to you as they are surprising.

THE QUESTIONING PROCESS REFINED: FROM THE *WHAT TO THE* WHY

Maybe it's the very rarity of questions about attitudes that makes them so useful as probing tools. Buyers are accustomed to having salespeople ask them informational questions and, on many occasions, "closing" or "commitment" questions. But it's widely considered bad etiquette to talk about feelings. So when they do get asked an "attitude" question, Buyers often respond much more volubly than you might have expected. Rather than being offended by the supposed effrontery, customers are actually disarmed and pleasantly shocked–ready to release those personal and emotional insights that custom supposedly dictates they keep inside.

The facts coming in from the field are plain. When you probe for a Buyer's Wins, you do get responses–responses that are invariably useful in managing the sale. We believe that BFI manager Mark Starr is not putting too fine a point on it when he observes, "Sometimes a customer has got to spill his guts. If you listen then, that's a very useful experience."

AEI Music's Dave Duff makes a similar point. Acknowledging the difficulty of probing for "something as subjective as Wins," Dave says, "They're not so hard to determine once you ask. That's the only way you're going to find out what's really on the customer's mind. Almost nobody does it, but it works, and here at AEI Music we're way past the point of having it embarrass us. I ask people all the time, 'If we get this account, what will it mean to you?' You'd be surprised what people will tell you, if you only ask."

We'll let our own Joe White, who sells for us out of New York City and Scottsdale, Arizona, have the last word. In an article for our company newsletter, *Best Few*, Joe emphasizes the emotional side of selling–the side that is intimately connected to a Buyer's personal Wins. To be sure, Joe writes, Buyers are interested in Results. There is a "solid, rational component to each buying decision," and that component determines the "what" that a given Buyer needs:

> The "what" is the solution they believe your service will provide.... But the "what" people buy is only half of the decision-making process. It doesn't say "why" they chose that particular product or solution. It doesn't say "why" they chose to partner with that specific sales professional.... When only the "what" side of buying is considered, salespeople leave it up to their customers, or, even worse, up to the competition, to actively incorporate the personal Wins into the solution presentation.... If salespeople are to contribute to a customer's total Concept, they must tactfully, professionally, and with a touch of eloquence discuss the emotional side of the buying decision.

Joe acknowledges, as we do, that this isn't always easy, no matter how eloquent you are, because "people don't speak freely about their personal Wins." But it can and must be done, to secure Win-Win relationships. Joe offers the following four hints, to make the task easier:

1. *Talk about Wins outside the office, perhaps over a meal or on the golf course, where "you both can relax without the restrictive atmosphere of a corporate environment."*

2. *Don't inquire about personal Wins in front of others. Talk to each Buying Influence one on one.*

3. *Be sincere in your attempt to learn about personal Wins. In other words, if you don't really care, don't ask. "If you do not come from this position, then you will get defensive comments and negative reactions and will probably lose a customer."*

4. *"Prepare, prepare, prepare." This means: Come to the sales call with questions that "reflect your sensitivity" to the customer's personal concerns and that are likely to "promote the customer's openness." And come ready to use Golden Silence–ready to listen.*

To these excellent tips, we would make only one addition. Make the attempt to determine your Buying Influences' personal Wins a part of every single sales conversation. We say this because it's so easy to let things slide–to assume that a customer's personal comfort level is the same today as it was two months ago. Wins and attitudes are notoriously subject to change, so unless your typical selling cycle is two or three days, we recommend asking at least *one* "attitude" question every time you meet with a Buying Influence.

In phrasing such questions, we find that it's most effective to use the traditional journalistic openers *what, which,* and *how* in conjunction with phrasing that tries to elicit a value judgment. For example, "What's your reaction to this piece of the proposal?" "Which of these solutions do you find more appropriate?" And, most useful of all, "How do you *feel* about . . . ?" The use of the common opener "Why?" we have usually found less effective, because it runs the risk of being heard as judgmental. "Why did you choose plan B?" has an edge. "How did you choose plan B?" doesn't.

One final warning. In response to such questions, don't expect to get the Buying Influence's life story or the murky reasons that she hates her Uncle Clarence. In bringing Wins to the surface, you're interested in how a customer feels about your proposal and its Results. It's not your job, and it shouldn't be your goal, to act as either Sherlock Holmes or Sigmund Freud. It may be helpful to know that Jack has a "need for recognition"–if the Results you're delivering are likely to deliver that Win. It's less essential, probably, to trace that need to the inadequate support he got as a child from his father.

In other words, it's not always essential to articulate the *how,* the down-and-dirty specifics, of people's Wins. It's always essential to verify *that* they will Win–and to show them that you and your company are the ones to make that happen. That's the only reliable process for overcoming objections, and for turning the pickiest of customers into your partners.

MANAGERS' CHECKLIST 2: THE CUSTOMER'S CONCEPT

To be sure that your sales force is positioning your products or services effectively from the customer's point of view, ask the following questions:

1. *In our current sales objective, what is each Buying Influence's mental image of a satisfactory solution? Are we sure we fully understand what each person expects the sale to accomplish?*

2. *Has each Buying Influence been permitted to think through the three essential steps of the decision-making process? What evidence do we have that they all understand the situation, have considered alternative solutions, and are ready to choose our solution as the best one? Are we confident that we haven't "slam-dunked" any of them into a hasty decision?*

3. *Is our solution the best one? Are we confident—and are all the Buying Influences confident—that we're not offering them merely an "acceptable" or "good enough" solution?*

4. *For each key decision maker, what are the concrete business Results that he or she wants to achieve?*

5. *How will each person's subjective self-interest be served by the delivery of the desired Result? How will each key player Win? If we're not sure about this critical "emotional side" of the sale, what steps can we take now to clarify the Wins? Who is in a position to give us Coaching?*

6

CAN'T YOU COME BACK TOMORROW?

"Strike while the iron is hot."
—English proverb

"Commitment isn't something extra. It's the whole point of going into a sales call. If you walk away and you don't have some level of commitment, your selling is reduced to a chumming exercise."
—Mike Joyce
Sales Consultant
Miller Heiman

ACCORDING TO BILL O'CONNELL, COAUTHOR OF *Sales Reengineering from the Outside In*, in the past two decades the cost of the average business-to-business sales call has been rising by over 10 percent a year. Today, sending a national account manager out for "face time" with a customer might cost your company $500 an hour.

You might quibble with these figures. Depending on your industry, the conventions of your type of business, and the liberality of your expenses system, the going rate of your calls might be a little higher or a little lower. But there's no question that paying for time with customers is a major business expense. It's so much of a burden to many companies that they're moving more and more toward telephone qualifying and selling as less costly, while even in companies that aren't that technologically sophisticated, accountants are looking long and hard at rising selling costs.

These are facts, plain and simple, although increasingly they're not so simple for companies to contend with. Authors Mark Blessington and Bill O'Connell understate the case when they say, "Few companies have succeeded in trimming costs per salesperson while maintaining the same level of effectiveness." In our experience, very few companies indeed have made much recent headway with the problem of cost of sales calls. In this chapter we explain one major reason why this is so—and point the way to a process-oriented solution.

THE PROBLEM BEHIND THE PROBLEM: IS THIS TRIP NECESSARY?

During World War II, when fuel was rationed, a government poster suggested that whenever they were about to get into their cars, Americans should ask themselves, "Is this trip really necessary?" The idea then, as during the oil crisis of the 1970s, was to minimize the number of times you wasted precious fuel on marginal or nonessential journeys. It was a good suggestion then, and it's still good now. Unfortunately, a majority of businesses tend to ignore it, prodigally sending their people out to beat the same bushes over and over again even when it's clear that the game there has long since left town.

In doing this—in sending their people out on multiple calls to the same unresponsive prospects—they are setting up the problem behind the problem of the high-cost sales call. It isn't simply that individual calls cost too much–that's a debatable point on which reasonable people might disagree. It's that we go out, come back empty-handed, and go out again. The real financial killer is the "one more try" routine that sends professional sellers scurrying again and again down dry holes. It's the series of high-cost calls that's the real budget-buster.

In saying this, we're aware that we're bucking one of the most cherished of all sales traditions: the belief that the key to success is "Never say die," that a salesperson's single greatest tool is a positive attitude. Among professional sellers, it's an article of almost religious faith that if you keep on pushing long enough, hard enough, with enough determination, the bricks will begin to crumble and the wall will fall down. It's heresy to hint that any other attitude is acceptable.

We're not knocking positive attitude. Certainly, a negative attitude can be disastrous, in sales as in anything else, and yes, other things being equal, tenacity can work wonders. But positive thinking alone just isn't enough. Not any longer. And when your tenacity is costing your company hundreds of dollars a call, it had better be paying off in more than good intentions. Too often, unfortunately, it's not. And companies are being bled dry from those "Come back tomorrows."

In the everyday world, the futility here would be obvious. Suppose you send someone to the store to do some shopping. You give the person the keys to your car and a shopping list: apples, flour, milk, tofu, a screwdriver. In the ideal scenario, the person returns shortly with all five items and your change. That's what you want, and what you expect. Everything done in one clean trip.

But suppose the person returns with only the apples and the screwdriver? In that case, he or she will have to return to the store to get the missing items, at a cost in your inconvenience and more fuel. Say that this second time your shopper gets the tofu but not the flour or milk. That means a third trip, with more cost and more annoyance.

Now, suppose further–and here the analogy with sales calls will become clearer–that your surrogate shopper isn't merely forgetful. Suppose that he or she returns from these less than satisfactory journeys saying that it was the storekeeper who made it impossible to get what you wanted: "Said they were out of tofu. Hid the flour in the hardware department. Flat-out refused to sell me any milk." Faced with explanations like that, you might reconsider the situation. Maybe your friend isn't an idiot after all. Maybe the problem was the store that you chose.

Going into a sales call is a far more complicated "shopping" trip than going into a market. Yet we usually equip our salespeople with little more than a sketchy list–and give them no defense against the shopkeepers who hide the flour in the hardware or refuse to release the milk. This chapter provides a new way of going about this–a way that will help you determine, before you've trekked to the Swinging Door Grocery a hundred times, whether or not it's a door that's really worth knocking on.

In our system for minimizing the number, and maximizing the effectiveness, of sales calls, the fundamental goal is to keep the sales process moving forward, toward a conclusion that is mutually satisfying and that builds long-term business. That's an undebatable premise, the foundation of our business philosophy. A related premise is that this is a two-way street. The people you sell to must treat you like a partner, not a patsy, if they (and your company) expect you to go back again.

The system itself–the shopping list, if you like–has three sequential, interactive components. Because the point of these components is to help you distinguish between the truly good prospects and the grocers from hell, you can think of them not only as measurements but as qualifying tests.

1. *In the first test, you assess a Buying Influence's level of receptivity by checking for the presence of an essential* **discrepancy.**

2. *In the second test, you screen your prospects and even your customers against an* **Ideal Customer profile.**

3. *In the third test, you determine your customer's willingness to act (rather than just talk), demanding and securing some level of solid* **commitment** *on each sales call.*

THE DISCREPANCY TEST: THE IMPORTANCE OF TIMING

A friend of ours whom we'll call Frank once sold charcoal to grocery stores. It was an entry-level position, involving less selling than delivery, but two aspects of the job gave it a sales spin. For one thing, Frank had to negotiate six days a week with store produce managers to find suitable display spaces for his product that would provide both the stores and the charcoal company with solid revenue. For another thing, he earned commission on what he delivered–fifty cents for every carton of four bags.

Thus Frank was confronted with the classic salesperson's decision: whether to go for the numbers and push as much product as possible into every store, or to adjust his delivery goals–in some cases downward–to reflect the differing needs of individual stores. Since more cartons meant more commission, his natural tendency was to push the product. One hot day toward the end of June, he learned how counterproductive that tendency can be.

"It was my biggest store," Frank recalls. "With the Fourth of July weekend coming up, I wanted to be sure it had a huge display, and extra stock in the back. It looked like exactly the right time and the right place to make a record delivery, but unfortunately the produce manager didn't see it that way. He had a dozen boxes of bananas blocking one aisle, half of Idaho's potatoes in another, and lettuce coming out of his ears. The last thing he wanted was more cartons."

As Frank tells the story, he went on for fifteen minutes in the traditional "Don't take no for an answer" style, using everything from logic to cajolery to convince the manager that somehow the space would open up, so that his shoppers would have what they needed on Independence Day. "The thing is," he pleaded with the manager, "we've found that the larger the display . . ."

"The thing is," the manager cut him off, "I can't squeeze in one more briquet. Now, don't you have other stores to go to?"

And Frank shambled off, having succeeded not only in talking himself out of a commission, but in turning a reasonably friendly relationship into one of antagonism. Why did this happen?

One answer relates directly to the importance of *Concept*. The central mistake that Frank made here was in assuming up front that his solution image was identical to that of the customer. Faced with the biggest charcoal-selling day of the year, surely the produce manager would want a gigantic display. That was only common sense. It was so commonsensical, in fact, that Frank felt he didn't even need to ask the produce manager about it. Predictably, this imposition of "logic" on the customer led to the loss of a sale.

But the second reason that Frank ended up, on that potential banner day, with no commission had to do with timing. Frank was only half right in assessing the situation as "the right place and the right time." At some other time, the produce manage might well have been receptive to Frank's argument. On that June day, though, Frank was in the right place at the wrong time. Whatever he said on that day, this manager was in no mood to buy.

We've all seen this a hundred times, with a thousand variations. The customer who, like the produce manager, is in "inventory gridlock" and just can't take on any more product. The vice president who, as you make your perfect presentation, is daydreaming about golf. The company that "really wants" to do business with you but is temporarily prevented from doing so by budget restrictions. What's common to all these scenarios, and to many more, is that the customer's mood is incompatible with a buying decision. You've hit him or her at such a bad time that, no matter what you do, there will not be a sale.

Many salespeople, when confronted with these scenarios, do what Frank did: forge ahead in the hope that glibness and perseverance will turn things around, will change the negative mood to a positive one. In our experience, that is almost always a waste of time. Frank wasted only fifteen or twenty minutes in this fruitless endeavor. In larger, more complex sales, the time drain can be much more substantial, as salespeople tot up those thousand-dollar-a-day no-win journeys.

It's to help you avoid this time drain that we recommend applying our first qualifying test–the test of discrepancy–as early as possible in the selling cycle and with every Buying Influence you call on. In Chapter 2 we noted that people buy to overcome a perceived discrepancy between where they are right now and where they want to be. If Frank had listened carefully to what the produce manager was saying, he would have realized that there was no such discrepancy here–and that all the talking in the world would not make it appear.

When You Can Sell—and When You Can't

In our Strategic Selling programs, we describe four types of receptivity, or Buyer Response Modes, that a Buying Influence might exhibit at any given time. These modes are (1) *Growth*, (2) *Trouble*, (3) *Even Keel*, and (4) *Overconfident*. Modes 1 and 2 pass the discrepancy test. Modes 3 and 4 don't.

When Buyers are in the Growth mode, they want to do "more and better." They perceive current reality to be less than the results they require, and they are therefore highly likely to approve purchasing proposals that promise to move reality up to those results.

A Buying Influence in Growth mode is like a ship's captain who is trying to break a speed record. The vessel is shipshape, running smoothly, and on the right course. What the captain wants is more power. If you're the vendor who can supply it, you're in a position to overcome the discrepancy, and in the process make a sale that will be to your mutual advantage.

When Buyers are in Trouble mode, they want to fix or improve something that's not working. Again, there's a gap between results and reality that you might fill. Finding a Buying Influence in Trouble is just as desirable as finding one in Growth. There's nothing cynical about this. If the point of selling is to solve customers' problems, the perception of Trouble is an opportunity for both buyer and seller. Your job here is straightforward. Make the Trouble go away.

In most cases this has to be done ASAP, and that points to the primary difference between Growth and Trouble. While Buyers in Growth may be looking for incremental improvement, Buyers in Trouble want their problems fixed now. There's an urgency about Trouble that makes it especially painful for the customer—and provides an attractive opening for the seller with a solution.

The Buying Influence in Trouble is like the captain of a ship that has just sprung a leak. No matter how clear its course and no matter how smoothly it had been sailing before the leak, the captain's first priority now is damage control. The contract will go to the company that can provide it most quickly.

When Buyers are in Even Keel mode, they want to maintain the status quo. They're like the ship's captain who is cruising blithely on a calm sea. They see no need for more power, and no storms on the horizon. Seeing no discrepancy between results and reality, they are unreceptive to change. Your chances of selling to a person in Even Keel are therefore slim.

Buyers in Overconfident mode also want to maintain the status quo. They're like the captain of the *Titanic*, who thought he was on an even keel. Although the "real" reality is that these Buyers are in deep trouble, their perceived reality says that things couldn't be any better. Even though this perception may be disastrously wrong, it's still the perception that counts. No *perceived* discrepancy, hence no sale.

What does this mean to you? It means that an initial key to avoiding Frank's frustration is to listen carefully to your Buying Influences' signals about their receptivity. If you're hearing some variation on "faster," "better," or "fix it," then you know that there's an opening for your business, at least as regards receptivity. If you're not hearing those signals, you should consider whether your time might be better spent elsewhere.

In general, you might say that the best strategy to adopt with a Buying Influence in Even Keel or Overconfident is to take the produce manager's advice and come back another day. But two peculiarities of receptivity make this advice tentative. Receptivity is *personal*, and it's *unstable*.

The Personal Factor

While companies as a whole may have their own personal "expansion" or "contraction" profiles—as measured, for example, by capital investment or stock price—this is *not* the receptivity that determines selling outcomes. You make (or break) your sales not to the Azdak Company or the Wrigley Group's manufacturing division, but to individual Buying Influences within those organizations, and it is the responsiveness of those individuals that is critical. Azdak's stock price may be soaring, but if key User Buyers there feel that the company or their departments are overextended, then the expansion profile doesn't apply to them—and ignoring their Even Keel mode will probably be a dead-end game.

By the same token, however, it's possible to sell even into a severely contracted company if critical Buying Influences are in Growth or Trouble. In fact, it's rare for an entire account—that is, all the Buying Influences—to be in Even Keel or Overconfident at the same time. Tina Aiken, who sells anesthesia monitors for our client Datex-Engstrom, Inc., makes this point well.

Tina deals most directly with physicians and anesthesiologists, but also with administrative and information systems personnel. "The people in the operating room may be perfectly happy with their current system," she says, "while an information systems manager could be concerned with the fact that the system is not providing complete documentation for all changes—thus losing the hospital money. Here the User Buyers are content with the established system, but you have an opening in that one disgruntled Technical Buyer, especially if you can turn her into a Coach. That's not a rare scenario. No matter how Even Keel the picture may look as a whole, there's almost always *somebody* in Growth or Trouble." A good selling strategy leverages those individuals against the rest.

Instability

It is not business conditions per se that determine whether a given Buying Influence will be receptive to your proposal, but that person's perception of *changing* conditions. Hence our four Response Modes should be viewed as reactions to specific business situations; they are not personality types. Most of the time, for example, Frank's produce manager was welcoming and jovial. His negativity that day was situation-specific. Strategically astute sellers don't brush off any Buying Influence as congenitally Even Keel. They track each customer's level of receptivity as business conditions—and resulting opportunities—change.

THE SCREENING TEST: YOUR IDEAL CUSTOMER PROFILE

Traditional selling, which sees the profession as a numbers game, tends to envision customers like cats: all of them, according to the proverb, are gray in the dark. That's fine if you don't mind selling in the dark. If you sell with your eyes open, you know that's not true. One of the first things you learn about customers, in fact, is that they are as different as cats and dogs—or apples and screwdrivers. Some are consistently a pleasure to do business with, while others make you daydream about becoming a beach bum.

Everybody has sold business that looked like a necklace but that turned out to be the rope you hang yourself with. Our second test helps you avoid that business. It helps you concentrate on customers who are as committed as you are to Win-Win outcomes, while screening out the turkeys who have taken corporate vows to make you miserable. We call this screening device the *Ideal Customer profile.*

The Ideal Customer profile is a checklist of characteristics that you and your company have consistently found in the customers that you most enjoy doing business with. By your Ideal Customer, then, we mean your company's ideal—the model of the customers that your salespeople would most like to sell to again. By implication, this list of characteristics is also a "negative image" of the prospects and customers you'd probably do better avoiding.

Constructing your company's Ideal Customer profile is basically a matter of distillation. Think first of the characteristics that are shared by your best customers—actual customers, not prospects. You determine the criteria for what's best. Think of the customers who have made you leave the sale singing, with whom you would do business again with no hesitation—not everybody you feel OK about, just your prime accounts. Think of what characteristics appear again and again with these Win-Win accounts, and jot them down. Next, think of your worst customers—the people you would cross the street to avoid, who would make you think about starving rather than do business with them again—and jot down a list of their most frequently observed characteristics.

In making these two lists, we urge you to look not only for the obvious "hard" features such as need for your products and financial solvency, but for "psychographics" having to do with values and attitudes. Trustworthiness, dedication to quality, personal integrity, responsiveness—these are examples of psychographic characteristics that our clients often identify in their best customers. In making your list of "best" traits, you should include those values and attitudes that are most important to you and your company.

Similarly, focus on psychographics in making up your "worst" list. In the workshops where our clients construct their Ideal Customer profiles, participants frequently name things like lack of loyalty, rigidity about prices, a confused buying process, and a suspicious, closed attitude toward relationships with vendors. Write down whatever irks you the most, the patterns of behavior that make you feel you're losing.

Finally, distill from these two lists the most significant characteristics that you seek in an "ideal" customer. These would be the most common traits in your "best" list and the *opposite* of the most common traits in your "worst" list. In our workshops, we have clients hone down their final lists to five Ideal Customer traits. In your business, you may find a four- or six-item list to be more appropriate. The number isn't etched in stone. The idea is to translate your gut feelings about your customers into a small cluster of concrete, clearly definable "performance measures" against which you can test the suitability of future business opportunities. However many traits you decide are appropriate, write them down, in the order of their importance to you. This final, distilled list of characteristics is your Ideal Customer profile.

Screening for the Best: Real-World Examples

What do you do with this profile?

The best way for us to answer that question is to share with you a number of actual profiles, beginning with the one that we use at Miller Heiman. Here are the five characteristics that, after some years of retooling and refining, we have found to describe the companies we consider our best—that is, the customers that we are most confident and comfortable doing business with:

1. *Their management wants a permanent change in the sales process, not just a two-day training workshop.*
2. *Their management places value on developing people.*
3. *They play Win-Win with their vendors, their employees, and their own customers.*
4. *They have a Complex Sale.*
5. *The company has at least 75 to 100 salespeople.*

The first three characteristics of this profile, all "psychographics," follow logically from what we have already said. They reflect, respectively, Miller Heiman's dedication to process, our belief in sales as a profession that deserves professional development, and our often stated commitment to mutual satisfaction as the linchpin of every solid business relationship. In utilizing the profile, we very seriously measure prospects' likelihood of fitting these characteristics, and we are extremely reluctant to pursue business where there isn't such a fit. We might be able to make a sale, for example, to a firm that wanted merely a two-day training program. But we would be making it under false pretenses, because that's not our expertise—and to do so would severely diminish the value of our services. So in cases where we're asked for "just training," we typically say no.

The fourth and fifth characteristics are more "demographic" than "psychographic." They reflect the fact that our client base is corporations who have the complexity to require our consulting, and the resources to profit from it. Our best clients work exclusively in what we call Complex Sales, that is, sales in which multiple parties have to say yes; and they conduct their business, generally, with fairly large sales forces. Again, we could target smaller firms, but our experience has shown that the larger companies use us most effectively, and we use that experience to screen out prospects that we can't serve as well.

This doesn't mean that we won't deliver programs to smaller companies. It means that we think twice, and carefully, about targeting smaller prospects.

It's important to emphasize that, although our company as a whole has established stable qualifying criteria that reflect our business philosophy, the Ideal Customer profile is also a very personal thing, and it may be utilized slightly differently by different members of the same company's selling team. Mike Joyce, for example, is a Miller Heiman field representative based outside of Chicago. His Ideal Customer profile derives from ours, and it's certainly compatible with it (if it weren't, he wouldn't be selling for us), but Mike has also modified the defining characteristics to suit his prospect base and his own personality.

"My Ideal Customer profile," Mike explains, "is a version of the Miller Heiman profile, with a few personal twists, based on the business contacts that I have and that I like to have, based on my experience, and based on my personal style. I've found that there are five things that I look for in a customer.

"First, I want to do business with people who are open, honest, and up front—people who have a Win-Win focus. Second, I want customers who are looking for process, not just training. Third, I want to work with companies who believe that developing their own people is a worthwhile investment, not just an expense. Fourth, my Ideal Customers have money to pay for quality, and they're willing to spend it. And fifth, they have a demonstrated commitment from senior management to the implementation of the process I'm trying to sell them.

"When you're in the early stages of a sales process, just developing contacts, you really need something to help you focus on the best possible business, and these criteria help me do that. I've learned to trust my Ideal Customer profile. Sitting down with prospects, I can tell pretty quickly now how close they are, or how far away, from what I'm looking for.

"Eventually it's a question of credibility. You can look at my criteria, and you'll see that. I want to work with people who trust me, and who trust me to bring value to their organizations. Over the years you learn to spot when you have credibility and when you don't.

"You ask yourself how prospects are dealing with you. Do they return your calls? When you're face to face, are they interested in really speaking with you? How are their questions phrased? Are they only looking for numbers and price comparisons, or are they willing to talk, to explore, to have a Win-Win focus? The answers to those question help you see beyond the dollars and cents of the situation. They help you see what kind of business you can do, and can't do, with these people."

An Environmental Criterion

Here's a client example that reinforces Mike's observations. Christine Jernigan is a sales manager for Browning Ferris–BFI, a world leader in waste-handling management. The town where she works, Elkhart, Indiana, is known as the "RV capital of the world," and the bulk of Christine's business is with local manufacturers of trailers, campers, and other recreational vehicles. Selling waste disposal systems to this particular customer base obliges her to be attentive to two criteria: financial stability and environmental responsibility. You'll note that the first is a demographic characteristic, the second a psychographic characteristic.

"Financial health is an obvious enough benchmark for us," Christine says, "because the semiluxury nature of our market makes it very elastic. People will go shopping for RVs or pleasure boats when times are good, but with any kind of economic crunch, the dealers suffer badly, and we have to be alert ahead of time to a customer's potential problems. You never know when an RV place is going to go belly-up.

"The environmental criterion may not be so obvious, but it's important to us as a company. At one level, of course, it's a matter of our own self-interest: We encourage recycling because it can be good for our business–recycling is a part of the package that we can offer customers. Beyond that, though, we're professionally committed. BFI is a contributor to the nation's cleanup efforts, and we don't feel very comfortable doing business with firms that don't value and respect that.

"That happens more than you might expect. Plenty of manufacturers are very aware of environmental issues, and they work with us well–

because of their attentiveness in this area, they provide a good fit to one important element on our Ideal Customer profile. But it's been a long hard road to get others to see things that way. A lot of places still do indiscriminate dumping of paint and solvents, and you've got to ask yourself, when that happens: Should I even be in this? Is this business worth it?

"Actually, though, it very seldom gets to that. We've turned down business, of course, because the prospect had no credit, or because the financial information we got made us too wary. But on environmental grounds? I don't think we've had to make that choice. With a firm that doesn't think twice about dumping, it wouldn't get that far with us. You know your local reputations, and you just find out. With a prospect whose basic social attitudes are so different from BFI's, we just wouldn't get started."

And in cases like this, not getting started can be a plus. The lesson is that your Ideal Customer profile can save you time and money by screening out "opportunities" that would probably bring you more grief than satisfaction in the end.

Looking for a Match, College Style

A third example illustrates that the Ideal Customer principle can also be applied to situations outside of selling. A friend of ours whom we'll call Fran recently finished a doctoral degree in the social sciences and, along with thousands of other new Ph.D.s, began looking for a teaching job. The usual "method" of doing that, she explained, is to scour the professional newsletters for available openings, and then apply for anything and everything advertised in your field. "You fire the shotgun into the air and you hope for the best."

Luckily for Fran, she didn't buy into this "marketing blitz" method. "Instead," she said, "I adapted the Ideal Customer idea, and saved myself an incredible amount of time by applying only to those places where I really wanted to work—where there was a real, measurable match between my values and theirs. I didn't even look at job postings. I researched the departments and the faculty in about 200 schools. Then I sent out customized letters to about 60 where I knew I had something to contribute to the work they were already involved in."

In narrowing the collegiate universe down to that 60, Fran used both demographic and psychographic criteria. Demographically, she wanted a small college and a medium-size department—one, as she put it, that was "small enough so I wouldn't get lost but large enough so I'd have somebody in my field to talk to." Her psychographic requirements were that the faculty be committed to teaching rather than research, and that its political orientation be "flexible rather than ideological."

"A lot of my friends thought I was being way too picky," Fran told us, "and they questioned the wisdom of putting so many limits on my opportunities. But the narrowing process really worked. I didn't waste time looking at places where I didn't want to teach anyway, and in the end I got five different interviews from my narrowed field of sixty. Out of those interviews, I ended up with three job offers. One in twenty might not sound spectacular, but in this job market it really is. I know somebody who sent out three hundred letters and got a preliminary interview from *one* school."

This lesson from the ivory tower is also true in business. Don't waste your time making connections that you don't really want. Maximize your time and your opportunities by zeroing in on those places where the match is real.

THE FINAL TEST: WHAT WILL THEY DO?

Your customer can have the greatest discrepancy in the world between reality and results and may be perfectly matched, item for item, with your Ideal Customer profile. None of that will mean anything if this customer won't or can't commit to *actions*—to concrete, measurable steps that will move the buy-sell process forward. Unless your customers are willing and able to commit to mutually beneficial actions, you are or soon will be back at square one, no more effectively positioned in the sale than you were at the beginning. A failure to act simply translates as "Come back tomorrow."

When we discuss *Action Commitment* in our workshops, we usually begin by discussing the "target" of the sales call, that is, where you want to be at the end of a call. There's a lot of traditional confusion about this concept, because salespeople typically define the target or objective in terms that are (1) too general, (2) too unrealistic, and (3) too focused on what the salesperson is expected to do. The third failing here is as significant as it is generally unrecognized. Whether they're extremely vague, like "Get him excited about this proposal," or extremely precise, like "Review the preliminary spec sheet," most targets share a common deficiency: they're not sufficiently focused on the *customer's* investment in a process that has to be mutually owned, and that is supposed to leave you both feeling satisfied. Most sellers, in short, assume that the sale is their responsibility, and theirs alone. The underlying idea is that if customers don't want to commit, maybe they will next time.

This approach is a distorted example of the idea that the customer is always right. We won't reiterate our disagreement with that cliché, except to say this: just as a successful sale is the result of mutual commitment, a successful call is the result of mutual investment. We couldn't agree more with Mike Joyce's assessment at the beginning of this chapter. If you leave a call and you don't know what the customer is going to do next, you might as well be aimlessly chumming for leads.

To place half of the responsibility for the sales call on the customer, where it belongs, we recommend using a technique that we call *bracketing*. Before you go into the call, *bracket* the possible outcomes clearly in your mind between the high and low end of a possible commitment by the customer. To use our Conceptual Selling terms for these high and low ends, we recommend that you define two concepts precisely:

- **Best Action Commitment**–*the highest level of commitment you can reasonably expect the Buying Influence to make as a result of this sales call*

- **Minimum Acceptable Action**–*the least that you will settle for and still be willing to "come back tomorrow."*

In defining a Best Action Commitment, you want to aim for actions that are specific, measurable, and tied to a time line. That's a lot of precision to ask for, but if you don't demand it, the backslide into fuzziness is virtually guaranteed. So, for example, "Get Jack to read my prospectus" is specific enough, but it doesn't say how Jack's reading is to be assessed, that is, how you can be confident that this action will get done. "Get Jack to respond in writing to the prospectus" is better–it provides a framework by which you can measure his reaction–but its vagueness about timing still leaves you open to another round of "Come back tomorrow." A properly phrased Best Action Commitment would go something like this: "Have Jack agree to a May 15 meeting at which he and I, along with other key players, will review the validity of my prospectus." That gives you, unambiguously, the *what*, *who*, and *when*.

But these specifics, of course, must also be realistic. May 15 has to be a date that Jack not only will commit to but will be able to meet, given his level of authority and his other responsibilities. Your goal is to move the sale forward by incremental commitment–not to set the bar so high that you're constantly jumping into it.

As for the Minimum Acceptable Action, that too must be specific, measurable, tied to a time line, and realistic. With "realism" as the watchword, there's some flexibility here. Our clients and colleagues who use the bracketing system can tell you that setting and resetting Action Commitments is the rule rather than the exception. After all, nobody can afford to cut and run at the first sign of a customer's reluctance to commit. Demanding commitment on each call doesn't mean holding your customer's feet to the fire. It means taking a judiciously flexible approach to the whole idea of "partnering"–expecting the best from your customers, but giving some leeway and being willing to adjust your expectations if the situation requires it.

"I never like to leave a call without *some* commitment," says Sam Abia, a marketing analyst for our client company SAS Institute. "But I also don't want to put the customer in a box. When I'm asking for commitment, I like to give him options. After all, he's only one person. Maybe he'll agree to something in good faith and find out later that his boss won't stand behind it.

"Say I've got a commitment from someone that he'll take my proposal higher up, to his manager–somebody with discretionary power, an Economic Buyer. My Best Action Commitment might be for him to let me make the presentation with him. If he's not comfortable with that, I try to find out what other options he would consider. Can I provide him with product literature, references, or other information that would make his presentation smoother? Would he like me to set up a demonstration? Or at least: 'Before you present this, would you be willing to let me give you some Coaching?' They're all options. What he'll commit to–and then actually do–depends on a lot of factors. You want him to commit to actions that demonstrate he trusts you and wants to move things forward. But you don't want to box him in too soon."

Our man in Seattle, Robert L. Miller, agrees. "You don't set commitment parameters in a vacuum," says Bob. "When you go in to a call, you have to remember where you are in the sales cycle, who you have on your team, and the authority level of the person that you're going to meet with. You try to set your Best Action Commitment within that framework. What's the greatest commitment I can get from this person at this time to move the selling process forward? The answer has to be logical, realistic, and nonthreatening.

"Sometimes you find that the person you're talking to just doesn't have the authority to do what you'd like to see done. All right. What *can* that person do? Suppose you want her to sign off on a delivery schedule, and she's not able to take on that responsibility. Can she commit to bringing you, or bringing your proposal, to the person who *can* sign off? Maybe your Minimum Acceptable Action becomes 'Get the delivery schedule on the desk of the Economic Buyer.'

"Too many people," Bob says, "go into calls thinking it's all or nothing. They've got their sights set on a very specific commitment from the Buying Influence, and when they don't get it, they slink away like a puppy dog, defeated. You've got to be more flexible and more pragmatic than that. You've got to be ready to accept a fallback position that will keep the process moving in the right direction. Maybe not as fast as you want, but still moving."

A "fallback" position, in other words, isn't necessarily a retreat. It's resetting the clock so that next time, you'll get that Best Action—or another Best Action which your reassessment of the situation tells you is more realistic. Bob very deliberately chooses Minimum Acceptable Actions that are stepping-stones, as it were, to his "failed" Best Actions. "Say the focus of the meeting is to discuss implementation of a series of Strategic Selling programs," he explains. "My Best Action Commitment might be to have us develop a schedule of dates and locations. If I find out once we start talking that that's not going to happen, then my Minimum Acceptable Action may be to have them agree to a pilot program, which will lay the groundwork for the more extensive schedule."

An alternative to this stepping-stone approach, when you fail to get a minimum commitment, is to take a hard look at your position with the Buying Influence and determine whether you're as solidly positioned as you thought you were. When you leave a sales call without getting any commitment, the least you should do is to seriously critique that last encounter. Ask yourself honestly where you stand in the buy-sell process, what information you have (and don't have), and how realistic you are being in pursuing this opportunity.

Setting commitment goals is not only incremental. It's also a process with occasional fits and starts—one where the goal is clearly marked, but the path to it may not be. You know the old railroad expression "You can't get there from here." A novice passenger might ineptly conclude, "Oh my God, I'm stuck in this mudhole forever!" The seasoned traveler knows that, wherever you are, some series of connections can get you home. You can't always jump from alpha straight to omega. But it doesn't follow that omega is an unreachable destination.

The Immediate Payoff

The long-term benefits of getting commitment on every call are distant but obvious. Securing commitment ensures that your customer is a partner, and that you are building the kind of relationship where both your firms prosper. But there's an immediate payoff as well, in terms of time saved. Another one of our colleagues, Brian Polowniak, makes this point convincingly when he contrasts the traditional disjointed call with the one that is tied to a goal that is understood—and publicly stated—ahead of time.

"For me," Brian reflected recently, "the major benefit of this piece is greater discipline and more efficiency. You can call it Best Action, Minimum Acceptable, or just plain commitment. Whatever the name, if you don't know what you want as you're going in, at the end of the call you're going to be disappointed. Without a clear picture of the outcome, you've got nothing to drive the call toward, so you revert to a shotgun approach, trying one thing after another. The call gets disjointed because it has no direction.

"When you do have a idea of what you want, the call is focused; it's moving somewhere, and you both know where that is. Not only does that make for shorter calls, saving you time and money. It also provides a common sense of closure.

"You know how unplanned calls come to closure? You drift toward the end of the hour, the Buying Influence fidgets, looks at his watch, and finally blurts out, 'I gotta go now.' When you've got your commitment goal in mind, that doesn't happen. When the desired outcome is known, both people know when to end the call. There's no divergence or embarrassment."

That commonsense ending doesn't just happen. Contrary to the popular wisdom that you shouldn't "give away your game plan" to the customer at the outset of the call, Brian recommends doing just that. "Hey, I give the commitment question right up front—tell him exactly where we are now and where I want to be sixty minutes from now. 'Jeff, we agreed last time that you would consider running two Conceptual Selling programs sometime in the spring. We were going to discuss scheduling today, and I'd like to hear about any difficulties or questions you might still have. But I'd like to leave here today with a confirmed set of dates.'"

How do Buying Influences react to this straight-from-the-shoulder approach? "In ninety-nine cases out of a hundred," says Brian, "the reaction is positive. Maybe you'll get the dates and maybe you won't, but I'll tell you one thing. You won't waste each other's time dancing around the issue. That's important to your customers, especially at the higher levels of the organization.

"The higher you go in an organization, the less time people have to spend. If you're like me and you do a great deal of selling to Economic Buyers, you're one of ten meetings he has that day. Laying your expectations out up front saves him time. Economic Buyers especially appreciate that."

The "No Commitment" Decision: To Walk or Not to Walk

What if you can't get even your Minimum Acceptable Action? We're still asked that question in every Conceptual Selling program, and our answer remains the same as it has been for over a decade. If you've truly established a reasonable minimum action and the customer still won't put out any investment of his or her own, then unless you're a lifelong masochist, you've got three choices:

Ask what's up. You can ask Buying Influences directly why they won't give you anything. In Conceptual Selling, we call this probing for Basic Issues, that is, searching for underlying and unspoken difficulties that the Buyer may have with you, your company, or your proposal. It's not a happy prospect to have to ask such a question, but if your sale is so badly stalled that you can't even get the minimum, what do you have to lose? That's option 1: "Jay, there's obviously an issue here that I don't understand–something that is making it impossible for us to move forward. Is it worthwhile our discussing this, or should I move on?" Whatever the answer, you're better off than remaining in "park."

Revise downward. Sometimes you misread the basic situation so badly that the Minimum Acceptable Action you've devised is just ridiculously out of the customer's ballpark. You'll usually get a hint that this is the case when you open the conversation trying to confirm some basic understanding–"We're here to discuss contract terms, correct?"–and the response you get is equivalent to "Hell, no!" Misunderstandings do occur, in even the best-managed sales, and we would never advise you to stick rigidly to a Minimum Acceptable Action if you come face to face with a surprise answer like this one. A caveat, though. Be wary of revising downward too quickly or too often. If you're that quick to settle for less, you'll soon have nothing.

Walk. The ultimate negative response to a negative response: close your briefcase quietly and say good-bye. We realize that this option is neither conventional nor desirable. We agree with Sam Manfer, who does selling for us from the West Coast, that sales professionals by nature "have trouble walking away."

"The whole idea is counter to our nature as salespeople," Sam says. "In fact, the common response, when you're not getting the commitment you had hoped for, is to keep plugging. I ask program participants all the time, 'If you got no commitment at all on a call, what would you do?' The usual response is 'Well, I'd keep trying.'

"One more try. One more follow-up call. Most of us are like that.

We hate to let things go. Partly, it's that we don't want to admit we've wasted our time–so we keep plugging, trying to justify the investment by throwing good time after bad. Partly, it's psychological. You don't want to admit that you've failed, that you've been rejected by a prospect, for whatever reason. But partly, also, it's a practical matter. We don't want to let things go because we don't have anything else waiting in the wings. There's not enough stuff coming into the pipeline, so we're afraid of watching the entire thing run dry."

We'll return to this painful "dry pipeline" in Chapter 10. Here the pain is more immediate and more palpable. In Sam's pungent terms, meeting the "no-commitment" scene is like being turned down by a prom date again and again. Painful, yes. But just because it's painful doesn't mean you shouldn't respond appropriately. In certain situations a mannerly retreat is exactly what's called for. If George Washington hadn't understood that critical piece of strategy, the United States might be known today as the fifty British colonies.

The lesson is applicable to areas other than sales. A colleague of ours has a photographer friend who for years has been creating a portfolio of local musicians' portraits. Recently she received a grant from a state historical commission to exhibit them in a major retrospective. She was pleased at the opportunity and saw only one glitch: the most famous musician in the state, an elderly jazz bassist, was so camera-shy that he had backed out of several appointments to sit for her, and as the show approached he was not even returning her phone calls.

"Not having this guy's picture in the show would be a major omission," she told our colleague. "But after six meetings with him fell through, I saw that I was cutting my own throat, neglecting everything else to get this one missing piece of the puzzle. There are only so many times you can hear 'Come back tomorrow' before you realize that what he's really saying is 'I'm not home.' It took me weeks to get that message, but it finally sank in.

"The show was two weeks away when I made a decision. I asked myself if it was worth giving it one or two more tries, even though that meant taking time away from the rest of the show. How big a coup would getting him be, and was it worth giving less than my best to the rest of the subjects? When I thought about it that way, the answer became clear. I wrote the bassist off as a lesson in frustration, and put the show on without him–to really good reviews."

In photography as in business, the lesson is the same. When you've "come back tomorrow" to the same person several times, there's nothing shameful in saying "That's enough" and in seeking opportunities where the grass is greener–and more welcoming. Sometimes, in fact, it's the only way you can Win.

Winning by Walking

Mike Joyce tells a story about himself that illustrates this well. "For me," he says, "getting commitment is just the way I work. When I get through a sales call and I don't get it, I realize there's been a disconnect somewhere and I have to reassess that customer. Sometimes, too, that means walking away. Not much fun. But there's too much good business out there to waste your time on long shots.

"I followed a lead to Milwaukee recently, where there looked like the chance for some significant new business. When I got to the meeting, there were six unknown faces there, including one guy who had just become the company's new VP of sales. This was a very measurement-conscious company, and the only question he had was this: 'How can you guarantee the results that your program will deliver?'"

"He wanted figures, revenue reports–the kind of stuff that few companies make available to anybody outside of their own boardrooms. I told him that we might be able to supply him with some of that, not to mention plenty of client testimonials, but that I was curious about the genesis of the question.

"I figured he had probably had some negative experience with another company promising and not delivering, and I wanted to focus the discussion on what problems that had created. So I tried to get at their current system of measurement. How do you track results under your current system? What's the baseline? What am I trying to sell in to?

"All pointless. We went back and forth for a bit until the realization hit me that he wasn't interested in playing a Win-Win game and he wasn't interested in hearing about process rather than training. Points one and two on my Ideal Customer profile–this particular VP and, maybe, his company weren't anywhere near the profile that I had set up. In addition to that–let's be honest–sometimes there's just a style difference between you and the customer, and it's not going to work no matter what figures you come up with. That was the case here. So, without wasting more of both our time, I bowed out and left.

"From what I know of your company," I told the vice president, "I believe that the Miller Heiman programs would address your problems very effectively. We're not hitting it off, though, and we both know that. If you agree but want to know more about our programs, I'll call our Reno office and ask for someone else to come talk to you about what we do."

This decision to walk was undoubtedly painful, but Mike remains convinced that it was the best step he could possibly make. "Playing games," he reflects, "would probably have gotten me that account. I knew what the guy wanted to hear, and after twenty years in this business, I knew how to phrase it. But I'm really not interested in working up that kind of business."

Does this attitude eventually pay off? Absolutely. Partly because you don't waste valuable selling time drumming up scores that will come back to bite you in the end. Partly because the word gets around that you're not interested in playing games—and you make up, tenfold, in good new leads what you've lost in poor business.

Like other Miller Heiman salespeople, all of whom follow the rule of "better, not just more" clients, Mike's customer base has dramatically expanded as he has become more and more selective about whom he lets in. "I'm getting more and more business," he tells us, "and increasingly that business is coming not from corporate leads, but from satisfied customers who have provided me with referrals."

That's not an outcome that would have happened if he had "sold" the Milwaukee company, but it's one that is perfectly consistent with a Win-Win philosophy: a philosophy in which everybody's time is considered equally valuable—and in which mutual ownership of the buy-sell process is the way to make it pay off.

MANAGERS' CHECKLIST 3: THE CUSTOMER'S COMMITMENT

On sales where one or more members of your sales team are constantly being asked to "come back tomorrow," managers should clarify the reason for the stalled cycle by proposing the following questions and suggested actions.

1. *Is at least one Buying Influence at the customer's organization in Growth or Trouble? How do we know? Do we have access to these key players?*

2. *What signals have we had regarding their receptivity? Have we verified those signals with at least one Coach?*

3. *Can we leverage the Buying Influences in Growth or Trouble against those in Even Keel or Overconfident mode? If not, why are we in this account at this time?*

4. *How well does this prospect or customer fit our Ideal Customer profile? Is there a solid fit on at least three of our criteria?*

5. *At the very least, whether it's on our profile or not, are we confident that this customer wants to be partners with us? What evidence do we have that this customer is committed to Win-Win outcomes?*

6. *If the customer or prospect isn't a close fit on at least three of our Ideal Customer criteria, is the business potential here so lucrative that we're justified in making an exception here? If not, what are we doing in there?*

7. *On the last sales call to this customer, what were our Best Action Commitment and our Mimimum Acceptable Action? By the end of the call, did we get at least the Minimum Acceptable Action? If so, on the next call we should (a) verify that the Minimum Acceptable Action was actually completed, and (b) reset our goals.*

8. *If we didn't get at least our Minimum Acceptable Action, what questions have we asked to find out why?*

9. *Can we use our Coach or other Buying Influences to leverage the Buying Influence who won't commit? If not, what is our justification for staying?*

10. *Each call we make on a customer is a costly investment. On the basis of the reciprocal investment we have received on the last sales call, are we confident that this customer is committed to Win-Win?*

7

IS THIS REALLY YOUR ROCK-BOTTOM PRICE?

"Price might fertilize the argument, but in the end it's always value that matters."
—Mark Starr
District Sales Manager
Browning Ferris-BFI

"Customers want the same thing that we do. We're not necessarily looking for the 'best' automobile repair shop or the 'best' barber. We're all looking for somebody we can trust."
—Bob Stewart
Vice President, Sales
American Teleconferencing Services

RECENTLY OUR COMPANY RECEIVED A REQUEST for proposal (RFP) from a large communications firm that was anxious to increase its business with major customers and was inviting proposal bids from leading sales consultants. As is the case with many RFPs, this one included a list of weighted criteria on which the submitted proposals would be assessed. Among the criteria was budget–a factor which, the RFP indicated, would figure in as 25 percent of the assessment.

Nothing said flat-out, "We're going to look more favorably on low-bid proposals," but the implication of that 25 percent was clear. No doubt the communications firm, a solid, respected player in its industry, wanted a high quality sales enhancement program, but as the numbers showed, the cost of the program was also a major consideration. As a result, it was clear to us, as it must have been clear to competing vendors, that we were being invited to play the "blind bid" game.

Traditionally, companies respond to such invitations by adopting one of two strategies: they play "lowball" or they emphasize "price performance."

In "lowball," you try to guess the lowest bid another vendor might offer, and then undercut it–even if this means discounting yourself out of a profit. The idea is that, in a world of cutthroat competition, business you get by cutting your own throat is preferable to no business at all–especially if you use it as a loss leader that you expect to recoup down the line. The problems with this type of self-sacrifice are that it's nonsustainable, it tells the buyer you come cheap, and it implies that the quality of your goods is also cheap.

When you emphasize "price performance" rather than price per se, you try to convince the buyer that what you're offering is so superior in terms of features and benefits that it more than justifies the inflated sticker you've slapped on it. This may be fine if your product or service really is dramatically superior to your competitor's. But in most cases today, that isn't so, and even when it is so, you can't rely on the customer to make that assessment, because (as we discussed in Chapter 2), people buy expectations, not products per se.

Because of the hazards inherent in these traditional responses, we shy away completely from the blind-bidding game. Instead, we conduct our business at a totally different level–a level where price, while a factor, is never the decisive factor, because we've worked with our clients in advance to forestall bidding wars and to position ourselves as the provider of "priceless" solutions. We don't try to drum up business by offering cheaper programs, because we think a "cheap" program would be the equivalent of a three-wheeled Cadillac. It might still look like a Cadillac, but it wouldn't perform like one.

So, in the scenario we've just outlined, the mere fact that we were being asked to play the bidding game made our decision relatively easy. We decided not to send in a bid. Instead, we wrote directly to the communication company's CEO, expressing Miller Heiman's interest in addressing its sales development problems and suggesting a top-level meeting between our companies' executives where we could discuss those problems in detail and determine Miller Heiman's ability to provide solutions.

This admittedly unorthodox response illustrates a number of critical principles.

First, it reiterates what we have said in previous chapters about the importance of understanding your customer's Concept *before* you try to pitch your world-class product. As we explained in our letter to the CEO, we felt it would be a waste of his time and ours for us to present a solution to an undefined problem; we needed the customer to sketch out his own solution image before we could spell out how we would color it in. All of this tracked our commitment to customized solutions, and our lifelong professional dedication to Win-Win relationships.

A second principle that our letter tried to put into play was our company's commitment to developing Ideal Customers. As we explained in Chapter 6, we seek business only with companies that are as dedicated as we are to Win-Win relationships, and to "full organizational commitment" to carrying them out. In approaching the CEO directly, we were saying in effect, "We're not interested in selling you. We're interested in improving the quality of your business." If this direct appeal elicited a negative response, so be it. We would then know that the communications firm was not our kind of customer.

The third principle was the underlying theme of this chapter. It's that—contrary to conventional wisdom—price doesn't matter.

All right. That's a little overstated. Of course price matters. In most sales situations, it matters a great deal more than 25 percent. But (1) it never matters as much as the bidding wars suggest, and (2) you have much more control over the impact of price than you might imagine. In fact, if you follow the guidelines that we lay down in this chapter, in most scenarios you can *almost* make price go away.

STUCK IN THE PRICE BOX: THE REAL REASON WHY

To most people involved in sales, this idea is anathema, because everybody "knows" that price is always decisive. How many times have you heard one of your colleagues, after losing a major deal to the competition, offer one of these explanations, based on the idea that "price is the driver"?

> *"I had the commission practically in my pocket when the competition oozed in with a rock-bottom bid."*
>
> *"We had the better product. They had the numbers."*
>
> *"You might as well fight city hall as argue about budget. If they don't want to spend the money, lowball wins."*
>
> *"The sticker price was the only thing they saw."*

We don't deny that price is often a factor in determining which competing vendor gets a bid. But the above explanations, like dozens of similar ones, give the impression not only that price is inevitably and always a decisive factor, but also that buyers, in making their purchasing decisions, use price rationally as a cudgel for vendors—that they maintain control by gleefully forcing prices downward.

Neither of these impressions is based in fact. The truth is that price becomes a decisive factor only in those scenarios when buyers have nothing else to look at—when they are at a loss for rational reasons to decide and look to price as a last-ditch default mechanism.

In Chapter 5, when we discussed the decision-making process, we said that buyers make good purchasing selections only after they have gone through "divergent thinking." Another way of saying this is that they base their final decisions on *differentiation*—on the distinctions they perceive between one solution and another. And, since what they want from a solution is either to improve or to fix a process, it's effectiveness, not simple cost, that primarily drives their choices. In fact, if your solution most effectively solves the customer's problem, price will seldom turn the tide toward your competitor.

But that's the case only when the buyer perceives a distinction, believes in it, and accepts it as important. If there's no clear difference between your solution and your competitor's, then the buyer will, quite rationally, force a distinction. Since buyers are by nature concerned with saving money, the "forced" distinction will more often than not be the price tag. It's an easy distinction to focus on, and if it's all you give your customers, that's what they'll look at. They don't want to do it, but they will when you offer them no alternative.

When that happens, you end up going head-to-head with your competitors in the business world's equivalent of "low card wins." It's a game that no seller likes to play, because it's one where nobody wins for very long. Fort Howard Corporation's senior territory manager Dan Salbego explains why. "There are sales reps and there are quoting reps," he says. "Quoting reps walk in with a calculator, try to guess the other guy's lowest bid, and come up with a figure that just sneaks under it. The trouble is, this is incredibly unstable. If price is the only thing that you're competing on, somebody can always sneak under *your* low bid. So you can win the contract today and lose it tomorrow."

The lesson for a selling organization is clear. If you are to escape the box—and the boxing-in—of price, you must offer your customers something other than a low bid, to help them distinguish you positively from your competition. Otherwise they'll be in the position of a coffee drinker who is offered two identical medium cups of Starbucks' special house blend, one at $1.25 and one at $2. Yes, in *that* case, only idiots would pay two bucks.

LEVEL 1: AT THE BOTTOM OF THE BUY-SELL HIERARCHY— COMMODITY SELLING

At Miller Heiman we have a name for selling that fails to offer the buyer a clear differentiation between competing products. We call it *commodity selling*, because it reflects the way sowbellies and other commodities are sold. Unless you're a hog, one sowbelly is pretty much indistinguishable from another. Hence, the most attractive vendor of sowbellies is the one with the lowest price.

Commodity selling may be fine in the Chicago futures market. It's a disaster to apply its principles to other kinds of selling, especially in arenas where the competition is fierce. If you position your product as if it's merely a commodity—that is, if you neglect to show your customers not just how your product or service is different, but also how the difference will bring them value—then you have no choice but to play the low-bid game. You'll be forced into playing it whether you want to or not, because you'll have invited your customer into the default mode.

But pushing commodities isn't the only way to sell. In fact, in terms of what we call the *Buy-Sell Hierarchy*, it's only the lowest, and the least effective, way to position yourself with a customer. In our Large Account Management Process, we describe a pyramid of alternative positioning styles, starting at the bottom with *commodities* and moving on up toward the *consultancy* level, where you contribute to your customers' organizational issues–where what you deliver is infinitely more valuable than a "cheap" product.

BUY-SELL HIERARCHY
(Your position as perceived by the customer)

The figure above illustrates the Buy-Sell Hierarchy. We've just described what it's like to be stuck at the bottom: it's like being caught in a price box. The scenario improves considerably as you move up, beginning with the second level: *selling quality*.

LEVEL 2: SELLING QUALITY

On a *Seinfeld* episode a while back, the gags revolved around a neighborhood takeout spot that serves the best soup in the city. Customers line up for blocks to be waited on by a counterman whose manners are as chilling as his soup is warming. Irritable and inflexible, this so-called "Soup Nazi" demands that the lunch crowd refrain from chitchat, uttering only the name of the soups they want before moving silently to the cashier. When one customer, Jerry's bubbly friend Elaine, dares to violate this rule by making small talk, the counterman banishes her into the street, gasping and soupless. No one raises a murmur at this behavior. The Soup Nazi's bean with bacon makes all indignities bearable.

This story line might be a parable about selling quality. When you're positioned as a vendor of "quality," you offer your customers a product or service that is a distinguishable cut above the competition's—and that's about it. As a seller of quality, you're in the business of delivering the best. You know it, your customers know it—and there's the problem. Even if you're not in the same league as the Soup Nazi, a focus on quality can focus you so rigidly on the product that you forget what the product is supposed to do, which is satisfy the customer.

You see this all the time in high-tech sales, where salespeople's detailed product knowledge—their intimate familiarity with bells and whistles—often blinds them to the specifics of a customer's problem. If you know that you've got the "best" product, there's a deadly temptation to assume that this fact in itself is all that any customer should need to know. Because what customer, given the choice, would take less than the best?

Sam Manfer, who sells and runs programs for Miller Heiman out of southern California, sees this product-centered thinking as almost inevitable. "Consultative selling is a great idea that everybody wants to follow," Sam says, "but to do it right you really have to listen, and listening isn't necessarily what we do best. It's human nature to be into ourselves first, to look at things from our own, or our company's, perspective, and to assume that if the customer's perspective is different, he's missing something.

"You get it all the time in programs. You ask a group to identify a given solution's strengths from the buyer's perspective, and you get a whole list of strengths that only a salesman could love. Everybody's still very focused on product—'He should love this; look at the extras'—and they find it difficult to put themselves in the Buying Influence's shoes. That doesn't do much for your credibility in the Buy-Sell Hierarchy."

The subtle arrogance that is implicit in a product-centered approach is only part of the problem. The deeper problem is that, in putting all your faith in quality, you fall victim to the idea that "Good products sell themselves" as well as its even deadlier corollary: "If my product is good enough, *everyone* will want it."

A related problem is that *quality doesn't last.* More precisely, its power to differentiate you from competitors doesn't last. That was one of the sobering trends of the 1980s: copycat experts turning high-quality innovations into norms. With more and more rapidity, yesterday's gee-whiz product is becoming today's 'ho-hum' offering and (even worse) tomorrow's dustbin special. Everybody today is in the situation of the bus driver in the movie *Speed*: Take the pedal off the metal, and your company may be done for.

Eliot Axelrod, an Apple account executive whose major account is the University of Minnesota, articulates the problem with a pointed example. "Market dynamism makes our industry, like many others, inherently unstable," he says. "With technology moving so fast, and with markets maturing overnight, the benchmarks for competition change every day. It took Comet thirty years to overtake Ajax in the cleanser market; Windows overtook DOS in only a few.

"Where I sell, in higher education, a hot, emerging issue is multimedia capability. Eighteen months ago, my customers were asking '*Can* you produce all this on one computer?' A year ago, the question had become '*How* can we do it?' Today, the 'can' and the 'how' are givens. Universities now want to be connected to the entire world, instantly. So multimedia has to be on the World Wide Web. And these new rules have been written in less than two years."

This "keep up or die" trend is especially visible in gizmo-intensive industries like computers, but it's no less true where technology is relatively flat. Every increase in quality is sooner or later (and usually sooner rather than later) overtaken by another one—making the first one as exciting as unsliced bread.

The bottom line is that customers expect the best. Giving them less keeps you fumbling around among the sowbellies. But even giving them the best is no longer enough. As our client Dave Laabs, vice president for sales and business development at McFarland Office Products and Business Interiors, puts it, "You put all our products and all the competiton's products out in a pasture with the cows. At a distance they all look pretty much alike, so you can't get solid differentiation today based on product specs alone. We're way beyond the days of satisfying the customer. The opportunities now are in *delighting* the customer."

LEVEL 3: DIFFERENTIATING THROUGH SERVICE

More and more, that delight is built on service. Progressive companies now increasingly rely on service and support contracts to make their "best" products more attractive than those of the competition. Here are examples from a couple of our clients.

IBM. In high tech, IBM led the way with a "service and support" strategy years ago, when it began placing enormous resources behind a corporate Delta Force of service engineers—and earning a reputation as the computer company that you could rely on anywhere in the world for instant maintenance. IBM led the high-tech pack for decades not because its hardware was significantly different from, say, Hewlett-Packard's or Apple's, but because of Big Blue's reputation for responding to trouble calls instantly anywhere from the Amazon to the Antarctic.

AEI Music. As David Duff, a major acount executive with AEI Music, noted in Chapter 6, highlighting a relatively minor superiority in service capability can make the difference between getting and not getting a piece of business. In Dave's story about the toy company, you'll recall, he was able to unseat a competing supplier who had been entrenched for nearly two decades by offering the differentiating factor of regular, price-stabilized service calls. "There wasn't a lot of difference in terms of the product," he admitted. "To tell the truth, the toy firm was perfectly happy with their current music system. We edged them out by going beyond the product, by giving them an added value the incumbent hadn't thought of."

That added value, however, is changing, even in terms of service and support, and as a result what were once significant service edges are gradually eroding in the face of customers' demands. Just as customers now take quality as a given, they are beginning to feel the same about service and support.

Consider one ubiquitous example: the toll-free customer-service 800 line. As recently as ten or fifteen years ago, the only firms in the country that offered their customers such an "extra" were the credit card leaders and the consumer product giants: Procter & Gamble, in fact, had one of the first, and it was an innovation when it was introduced in the 1970s. Today, only highly localized mom and pop businesses can even think of competing without this add-on. You could no more reach a national market without a toll-free line than you could survive without a telephone itself.

The same point could be made about fax capability or availability of replacement parts or speed of delivery. Such elements are no longer part of "enhanced packages." They're part of the entry fee you pay to play the game. As Geoffrey Bloom, president of a giant footwear marketing firm, described his retail customers to *Business Week*, "They want resupply in twenty-four hours, they want computer linkups, they want sophisticated financial analysis of our product's potential.... That's what I have to do to be viable." Such service and support constitute a new, upgraded given. This means that, for real sales success, you have to move higher. You have to be able to offer something that's not yet a given.

LEVEL 4: GROWING THE CUSTOMER'S BUSINESS

You do that, ironically, by moving even further from the product—something that goes dramatically against the sales professional's grain. Our natural tendency as salespeople is to highlight our products, to keep hammering away at how spiffy our new line looks, and to forget that the only reason customers care is that they hope our line will help them salvage, or improve, their own.

At the fourth level of the Buy-Sell Hierarchy, you are perceived as making a concrete contribution to the same issues that give your managers nightmares: day-to-day operations and long-term profits. If you can concentrate on that while your competitors are knocking each other out trying to fine-tune their service capabilities, you will establish the differentiation you need.

We are sometimes asked if this isn't getting too far from the knitting. Isn't making a contribution to a customer's profit margin the role not of a sales professional but of a management consultant? And if you concentrate all that energy on growing their business, what's going to happen to yours? What about *sales?*

Our reply is that "sales professional" and "management consultant" are no longer two mutually exclusive terms. To sell effectively, you've got to be a consultant. Not because "consultative selling" is the latest fad in the now-you-see-it, now-you-don't world of corporate reengineering, but for a far more practical reason: it is what customers are demanding.

Here are the facts. Learning International is a Connecticut research firm that recently conducted a survey of customers' attitudes. When they asked corporate clients in the high-tech pharmaceuticals and finance industries what they valued most in a supplier, this is what they found:

- *The single most valued attribute was "business expertise," that is, awareness of the customer's business and the problems the customer was facing. Just under 30 percent of the customers surveyed identified that as a critical factor in vendor choice.*
- *Another 25 percent of the surveyed customers picked "dedication to the customer" as most important.*
- *The next most popular attribute—at 23 percent—was "sensitivity to the account" coupled with "guidance" for its problems.*

What links these top three attributes, it's easy to conclude, is the attention to customers' needs that we discussed in Chapter 2—an attention you can develop only if you take the customer's business, not your own, as the driver of your game, and if you do so even in scenarios where it loses you orders.

What about the product? What about all those features and benefits that most sales professionals think they're in business to deliver? The surprising answer is that, according to the Learning International survey, "product performance and quality" was a very poor fourth: only 10 percent of those surveyed mentioned it at all.

This finding reinforces our own. It's not that customers don't care about performance and quality. It's that they've come to expect both as natural—and as unproblematic givens. What they want in vendors, now, is something beyond this. They want quality backed by a professional who can help them grow their business. That's the type of differentiation the most competitive players now aim for.

LEVEL 5: STRATEGIC ORCHESTRATION

At the very top of the Buy-Sell Hierarchy, sellers are perceived as contributing not only to measurable revenue and profitability, but to broader and more diffuse organizational issues that have a less direct impact on the bottom line. The distinction is subtle, but it's instantly understandable to anyone who sees more in a business than quarterly P&L statements. At level 4, you are able to say to the buyer, "Here's a way you can make more money this year." At level 5, you say, "Where would you like to see this company five years from now? And what can we bring to the table that will help you get there?"

In "Death of a Salesman," a fascinating story on the "new selling" written for the September 1994 issue of *Management Review*, Catherine Romano sums up the picture succinctly, and in the process highlights the emerging importance of consultative, or partnership, roles. Referring to Miller Heiman's Buy-Sell Hierarchy, she writes that in climbing this ladder,

> Salespeople must adopt a different role, a part that bears no resemblance to Willy Loman. Buyers are looking for salespeople to wear three hats: long-term ally, business consultant, and strategic orchestrator. The role of strategic orchestrator, in which salespeople bring the resources of their company to client organizations, is the newest and most challenging aspect of a salesperson's new job description. Be forewarned: If your company's sales force is not effectively acting as strategic orchestrators, it's a sure bet that it soon will be—or the company will be losing market share.

That's an excellent brief description not only of the "new selling," but of the "new differentiation" that must accompany it. The lesson is clear. To be a player today, you need much more than a great product backed by great service. You need at the very least an attention to your customers' profit issues—and a willingness to cut judiciously into your own short-term profits to secure the long-term benefits of a business alliance. Beyond that, with increasing urgency, you need to position yourself as a member of the customer's own management team—as alert as he or she is both to market issues and to the internal bobbing and weaving through which those issues are addressed. In short, to use Catherine Romano's memorable phrase, you need to be a "diagnostician of the company's ills."

Bob Stewart, the American Teleconferencing Services executive whose epigraph on trust opens this chapter, recognizes that selling in this manner doesn't necessarily evoke instant acceptance. "One of our principal goals," Bob says, "is to demonstrate to the people who use our services that we can be one of the items in their "in" basket that they don't have to worry about—and that, in the process, we can make them look good to their own people as well as their own management. But they're not necessarily going to see that right off the bat.

"Initially, in fact, most prospects question your motives. Since most companies are in there for the quick sale, it may take months before a customer realizes you're different. It's great when you hear that click happen: 'These people care about my organization. They want to make me look good.' But it doesn't come overnight. You've got to work at it, and to be really successful you've got to understand your customers' business even better than they may understand it themselves.

"That's one of the great advantages that selling gives you: it forces you to take a broader view. I worked for IBM for sixteen years. I thought I understood what was important to them, but now that I'm engaging with them as a customer, I have a perspective on their business that I never had as an employee. A great sales organization has to have that. You have to know more about your customers than they know about themselves."

Michael Hammer, coauthor of *Reengineering the Corporation*, lucidly described one of the implications of this approach in a recent interview with the magazine *Sales and Marketing Management*. Recognizing the cross-fertilization that is increasingly a feature of the way leading companies plan their operations, he describes the emerging trend of "cross-company reengineering." Following this trend, executives at traditionally interlocked companies are being forced to say to each other, "We need to reengineer the way we work with you, and together we have to find new ways of streamlining the processes that connect us."

DOING IT RIGHT: LOCKING IN THE BUSINESS

One of the best descriptions of this streamlining that we've ever heard comes from one of the participants in our Strategic Selling program, Bruce Thrush, a national accounts director for Kwikset, the largest domestic lockset manufacturer. Last year a major Kwikset customer, Home Depot, challenged its vendors to produce new merchandising plans. "Our chief competitor," says Bruce, "came up with a plan, and as the market leader we were obliged to respond. But we wanted to get beyond price and old-fashioned head-butting. Instead of playing the 'My dog is bigger than your dog' game, we wanted to act as a consultant for Home Depot's business, to develop a marketing strategy for their whole lockset segment.

"To do that, we had to overturn some ancient assumptions about what a vendor and a buyer have a right to expect from each other. Normally, for example, we couldn't get our hands on sales data—even on what volume of Kwikset's own merchandise they were moving. The assumption was that this is proprietary information, so it shouldn't be shared with anybody outside the company.

"We felt that, to produce a solid marketing strategy for them, we needed to get basic figures on how we were doing, how the lockset segment overall was doing, and so on. At a start-up session with a dozen regional buyers, I laid that out. I verbalized the fact that we believed we had a fiduciary relationship with our customers, and that they should understand that we wouldn't use their data against them. This was part of being a consultant, not just a vendor. They saw the logic in that, and we got the data.

"Other assumptions we challenged had to do with design. Footage specs, for example, were a big nut to crack. The given wisdom in the warehouse-style retailing industry is that new vendors require eight-foot sections, or bays. Our proposal uncovered some hidden inefficiencies in that tradition, suggesting how changing the footage might help boost profits. We did the same thing with the visual appearance of the bays. Our thought was they should break them up with curtains, use a little more off-white in the color scheme, a little more of an open look.

"That wasn't an easy sell at Home Depot, where people are prouder of being orange than the Syracuse football team. But we talked it through, and found ways to modify their design so that our suggested new look would still be acceptably 'Depotized.' There's a lot you can accomplish if you don't allow your ego to get in the way, and we weren't trying to get our way, just improve the profit picture for a critical customer.

"And that leads to the most important assumption we challenged—

the assumption that every supplier lives for short-term profits. Floor managers and others at Home Depot had complained to us in the past that we were always asking for, and getting, too much display space. No doubt they make the same complaint to other vendors, but with this new merchandising plan, it focused on us. Wasn't our plan just a new way of getting Kwikset more space?

"It amazed them—and I think it really solidified the deal—when we explained that we would be willing to *give up* space, because we were committed to improving not just Kwikset's sales, but the profitability of their entire lockset business. That's not disingenuous, either. We were, and are, committed to that—for a very practical and ultimately very self-serving reson. If Home Depot's lockset segment stays flat, our lion's share of the shelf space isn't worth much. If our consulting plan helps to boost that segment overall, then we'll do better, even with a smaller shelf area.

"And this is true even before taking into account the long-term benefits of serving as their consultants. If our design for them works, and we believe it will, then they will see us as a partner, not just a vendor. When our analysis helps Home Depot's profits go up, sooner or later we will be neutralizing the competition, for a simple reason: the competition doesn't do that."

SURVIVAL OF THE "FIT THOUGH FEW"

Neutralizing the competition indeed. One outcome of the type of interaction that Bruce describes, as many corporation-watchers have pointed out, is a series of shakeouts that eliminates all but the most serious suppliers. Let's face it. Not everybody *wants* the partnering that we recommend. Increasingly, those who don't want it fall out of the race, and customers are left to choose among those "fit though few" suppliers with whom they are able to develop the most durable relationships. As Blessington and O'Connell observe about the widespread trend toward single-sourcing, "current procurement techniques" are geared toward "locking in the enduring value provided by a supplier relationship."

A second, corollary outcome is that those relationships can be based on premium exchange, that is, on higher price. Out of numerous examples we could mention, we'll cite only the case of one successful client, a regional manager for a national manufacturer of heavy machinery. The traditional competitive style in this arena, he told our newsletter editor Sally Glover, used to be "strictly equipment versus equipment. That was a problem for us, because we are significantly higher on price on one of our top pieces of machinery."

In a recent sale, however, he and his sales team adopted a consultative role, "studying the customer's operation and determining what was working and what wasn't." In "writing the specifications for the customer," the team effectively eliminated the competition even though its package was $130,000 higher. "In forty-one years of selling," the manager said, "I have never won a sale where I was $10,000 higher on price, let alone $130,000. Our consultative strategy helped the customer to realize that we were delivering something that went way beyond the cost of the order."

Michael Hammer, speaking to William Keenan Jr., gives a typically manufacturing spin to outcomes like this one, when he explains why higher price is often both inevitable and desirable: "When processes between customers and suppliers are streamlined, customers are often able to reduce their operating costs by having suppliers take on some work which used to be done by the customer. In many cases the supplier needs to recoup some of that additionally incurred cost in the form of higher product price. And the customer has to see that the higher price is, in fact, part of a lower cost."

We agree with this analysis, but it's important to add that the reduction of operating costs is not the result exclusively of a supplier's doing "more work." A customer's operating costs may also be reduced by the purchase of a product-service package whose superior capabilities brings him or her other, down-the-line added values: better quality control, for example, or reduced downtime, or an increase in end-users' satisfaction. In addition, customers may save operating monies by utilizing any number of "beyond the product" enhancements that a supplier at level 4 or level 5 may be able to bring.

That's the whole point of our injunction to "move up the hierarchy." In doing so, you can have an impact on your customers' overall cost of doing business. When they see you do that consistently, they will pay your higher price. That's the real opportunity, and the challenge, of being a "strategic orchestrator."

PRICE, COST, AND THE CHIVAS REGAL EFFECT

We're not suggesting that all premium pricing is benign. In a story in *USA Today* about the rising cost of college tuition, Frank Newman, the president of a Denver-based education commission, was quoted describing the "Chivas Regal effect." That effect is all too relevant to what might be called the "reverse price wars" in luxury and high-end markets.

Reflecting on his experience as director of university relations at Stanford, Newman described the Chivas Regal effect this way: "If Harvard is $400 more in tuition than Stanford, people are going to believe Harvard is better. So we better get our tuition up." The inflationary spiral that this kind of thinking encourages is all too well known to anyone putting a child through college—or buying a top-shelf Scotch. It's *not* what we mean to encourage when we speak about charging a premium price for a premium product.

Your company's pricing decisions are affected by numerous inputs—competitive pressures, material and operating costs, inflation, market elasticity, and a host of other considerations. Our point is not that you will be able to—or that you should try to—charge whatever the traffic will bear. It's that, in assessing the value of your product or services, you should also factor in such added value as the information and coaching you give your clients. If that's worth something, then it ought to be reflected in your product price. And increasingly, if you're not providing that added value, then you won't be able to call on the Chivas Regal effect anyway—savvy customers simply won't pay the freight.

The inanity that Newman describes, in other words, is an inflationary aberration in high-rolling markets. But even without this kind of false competition, people would still be paying premium tuition rates to the likes of Harvard and Stanford, and for the same reason, in the end, that they pay it to us: because those schools are providing more than excellent teaching and diplomas. Their degrees are perceived by customers as giving them a competitive edge in the business and social markets. That's why Harvard costs ten times as much as your local community college. That's why the top "education vendors" can command their top rates: they reduce their customers' sensitivity to price because those customers are convinced that the add-ons are worth it.

OTHER BENEFITS OF MOVING UP THE HIERARCHY

In addition to reducing price sensitivity, moving up the Buy-Sell Hierarchy also brings you three other significant benefits. Ironically, it shrinks the competitive field. It ensures healthier, more durable business. And it connects you with the key decision makers in your clients' organizations.

Competing with the Best

It's paradoxical but true. As you move away from providing commodities and toward providing solutions, the field of viable competitors actually shrinks. Everybody is prepared to go head-to-head with regard to product and service specs, but only a savvy few have come to understand the value of making contributions beyond the sale. This means that if you position yourself at the top, you'll be standing on a smaller platform and jockeying for sustained position with sharper, more aggressive rivals. It's not accidental that the hierarchy is drawn as a pyramid. The field of play at the top is smaller and more intense. There isn't really less competition, but there are fewer competitors, because most producers aren't ready to play in this league.

Managed Business Health

John Young, the former president and CEO of our client Hewlett-Packard, once paid us a welcome compliment when he described the Miller Heiman mission as helping customers to create "the kinds of partnerships that will last over the years to come." We do that in no small part by showing our clients the wisdom of "selling up"–of establishing themselves as level 4 and level 5 players, intent on securing their business not just by "selling" today, but by improving the health of those companies that will buy in the future.

Managed business health is what it's about. We've said that people buy to solve business problems–in terms of our metaphor, to make an "illness" go away. Many competitors don't even get this far. They're stuck in the selling profession's stone age, pushing their snake-oil cures to all and sundry, never bothering to ask about the client's symptoms. A precious few are taking a more therapeutic approach by talking to customers and trying to supply those solutions that will most quickly make their maladies disappear. That's good, but it's not enough. What we're recommending is a *preventive* approach to problems, to supplement the more conventional *curative* one. It's fine to "fix" a customer's inventory backlog. It's better to provide perspective on the customer's entire warehousing system, ensuring that there won't be an inventory "relapse" in the future.

In traditional Chinese medicine, the doctor is paid not for fixing problems but for keeping the patient healthy. When a patient falls ill, it's assumed that the doctor has been neglectful, and the fee is withheld until the patient recovers. This radically preventive approach is worth considering, if not as a practical alternative at least as a model of how vendors should be assessing the health of their long-term partners. Imagine how business culture (not to mention the reputation of "sales") might change if vendors were paid a retainer for contributing to their customers' profitability–and were denied this fee when profitability went down. That would be "cross-company reengineering" with a vengeance.

Selling at the Top

Last, but certainly not least, moving up the hierarchy allows you–or, rather, forces you–to position yourself with the leaders to whom business and organizational issues matter: the executives with responsibility over their companies' health. Presidents, CEOs, COOs, CFOs, EVPs, and vice presidents–all those movers and shakers whose authority routinely intimidates field reps, but whose involvement is essential to the building of the partnerships we're discussing.

Getting to see these people is not simply a matter of knocking. There are real difficulties that salespeople encounter in getting to Economic Buyers–difficulties having to do with identification, access, and intimidation. Nonetheless, having someone cover those high-level bases–whether it's a sales manager or a senior executive–is fast becoming essential in today's environment, because it's only these players at the top of the customer's buying hierarchy who can ultimately waive price restrictions and get you out of the box.

There's often a conflict between these people and the "purchasing agents" who ostensibly say yes or no. The reason is their difference in focus. Economic Buyers want to reduce their costs. In most cases, a purchasing agent–the classic example of the Technical Buyer–wants to reduce the immediate sticker price. Because many Technical Buyers (and User Buyers) are "measured only on product price" and not on "the total cost of that product to their company," they have trouble looking at the long term and growing the future. They're blinded by glasses that only let them see so far. It's the sales professional's task to change their prescription.

MAINTAINING YOUR FOOTING

If we've given the impression in this chapter that moving up the Buy-Sell Hierarchy is a natural, one-way progression, we should correct that impression here. The reality is that, with most customers, you have to fight, and fight hard, to demonstrate the benefits of cost-driven thinking over price-driven thinking. There seems to be, sadly, a kind of entropic drift toward "seeing only the sticker," and this means that the old injunction "caveat emptor" needs to be augmented by "caveat vendor." Given the chance, many buyers will try to push you down the hierarchy, because in their (shortsighted) view, it's easier to deal with a commodity pusher than a consultant.

Elizabeth Ngonzi, who sells cash registers and other point-of-sale equipment for Micros Systems, relates an experience that illustrates this "footing" problem—and how attention to added value can help to over-come it. "People will always try to push you downward," she says, "and if you're not careful you can get sucked in to the old bells-and-whistles, one-upmanship game. One of our main competitors, for example, offers a meal-ordering system with a color touch-screen. At Micros, we believe that color is a pretty gimmick that doesn't really add value, so we've stuck, at least up to now, with monochrome screens. Our competitor, of course, makes a big deal of the color feature, and there are plenty of customers who are con-vinced they've got to have it.

"I had a prospect last year, for example, who told me straight out that he was going to go with the competition for the simple reason that 'Micros doesn't have color.' When we began talking about why color was important to him, it became clear that he didn't really need or even want it—he was using our lack of that feature as a pricing negotiator, hoping that I'd offer our monochrome screen at a discount. In Miller Heiman's terms, he was trying to push me down the Buy-Sell Hierarchy, to position Micros as just another pusher of commodities.

"I didn't play the game. Instead of budging on price, I talked about the added value that Micros could bring to his operation. I stressed our his-tory of reliability, our service record, our belief in the value of building a long-term relationship. It turned out that those things mattered a lot more to him than spiffy graphics, and when he saw that they were central to our way of doing business, the issue of color never came up again."

One of our sales consultants, Mike Joyce, used a similar "refooting" technique recently when a client asked him to deliver a detailed compari-son between Miller Heiman programs and those of another consultant. The embedded message in this request was, "I want the two of you to fight for a toehold at level 2." Mike's response in effect was, "We don't do that. If you need to make a comparison, can you tell me what you want to com-pare and whom you'll be showing the comparison to? That will help me to identify your concerns more clearly." Mike may or may not get that piece of business, but if he does, it will be within parameters that he and Miller Heiman feel comfortable working with. If he doesn't, all we will lose is a poor-fit prospect.

We'll give the final word to Bob Stewart of American Teleconfer-encing Services. Bob's company arranges multisite telephone conferencing, mostly for Fortune 100 companies. "When somebody says 'Let me try your services at a discount,' I generally say, 'We'll let you use the services twice at a discount, but let's apply the discount on times two and three.' We don't want to be in and out. We want the chance to build a relationship, to understand the customer's Concept, to refine our operation so that, by the third or fourth meeting, we understand their needs better and we're able to give them much more than they asked for.

"You can't do that right at the outset. It takes time to understand your customers' particular problems, so you can show them that you're in business to make them look good. That's why we'll try to arrange for a package of three or four meetings. By the third one, you're on the way to mutually developing a solution. You've impacted the criteria that lie behind their buying decisions."

We take a different tack from Bob's toward the "freebie" approach to starting up a customer relationship. If a client asks us for a no-charge program, we're less likely to say "Later down the line" than "We're not a discount firm. Give us the chance to deliver, to tailor our presentation to your particular business needs. If we can't do it right, we'd rather you didn't pay us at all." But we're on exactly the same page as Bob is when it comes to having an impact on the customer's criteria for buying decisions. Making such an impact, in fact, is a primary index of success in today's selling world. If you're involved that deeply, and at that level, in your customers' decision making, you are well on your way to serving as a strategic orches-trator—and to freeing yourself for good from the prison of price.

MANAGERS' CHECKLIST 4: THE BUY-SELL HIERARCHY

Given that your company's position in the Buy-Sell Hierarchy is deter-mined by the customer's perspective, not the seller's, here are some probing questions to assess the stability of your footing.

1. *What is our current position on the Buy-Sell Hierarchy? Are we at the very minimum offering this customer excellent products and services that fulfill his or her perceived needs?*

2. *What's the concrete evidence that our offerings are better than those of the competition? What are our unique strengths vis-à-vis our nearest or most threatening competitor?*

3. *What specific internal business problem have we helped this customer to understand better? When was the last time someone from our sales team met with a manager in the customer's company to discuss that problem? What specific expertise or consulting capability did we bring? What ev-idence do we have that it was (a) understood and (b) appreciated?*

4. *Who is the highest-placed person in our organization who has met with a counterpart in the customer's organization? If we haven't established*

executive-to-executive contact at least at the vice presidential level, why not? Do we need Coaching on this score? Who can provide it?

5. What specific information have we brought this customer in the past ninety days to help its management understand industry trends better? If we haven't provided this kind of organizational support in the past quarter, who in our organization is best positioned to provide it now? Schedule a meeting to that effect, with accountability and timetable.

6. Have we recently lost business with this customer because of price sensitivity? If so, how can we reposition our products or services so that the customer will understand the cost-effectiveness of buying from us rather than from a "cheaper" supplier?

8

WHY DIDN'T WE SEE THAT COMING?

"The customers we serve are constantly undergoing M&As. If we hadn't adopted a systematic process for identifying Red Flags, we wouldn't be doing nearly as well as well as we are."
–Joel French
Vice President, Healthcare
Sentient Systems

"It is better to know nothing than to know what ain't so."
–Josh Billings

IN CHAPTER 4, WHEN WE DESCRIBED BFI REP-
resentative Robyn Crebs's record-breaking sale to a food warehouser, we
observed that her success could be attributed directly to her detailed plan
for covering the account's Buying Influences. In working through that plan,
she discovered a hole in her strategy that she hadn't recognized before: the
fact that the supposed Economic Buyer with whom she was talking lacked
the budgetary authority to release the needed funds. For Robyn, in other
words, it was careful analysis of the situation that made the difference between two years of butting into walls and the President's Club. What got
her the order, eventually, was *better information.*

Consider a "what if" variation on this scenario. What if Robyn had
not looked beyond the obvious? What if, in attempting to sell into this
mammoth, complex account, she had continued to rely on the salesperson's traditional gifts of instinct, known contacts, and perseverance? What if
she had assumed rather than constantly checking her information? What
probable outcome would she be looking at then?

The answer is implicit in her story. As she told us, before she applied systematic *analysis* to the account, she had been hammering away at
that door for over two years. The danger here was more than simple ex-
haustion. Not only was her perseverance getting her nowhere. She was also
leaving the warehouse opportunity vulnerable to capture by a competitor
who *had* performed the necessary analysis, and who could waltz in a door
that Robyn hadn't seen open.

In Robyn's case, this didn't happen. But scenarios like the one
we're describing are not hypothetical. They happen every day, as sales organizations watch deals they have worked on for years suddenly fall
through because they have been relying on things they know that "ain't so."

WHAT HAPPENED?
COMMON EXPLANATIONS—AND THE UNDERLYING CAUSE

When disasters like these occur, there is seldom a shortage of frustrated,
befuddled explanations. They usually follow one or more of the following
familiar patterns:

> *"Another week and we would have had the deal sewed up. They just
> came in out of the blue, and we got blindsided."*

"It turns out that we were talking to the wrong people all along."

"There was nothing anybody could have done. It was internal politics."

"We thought we had all the bases covered. Then their budget fell through."

"At the last minute nobody got the bid. They shifted resources around and did it themselves."

Notice two things about these explanations. First, they all assign blame for the loss of the sale to a source that is external and unmanagable, that is, beyond the reasonable control of the selling organization. We lost the sale not because of anything we did or didn't do, but because of a hidden competitor, or Buying Influences who misrepresented themselves, or a customer's decision to turn inward and freeze vendors out.

Second, in spite of the blame-fixing, every one of these common explanations for "why we blew it" reveals the same underlying cause. In every case, the business was lost because the selling organization lacked some essential piece of *information* about the account. Whether the identified culprit is a competitor or budgets or "politics," the sale was really lost because the sales team had incorrect information, or because they acquired the correct information too late to make a difference.

The lack of solid information is such a deal-killer that, in our programs, we call it an *automatic Red Flag*. We use Red Flag as a symbol to describe any area of account strategy or sales call planning where you're missing information, or where you're not absolutely certain that the information you have is accurate. Much of what we do in our two-day workshops focuses on the identification of these trouble spots—and on drafting strategies to eliminate or reduce their influence. *Not* doing this practically ensures that you will lose business because you don't "see something coming" before it's too late.

In the complex sales that are so common today, countless areas can turn into Red Flag zones. It would be impossible to list them all in a single chapter. What we can do is to outline the most common areas where our clients encounter an information blackout, and then show you how a detailed *Situation Analysis* can help you fill in the blanks, eliminate Red Flags, and minimize the chances of losing business because of imponderable "externals." That's what this chapter is about. It reviews everything we've been saying about the sales process up to this point and distills it into a modified version of the Situation Analysis worksheet that we present more fully in our corporate programs. We emphasize here exactly what we emphasize there: the fact that a good account strategy begins with under-standing your position, that it should be composed of concrete actions that leverage from your company's strengths, and that, to remain effective, it has to be continually reassessed.

POSITION: SUBJECTIVE AND OBJECTIVE TESTS

Remember Wrong Way Corrigan? He was the pilot who, in 1938, flew east-ward out of a fog from New York to Dublin, supposedly under the misap-prehension that he was headed for California. A perfect example of not understanding your position. In Corrigan's case, it worked out well: he got a ticker-tape parade in New York City. Don't count on that reaction in high-ticket selling. If you misunderstand your position in your market or with your customers, you're less likely to end up in Dublin than in the drink.

To help you avoid that problem, we recommend that you take fre-quent fixes on your selling position, both at the start of your sales cycle and periodically thereafter. Assessing your position, both subjectively and ob-jectively, is the only sure way to be constantly alert to "what's coming," and thus avoid losing business that you thought was in your pocket.

In the *subjective* assessment, simply ask yourself how you feel, at this moment, with regard to the sales objective that you're trying to accom-plish. Feelings are not in themselves a sufficient gauge of position, but they are a beginning, and failing to take them into account can deprive you of one useful source of information. In our Strategic Selling programs, partici-pants assess their feelings about their account situations by rating them on a continuum from "panic" to "euphoria." You can use the same continuum, or devise terms of your own, to measure how comfortable and confident you are at a given point in the sale. The point is to acknowledge the psychological factor—what Joe White called the "emotional side"—in your buy-sell encounters. That factor may be difficult to measure, but it's never irrelevant.

In the *objective* phase of assessment, we recommend that you ques-tion critically where you stand with regard to the elements of the sales process that we've already discussed. Ask yourself how solidly, or how ten-uously, you and your company are positioned with regard to the following six elements: (1) Concept, (2) Buying Influences, (3) Win-Results, (4) Re-ceptivity, (5) Commitment, and (6) the Buy-Sell Hierarchy.

Sales managers should be directly involved in this objective phase of Situation Analysis, and for that reason what we present in the rest of this chapter should really be seen as an expanded Manager's Checklist. It gives specific questions that we recommend managers ask to test their sales teams' position with regard to the six elements. It also provides, as you'll see, a detailed review of everything we've discussed so far.

MANAGERS' CHECKLIST 5: SITUATION ANALYSIS

Before we get to the checklist proper, let's address two questions that we're often asked regarding the use of these Situation Analyses. The first relates to when, and in what circumstances, they should be performed. Clients often ask us, "How often should we do an extended Situation Analysis?"

The only honest answer is, "As often as necessary." Some of our clients do an analysis of this type for each new piece of business with a new client. The sales managements of other clients require it only for their larger pieces of business—say, pending sales over $50,000. At Harris Corporation, management modifies that general approach by requiring analyses of objectives based on market potential. "Usually," says Harris's vice-president for international sales, Larry Smith, "a division will want an in-depth look only on sales over $100,000 or $200,000. But if it's going to lead on to major business in the future, the sale of a $50 widget might also merit a thorough pursuit."

Even when the market potential is not extraordinary, special situations may still indicate the need for Situation Analyses. Many client companies, at our suggestion, require them whenever an account is scheduled for transfer to a new representative, or when a manager will accompany the salesperson on a joint call. In other companies, management requires Situation Analyses periodically through the sales cycle—so that, in businesses with very long sales cycles, the team may do three or four such analyses between qualifying and the close.

In these days of endless mergers and acquisitions ("M&As") this latter case is often the rule rather than the exception. Joel French, vice president of healthcare for our client company Sentient Systems, observes that the current M&A fever has led to "unprecedented consolidation" in the healthcare industry—and that this in turn has driven his company and others to consider the need for frequent Situation Analyses. "In the wake of an M&A," Joel says, "you often lose the clarity that you thought you had. The number of Buying Influences might go up, or down, or they'll be clustered differently on the basis of the new organization. Sales often get stalled when that happens—which is why you've got to be constantly rethinking the situation."

In other words, you reassess according to need. The one reliable guideline is this: Do a Situation Analysis whenever urgency or uncertainty indicate that you need clarification of account information.

The second question we're often asked is what the role of the manager should be in Situation Analyses. Our answer is that the manager should be part team leader and part Coach–raising relevant questions to sharpen the team's understanding of the sale and (just as important) to highlight areas where better information is needed.

Here, by contrast, are some common managerial roles that you should *not* adopt:

- **Inquisitor-judge.** *Don't ask, "Why didn't you deal with this six months ago?"*

- **Answer giver.** *Don't say, "There's only one solution that makes any sense here."*

- **Storyteller.** *Don't say, "When we encountered a similar problem two years ago, here's how we handled it."*

- **Parent.** *Don't ask rhetorically, "How many times do I have to tell you not to do that?"*

The point, in short, is not to grill or interrogate your people, but to determine, through group analysis, where your company is strongly positioned and where it's not. If this analytical exercise reveals, for example, that nobody has yet contacted the Economic Buyer, the appropriate response is *not* "Why not?" or "What the hell?" The appropriate response is to identify that piece of the picture as a major Red Flag, as a trouble spot that, if you don't cover it, will send you reeling into the fog.

Having made these two clarifications, let's look now at the Situation Analysis in detail.

Process Element 1: Concept

The focus here is on selling effectively to your customer's solution image. Since that image varies from person to person, you should consider "the customer" in these questions as referring not to the buying organization as a whole but to each of its individual Buying Influences.

1. With regard to our current sales objective, what is this customer's Concept? What is the specific problem that the customer is facing, and what is his or her solution image for resolving it? We should be able to write this out as the customer would phrase it.

2. How will our product, service, or proposal close the gap that this person perceives between desired results and current reality? We should be able to write the answer out in the following form: "Our (name of product/service) will help (name of customer) accomplish (customer's Concept) by (method of accomplishment)."

3. Is the solution we're proposing really the best solution available for this customer's needs, or just the best that our company has to offer? Have we encouraged the customer to move from cognition to divergent thinking to convergent thinking—or have we "slam-dunked" him or her into our own best bet? Are we certain that we're not just selling what's expedient for us?

4. Even more important, is the customer certain of this? Does this person understand our commitment to helping him or her achieve the desired results? We must be perceived *by the customer* as a contributor to the best solution, not as a pusher of our own products or services. What evidence do we have that this is so?

5. Does the customer himself or herself fully understand the Concept? If not, how can we help facilitate the decision-making process? What consulting help can we provide that will help us develop the best available solution together?

6. If we have any uncertainty about the customer's Concept, what Coaching do we need to help us understand it better? Who can give us that Coaching?

Process Element 2: Buying Influences

The focus here is on identifying and covering the bases with all the players who can have an impact, positive or negative, on your sales objective. No matter how many of these players there are—and there may be many—each one plays one or more of four clearly defined Buying Influence roles.

1. Who is the Economic Buyer for this sales objective? Recall that, for each objective, there is only one person playing this role—and that the role may shift up or down the organization depending on the importance of the sale. To identify the Economic Buyer, we need to ask which person controls the necessary funds and will make the final decision—approval or veto—about the solution. We should also ask, "To whom do the people who will be affected by the solution report?"

2. Since Technical Buyers frequently masquerade as Economic Buyers, what evidence do we have that the person we have identified as the

Economic Buyer will in fact play that role in this sale? Is the evidence direct or indirect? If it's indirect, has it been corroborated by a Coach or another Buying Influence?

3. Have we identified all the players whose actual job performance will be affected by our proposal? In the department that we're selling into, do we know who will supervise the installation and use of our product or service? List all of these individuals as User Buyers.

4. Have we identified all the players with responsibility for judging and recommending our proposal on the basis of specifications? We should look for such individuals both in the buying organization and outside of it—for example, in governmental agencies. List all of these people as Technical Buyers.

5. Have we developed at least one reliable Coach to help guide us in achieving this sales objective? Are we certain that this person is not merely a friend or a source of information? To be a reliable Coach, the person must (a) trust us, (b) have credibility in the buying organization, and (c) want us to make this sale. What evidence do we have that this person meets these three criteria?

6. Have we adequately covered all of the Buying Influences? Field salespeople often cannot cover all key players themselves, so each Buying Influence should be covered by the individual best qualified to do so. That might be the salesperson, the Coach, or someone else in our organization. Write down who on our team we have covering each of the Buying Influences. What evidence do we have that all of these bases are covered well?

Process Element 3: Win-Results

We focus here on how well our proposal will deliver both the business Results that the customer needs and the personal Wins that the Buying Influences require.

1. Although "companies get Results," it is still individual players' needs that are satisfied by the delivery of those Results. In addition, our proposal, if accepted, will very likely deliver a variety of Results, and those Results will mean different things to different Buying Influences. Therefore, for each Buying Influence, we need to identify the specific business Results that he or she requires, and that our proposal promises to fulfill.

2. In identifying these Results, we should ask: (a) Which of the Buyer's business processes does this Result affect? (b) How does our proposal fix or improve that process? In identifying the type of Results that

each of the four Buying Influences typically looks for, keep the following general principles in mind:

- **Economic Buyers** *typically look for bottom-line Results such as low cost, good budget fit, increased productivity, higher profitability, and better return on investment.*

- **User Buyers** *typically want performance-related Results such as increased efficiency or reliability, more versatility, ease of application, superior service, and the opportunity to do their jobs better, faster, and more easily.*

- **Technical Buyers** *look for Results that affect "technicalities" including (but not limited to) product specs, delivery schedules, legal issues, technological requirements, and price.*

Coaches, in their capacity as Coaches, don't have their own business Results. By definition, the Result they want is to have you make the sale.

3. When we deliver these Results, how will each Buying Influence Win? That is, how will each player's individual self-interest be served by the timely delivery of these business Results? In considering this question, note that among the most common reasons that people Win are that the Results enable them to:

- *Gain control over others*
- *Become more productive*
- *Gain recognition*
- *Increase their self-esteem*
- *Gain more freedom*
- *Get more family time*
- *Remain in power*
- *Improve their skills*
- *Improve their social status*
- *Feel more secure*
- *Gain more responsibility*
- *Make a contribution*

This is but a handful of the countless ways in which Buying Influences, as unique individuals, feel that their self-interest is served. If we're not clear about how each individual Buying Influence will Win, we should (a) infer the answer from the person's required Results, (b) get Coaching, or (c) ask the Buying Influence directly.

4. For each Buying Influence involved in this sale, we should be able to write a "Win-Results Statement" in the following form: "(Buying Influence) will Win because our company's delivery of (Result) will provide him or her with (Win)." If we can't complete that statement with confidence, we may not adequately understand the Buying Influence's self-interest, and we should inquire further about it or seek further Coaching.

Process Element 4: Receptivity

Here we aim to clarify which of our Buying Influences are receptive at this time to considering change—specifically, to the change that our proposal implies—and which ones are not.

1. What is the current Response Mode of each Buying Influence? On our list of Buying Influences, we should identify each one's current mode as Growth, Trouble, Even Keel, or Overconfident.

2. For the Buying Influences that we have identified as being in the Growth mode, what evidence do we have that this assessment is accurate? Typically, when you speak to people in Growth, you'll hear the following phrases:

> *"We're upgrading our standards."*
>
> *"Tougher regulations are coming out of Washington."*
>
> *"We're on the verge of a real opportunity here."*
>
> *"Things are moving so fast that I'm afraid I'm going to lose control."*

If we're not hearing comments like this from our so-called Growth players, we need to reassess their receptivity. If we are, what specific information have we given them to demonstrate that our proposal will contribute to Growth?

3. Which of our Buying Influences are in Trouble? Check this assessment for each player by listening for typical Trouble mode comments like these:

> *"There's no way we're going to make that deadline."*
>
> *"The competition is breathing down our neck."*
>
> *"If we don't pull this off, my job's on the line."*
>
> *"I can see the brick wall coming, but I can't find the brake."*

Notice that all of these comments describe current problems. How will our proposal prevent things from getting any worse? What specific information have we given our players in Trouble to demonstrate that we can minimize further negative impacts?

4. Which of our Buying Influences don't want to rock the boat? Listen for comments like these:

> *"We're doing fine just as we are."*
>
> *"Try my replacement after I'm transferred next month."*
>
> *"My boss says this is a low priority."*
>
> *"There's no room in the budget for this right now."*

For everybody who's talking like this, we should note that he or she is in Even Keel, and is therefore minimally open to making any changes. Mark this as a Red Flag. Which of our Growth or Trouble players can we leverage with to turn the Even Keel player around?

5. Are any of our Buying Influences arrogantly Overconfident? To spot people with their heads in the sand, we should listen for comments like these:

> *"We already do that better than anybody else in this industry."*
>
> *"That problem has already been solved."*
>
> *"Not in my department, you don't."*
>
> *"If it ain't broke, don't fix it."*

Mark all Overconfident players as Red Flags. Consider these strategic options: (a) leveraging from a Growth or Trouble player, or (b) waiting for the arrogance to lead, inevitably, to Trouble.

Process Element 5: Commitment

The point here is to "prequalify" our leads so that we focus on our potentially most reliable customers—and then to "requalify" them throughout the selling cycle, to determine that they're actually playing Win-Win.

1. Refer to the Ideal Customer profile that we created in Chapter 6. How well does the customer we're trying to sell to now match the five criteria we established there? If there's not a good match with at least three of our criteria, have we considered whether we really need this business?

2. Our commitment is to achieve mutually satisfying, long-term, Win-Win relationships. What evidence do we have that this is also our cus-

tomer's commitment? What has the customer done recently to demonstrate its ownership of the buy-sell process?

3. On our last sales call to this customer, what was the salesperson's Best Action Commitment? What was the Minimum Acceptable Action? Was either commitment met? If not, were there factors that made that lack of commitment understandable?

4. If we're not routinely getting at least the Minimum Acceptable Action on sales calls to this customer, we should be asking Basic Issue questions to find out why. Was that done on the last sales call? If not, someone needs to do it the next time we meet this customer. If this doesn't result in a clarification of the customer's lack of commitment, we need to rethink how important this business is to us. Should we accept the slow progress, or should we walk?

Process Element 6: The Buy-Sell Hierarchy

The focus here is on our company's position vis-à-vis the customer's company. We're looking for a fix on where we stand in the customer's eyes.

1. To keep ourselves out of the price box, we need to be clearly differentiated from the competition. What unique strengths can we offer this customer that the competition can't? What evidence do we have that the customer understands and appreciates our uniqueness?

2. How well do we understand this customer's industry and general business problems? Have we met recently with its senior management to discuss its business concerns, not our products or services?

3. What is the highest level at which we have established contact between our two organizations? What Coaching do we need to build a stable relationship at the senior management level? Who is best positioned to provide that Coaching? Who in our organization is best positioned to contact the potential Coach?

LEVERAGING FROM STRENGTH

The second step in improving your position, after you've gone through this checklist, is to protect yourself from the unexpected by attacking the Red Flags you've discovered. There are two basic approaches to this task, only one of which is likely to get good results.

The traditional approach is to attack the Red Flags head-on, to hammer at them directly until they disappear. You've left four phone messages for Ellen Chalk, the Economic Buyer, and she's never responded? Leave her a fifth message. Dan Deleone, a key User Buyer, is deeply entrenched in an Even Keel mode? Convince him that what he ought to be feeling is Growth. Frank German, a Technical Buyer in finance, says that your service package is more expensive than the competition's? Offer him a discount. If the Red Flag is the problem (so goes the traditional logic), pull it up. Just do it.

As we've said before, there's nothing wrong with optimism. But in and of itself, it won't get the job done. Let's face it; some Red Flags are so firmly impacted that all the king's horses and all the king's men couldn't budge them—not when they go at the problem head-on. Some flags are stuck in so deep that you have to *lever* them out. That's exactly the strategy that we insist on. To get rid of a Red Flag, use the leverage of your company's strengths.

Look at the examples we've just mentioned, from the "strength" perspective.

If Ellen Chalk has failed to respond to four phone messages, the chances are good that you haven't established enough personal credibility with her to get your calls returned. That's your problem—lack of personal credibility—and it's working from weakness to think that perseverance will overcome it. In this situation, we'd recommend looking for someone else—a senior executive in your company, a Coach—who does have credibility with this Economic Buyer, and getting that person either to set up the meeting you want with Chalk or to cover her directly. That would be using a strength (your colleague's credibility) to offset the influence of an "immovable" Red Flag.

In the second example, if Deleone is Even Keel, your need to make a sale will not convert him suddenly to Growth. Even Keel is a personal feeling, and you can't dislodge it by dismissing its validity. That strategy works from weakness. But recall what Datex-Engstrom's Tina Aiken said about levels of receptivity: "There's almost always *somebody* in Growth or Trouble." If another Buying Influence fits that picture, that's a strength. One strategy which leverages from strength would be to get your Growth or Trouble Buyer to demonstrate to Deleone that his company as a whole will profit from your solution.

In the third example, Frank German is asking you to play the pricing game—to accept a position at the commodity level of the Buy-Sell Hierarchy. By agreeing to discount your service, you've accepted that invitation, which—even though it may get you the business—is a strategy built on weakness. Presumably your company developed its pricing for good reasons, and a strategy built on strength would demonstrate those reasons to this Technical Buyer. Superior service, greater reliability, a history of top-notch consulting advice–whatever your particular strengths may be, they are what you should emphasize in eliminating the Red Flag of price competition.

ACTIONS: WHAT, WHO, AND WHEN

The third step is to set actions–concrete, measurable "to do's" that will improve your position. In setting these actions, you should be guided by the questions that we outlined in the preceding section, deciding upon actions that will resolve the difficulties identified there. In addition, you should keep the following criteria in mind:

- *Each action should indicate what is to be done, who is to do it, and when it should be accomplished.*

- *Each item on an action agenda should capitalize on a strength, eliminate or reduce the impact of a Red Flag, or (ideally) do both at once.*

- *If a given action is contingent upon Coaching information you have yet to acquire, your action agenda should also indicate that: it should say what information is missing, and who is to supply it.*

Returning to the first of our three examples, let's suppose that, in your team meeting, team member Lynn Shields mentions that Chalk, the unresponsive Economic Buyer, belongs to the same charity board as Will Fairlane, one of your own company's vice presidents. One reasonable action then might be: "Have Lynn Shields ask Fairlane by next Tuesday if he can arrange a meeting with Ellen Chalk." That leverages a strength (the charity board connection) against a Red Flag (Chalk's unresponsiveness), and it specifies *who* (Lynn Shields), *what* (ask Fairlane), and *when* (Tuesday).

For the second example, say you discover that Dan Deleone's Even Keel mode is related to his fear of change–specifically, his fear that company expansion will make his own tight little department less manageable. To eliminate that Red Flag, you need to contact somebody who is in Growth or Trouble–but you don't know who in Dan's company fits that bill. Here you've got a "missing information" problem that compounds the original Even Keel mode. So a sensible action would focus on getting that information: "By the end of the month, I need to find one Buying Influence who is not Even Keel or Overconfident."

In the third example, you could meet German's price objections by emphasizing your company's unparalleled record for on-time service. Maybe he would buy that advantage, and maybe not. But at the least it would constitute a bid to be a noncommodity player—and show him why you believe your (higher) pricing is warranted. A reasonable action here might read like this: "Prepare two-year history of flawless service to show Frank German at our March 30 meeting."

All such actions, it should be emphasized, are steps along a path to an improved account position. In the sales process there's no such thing as a definitive position, or a strategy that's so impeccable it never fails. If in Hollywood you're only as good as your last movie, in sales you're only as stable as your last meeting with your customer. When we speak about setting a strategic plan, therefore, what we really mean is the ongoing process of reassessment and repositioning. Unless your positioning stays active—unless you stay alert to current and potential changes—you're opening the door to lost information and lost revenue.

That's why, in the accompanying diagram of the complete Situation Analysis, we include a reassessment *feedback loop*. That loop goes from your "final" step of strategy, the setting of actions, back to all the individual process elements that you took into consideration in determining those actions. It has to. If you don't apply this kind of constant reassessment, inevitably you're going to end up taking for granted something that, in the words of the humorist Josh Billings, just "ain't so."

Or, as one of our colleagues in the communications industry puts it, "When you think that you've got the business locked, it's time to check your key."

A FINAL TIP: THE "OPEN KIMONO" PRINCIPLE

We end this chapter with a piece of unorthodox advice. One of the cherished principles of business operation is that you play your cards close to your chest with your customers as well as your competition, sharing with them only what you can't avoid revealing. That may have been fine for the days of selling as mortal combat, where customers were considered marks to be tagged and deluded. As we enter this revolutionary era of the sales process, however, it's a principle whose fundamental flaws are being everywhere revealed.

Today, the most progressive sales organizations, the most successful consulting groups, are taking exactly the opposite approach, opening their minds and strategies to the companies they do business with, because

SITUATION ANALYSIS:
The Complete Picture

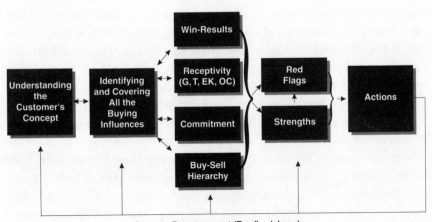

Constant Reassessment (Feedback Loop)

Three questions to ask every day:
1. How are we currently positioned in the <u>customer's</u> eyes?
2. What further or better <u>information</u> do we need?
3. What <u>Coaching</u> do we need?

they understand that this is essential in Win-Win relationships. This doesn't mean necessarily that you have to open your books to your customers, or that you share with them every minor glitch in your own organization. It means that, in those areas where you and they share a vested interest, you make "partnership" a reality by letting them know what you think–and especially what you think about doing business together.

Mike McCarver, vice president of corporate sales for KLA Instruments, calls this the "open kimono" approach. The idea behind it is mutual self-interest: the conviction that when your best customers understand how you want to conduct business with them, both your firms profit–and that a certain amount of "card showing" is therefore essential.

In accordance with this principle, our recommendation is that, when you're dealing with a customer whose business is important enough to you to justify doing an extended Situation Analysis, you consider sharing that analysis with its subject. If the customer is truly a partner, you won't lose by doing so. If, on the other hand, you see this as tipping your hand or giving away trade secrets, then you probably don't have the kind of relationship with this customer that we're recommending.

You may recall what one member of our field staff, Brian Polowniak, said about sharing information in Chapter 6, on customer commitment. To Brian, it's simply part of a sensible, open strategy to tell his Buying Influences, at the beginning of each sales call, what commitment he hopes to get from them by the end of the meeting—as well as what he's ready to commit to in return. "Laying your expectations out up front," he points out, "saves the person what he probably needs the most, which is time." Brian also shares his Ideal Customer profile with prospects. "Usually I'll do that right at the beginning, on the phone," he says. "I spell it out. 'Here's what we're looking for in our clients. Here are our best fits.' If he connects with that, you've both saved time. If he doesn't, it probably doesn't matter."

Mike Johnson agrees. Mike started using our sales processes while he was at Siemens some years back. He is now vice president of customer alliances at Becton Dickinson Infusion Therapy, and he has been profoundly influential in making "mutual vested interest" part of both companies' philosophies. "When we're dealing with our top-tier customers," Mike says, "the movement is toward 'You open your books and I'll open mine.' The trust factor is central. And the real courage comes when you sit a customer down with an account analysis and show him where the shared interests are, and where there are problems.

"We come right out and say it. 'Here, Jim, you can see that we have you down as a Red Flag. I just don't feel that your palm tree and my palm tree are the same. What can we do to understand your Concept better?' It's a revelation, believe me, when they see that. They might be shocked or confused, but it confirms the trust factor, and so it keeps you moving in the right direction."

What you share with your customers—how much or how little—depends on you. We won't presume to give you specific guidelines on how to enter this admittedly touchy area. But one thing has been proved again and again in our dealings with our own customers. The most productive and stable relationships we've ever developed have rested not on willful ignorance but on mutual education. If you're working with people, not against them, you begin on the same page.

"Same page" or "open kimono" relationships are what we at Miller Heiman call *joint-venture partnerships*, and what Mike Johnson's company calls customer *alliances*. Such alliances are increasing in popularity every year, and because they are so important to revenue, protecting them against erosion is a business necessity. In our final "deadly scene," we look at how that is done.

9

HOW DID WE
LET THEM GET AWAY?

"The only thing more dangerous than total defeat is total victory."
–Daniel Lazare
The Frozen Republic

"It's real simple. If you want to maintain a customer, you've got to show sustained interest in his business. None of this stuff is exactly rocket science."
–Robert L. Miller
Miller Heiman
Sales Consultant

A S DISAPPOINTING AS IT IS TO MISS OUT ON new business that you thought was about to close, it's even more painful to lose an old account that your company has come to think of as a sure thing. We mentioned this deadly scene in Chapter 1, when we described a manufacturer being outsold by foreign competition. In cases like this, financial distress is compounded by emotional shock, as you realize that, in business, nothing is ever fully tied down–that even the oldest of your accounts may be subject to erosion.

At Miller Heiman, we provide two interrelated solutions to this problem. One is the Situation Analysis that drives Strategic Selling. The other is our Large Account Management Process, or LAMP. This chapter presents the highlights of that process. By incorporating it into your overall sales operating process, you can ensure that "long-term relationship" becomes more than a faddish phrase, and that the revenue stream you most rely on remains steady and strong.

That stream, as we stressed in the Introduction, flows directly from attending to your important accounts. In LAMP, we sharpen the point of that observation by noting that, in most corporate environments, the bulk of the revenue comes from a very few accounts. We don't mean to diminish the value of any single customer, even your smallest, but it's becoming clearer and clearer in these days of single-sourcing shakeouts that steady revenue comes not from giving "good enough" attention to everybody, but from giving superior, exceptionally focused attention to your most reliable customers–the ones who best match your Ideal Customer profile.

Over the years we've found that these customers seldom amount to more than a tiny percentage of your total client base. We call this finding the *5 percent pattern*: 5 percent of your customers typically bring in 50 percent or more of your business. Another 15 or 20 percent may account for another 25 percent, and beyond that there is usually a small cadre of potential Ideal Customers who, if properly managed, might provide significant additional input to your revenue stream. Taken together, the customers who fall into these three categories are what we refer to as *Large Accounts*. In your industry they may be called "key" or "national" or "major" accounts. The terminology is immaterial. What counts is the major business that these customers bring in–and will continue to bring in, indefinitely, if you don't drop the ball.

We consider these large accounts so critical to the effective management of every sales-driven business that we call them not just accounts but *external assets*. They represent revenue that is sitting out there, ripe for somebody's taking—revenue that can make or break your business, depending on how you approach it. We believe that you should give as much attention, and as careful attention, to these external assets as you would to internal assets like capital equipment, inventory, or your own personnel.

In fact, given the critical importance of your largest customers to your revenue picture, it's surprising that businesses don't universally understand Robert L. Miller's dictum: it is common sense to sustain the interest of the folks who sustain your business. Not to do so is like setting a match to your own inventory.

Companies fail to do this, however, with appalling frequency. You can't pick up a copy of the *Wall Street Journal* from one day to the next without reading the sad tale of an industry leader who has just lost its oldest client. Everywhere you look, companies who have had ten-year honeymoons with certain key accounts wake up amazed to discover that those accounts have flown the coop. Why does this happen?

THE EXTERNAL REASON—AND THE REAL REASONS

The conventional answer to this question is "stiff competition." The Oak Group may have sold profitably to Acorn, Ltd., for twenty years; but when Maple Industries horns in on Oak's territory, with a better service package and a lower bid, Acorn instantly severs the old connection. Not only is this scenario not Oak's fault, but there's nothing that Oak could do (or could have done) about it.

Wrong. As we suggested first in Chapter 7, on price competition, solid business is seldom built on low bidding or discouraged by premium prices that purchase premium value. When an "old reliable" customer goes over to the competition, price competition may be the ostensible cause, but it's rarely if ever the operational reason. The real reasons behind this deadly scenario usually have less to do with finances than with psychology. Bob Miller's right: It's not rocket science. Good customers leave you, in most cases, because they don't feel that you are treating them like good customers. Let's break this root cause down into its most common manifestations.

Variant 1: Of Victors and "Spoils"

As Daniel Lazare's telling epigraph suggests, it can be as hazardous to win a battle as to lose one. The root cause is that victory has a tendency to make you complacent, if not actually arrogant, toward its fruits. When you've been comfortably delivering your products or services to a customer for as long as either of you can remember, you are apt to take this particular revenue-supplier for granted, to assume that he or she is satisfied with the arrangement, and to proceed as if your arrangement is perfect as it stands.

Even in a romantic relationship, this is a hazardous assumption—as the divorce rate among longtime partners sadly attests. In business, where your alliances are built more on pragmatics than on passion, this cavalier attitude is likely—indeed, is almost certain—to make the customer feel used, feel less like the fruits of victory than like the "spoils" of war. A customer who feels that, even transiently, is going to look for satisfaction elsewhere.

We saw this recently on a visit to a clothing supplier. The company has a virtual lock on the children's casual market, so much so that it is able to dictate to retail outlets exactly how much of its new fall line each one will get. Retailers are so eager to gain large allocations that, up until now, they have patiently accepted whatever the clothing firm gave out. But things are changing. The pressure of overseas competition and the rise of knockoff fashions have undermined the clothing firm's traditional market dominance, and it has started to hear nasty rumors that retailers are limiting their shelf space to make room for upstart brands with higher profit margins.

Here, the element of foreign competition was unavoidable. What was avoidable was the clothing firm's arrogant attitude: "We call all the shots." In effect this firm was telling customers, "It's us or nothing." This miscalculation is shaking its control of a once unassailable market—and threatening to turn it from an all-powerful victor into spoils itself.

Variant 2: "Been There, Done That"

In a second variant, salespeople—without ever consciously wanting to neglect their old accounts—gradually shift their attention to newer business, because the financial incentives for doing so are irresistible. Many companies today are speaking gingerly about adjusting compensation schemes so that "full customer service" is more adequately rewarded, but the plain fact is that, in even the most progressive-minded firms, the biggest rewards still go to the field people with the highest "kill ratios." Usually this means the people who have closed the most new business this quarter—whatever the shape of the accounts they closed last quarter.

We'll return to this issue in Chapter 14, where we review a debate that is currently raging in many sales organizations over the merits of skill-based and team-based incentives. Here we'll just make the basic point that salespeople who see that their bread is buttered by new closes will be likely to take a "been there, done that" approach to their older accounts. That leads to predictably meager results in terms of customer satisfaction.

Variant 3: Boiling the Frog

Variant 3 combines the underlying reasons, and the outcomes, of variants 1 and 2. In this third variant, the sales group fails to take adequate notice–or to take it early enough–of organizational changes in the customer's company, and as a result finds itself, months or years down the line, trying to sell into a situation that no longer exists.

In Chapter 4, on Buying Influences, we stressed the need to evaluate key players again and again throughout the selling cycle, so that you don't box yourself into a corner talking to someone who has long since passed the baton to somebody else. We reiterated the principle in Chapter 5, where we cited a customer's reorganization as an automatic Red Flag. Forgetting that principle can lose you more than the sales objective you're currently working on. It can lose you ongoing business with any large organization where administrative shifts and title changes are a regular occurrence–which means, these days, virtually every business on the map.

Apple account executive Eliot Axelrod sees this scenario as endemic in high-tech arenas. "Technology moves so fast," he says, "that marketing, and marketing management, is always playing catch-up. Customers and vendors alike all want long-term, stable relationships, but the instability of the market makes it difficult to commit, and this is compounded by the instability of upper management. When you move folks at that level around so fast, it's extremely difficult to sustain long-term relationships"–or, we might add, a solid fix on the relevant players.

"Why do couples dump each other after a while?" asks Robert L. Miller. "Maybe they grow away from each other because they're becoming different people. In business, when you first sell an account, there's a tremendous amount of excitement, of enthusiasm and anticipation. Later, the people you know there leave and they're replaced by new ones who don't know you, and who don't know why you were hired in the first place. Eventually, three or four years down the line, the account is still using you, but they don't know why, and maybe you don't either.

"It's like boiling a frog," he concludes with a slightly gruesome Aesopian parallel. "If you threw the frog directly into the boiling water, it would hop out screaming, shocked by the sudden change. But if you put it in tap water and turn the heat up gradually, it can't feel what's happening until it's too late. When you lose track of an account in sales, it's the little shifts that matter. There's been a little change here, a little change there, and one day you wake up and realize: A while ago we were the solution, and now we're the problem."

What do you do about it? There are a variety of answers, but they all go back, directly or indirectly, to what we said at the beginning of the book about integrating selling into business operations, or "full organizational commitment to the overall sales job." The best way we know to prevent account erosion is to recognize, at every level of your organization, that this task is not incidental: it's what you *do*.

FOLLOW-UP, OR "SELLING BEYOND THE CLOSE"

Preventing account erosion means going "beyond the close" to determine how effectively your products or services are performing what you expected, and promised your customers, that they would perform.

One of the simplest ways to do this is to run follow-up surveys. For example, one of our clients, a financial services company, sends its clients a "customer satisfaction questionnaire" that begins with the announcement, "Help us make sure that we're giving you the very best service we can." The questionnaire contains a detailed list of "performance checkpoints" on which the customer can rate the financial company's effectiveness, ranging from "soft" items like "sensitivity to your unique financial needs" to "harder" items like "technical expertise," "added value," and "reduction of costs."

One of the most interesting performance checkpoints is "characteristics of our personnel." Here the financial firm asks its customers to assess the effectiveness of the selling team. Were the team members "accessible and responsive"? Did they "explain our services adequately"? Did they "make dealing with us a pleasant experience for you"? The goal here is to fine-tune the sales process itself, by getting feedback on its professionalism and proficiency. But this fine-tuning also lets customers know that, in the eyes of the financial company, the relational aspects of selling are just as important as the more obvious nuts and bolts of quotes and contracts. The questionnaire as a whole also lets them know that our client is interested in building a long-term relationship.

At Miller Heiman, we follow up with our clients in a slightly different manner. Forty-five days after the completion of any of our corporate programs, we phone the participants to see how well their companies are implementing the processes. We've stressed that we sell process, not training events, and our client support callback program underlines that fact.

Our client support staff members, Holly Jenkins and Beth Rutherford, are on the phone every day moving our process "beyond the close" by making sure that clients are fully satisfied with what they've purchased from us.

To make a program like this work, "client support" has to be seen as part of the overall sales job, and the employees charged with that support have to understand the product or service as well as the field staff who sell it. Beth and Holly are so well versed in our processes that they are able to provide corrections and even mini "refresher courses" to participants who are having trouble with any of the concepts.

On one recent call, for example, an obviously confused client told Holly that he had more Buying Influences than he could possibly keep track of. By questioning him about the key players' roles, Holly determined that he had fused two sales objectives into one, merging the players together at the same time. She suggested that he break the scenario out into two separate sales objectives, and do a separate Situation Analysis for each one. "When I followed up with him later," she reports, "he said that splitting the account into two had been a great idea. The real opportunities there were different from what he had originally thought, but by using two analyses he had been able to clarify things and actually close two orders."

This anecdote reveals the value of *open-ended* follow-up with clients. Holly's coworker Beth reinforces this point in describing the variety she encounters in her client support calls. "There's really no typical pattern. We have a question guideline that gets things started, but after that it really depends on people's responses. We like to let them talk freely about whatever's giving them trouble, and we just have to listen before we give advice. We'll encourage that openness, too, with our phrasing. We might ask, 'Can you tell me a little bit about how you're implementing the process?' and the client will be off and running with a particular agenda."

As we put it in Chapter 2, you need to listen first, before you can understand the Concept that is in the customer's mind. We make that lesson part of the way everybody in our company conducts his or her work, whether the person is booking programs, covering the bases with Buying Influences, or making follow-up calls.

FOUL-UP: DEALING WITH MISTAKES

Following up on successes is relatively easy. Following up on foul-ups is a lot more touchy, but it's every bit as important in sustaining good business. A couple of our clients have given us especially good insights on this matter.

Tony Cueva, a Miller Heiman client associate who has introduced hundreds of his company's salespeople to our programs, is manager of national accounts for Ceridian, a major national payroll and human resources service company. "We do millions of payroll transactions a year," Tony says. "While we would like to say that we get every transaction correct, that would be naive, because of our industry. Nobody could. We don't deny that, and we don't try to convince our customers that we're infallible. We avoid giving references, for example, that will say we never make a mistake. We couldn't get that kind of reference without lying. Instead, we say: Judge us on how well we react when we do make a mistake. Talk to our references. Find out how well we fix something when it goes wrong."

Michael Johnson, a driving force behind Becton Dickinson's broad adoption of our sales processes, is his organization's vice president of customer alliances. Mike echoes Tony's observation, and he goes even further, suggesting that the best damage control of all may involve an almost unthinkable tactic: warning customers about problems *before* they occur.

"We develop new products every year," Mike says. "Sometimes they're not perfect. Sometimes we're still working out the bugs, or we're learning from experimental models. Faced with this type of situation, most companies hide the potential problem. We don't. If we know there's a quality problem, or a potential for failure with one of our products, we tell our customers up front—before we have to report it to the FDA.

"This approach is a matter of trust, and of building the trust you need to secure good business. We're always asking ourselves, 'How can we ensure that we're credible to our customers?' One way is to share the potential difficulties from the start. You have to ask, 'How can we talk to customers about that?' In the long run, this helps you rather than hurting you, because customers don't get angry about quality problems. They're realistic enough to know that such problems are inevitable. They get angry if you don't tell them that something might happen."

Sometimes this honesty leads to temporary setbacks, Mike admits. "But when that happens, when a customer backs off, we work with them to better understand their solution image. What can we do to work through this potential problem? How can we develop solutions that will benefit us both? Whether the individual sale is successful or not, we're continually moving toward maintaining those Win-Win partnerships."

INTEGRATED SELLING REVISITED

"Whether the individual sale is successful or not." This is a critical, and revolutionary, perspective—one that recalls the notion of integrated selling we introduced in Chapter 1. By way of revisiting that notion, here are the major implications that this perspective has for nurturing, and holding on to, reliable business:

First, sales must be seen as integral to, and integrated with, the broad business concerns of both organizations. It's not an isolated "function" or a "department," but the symbolic and fiscal heart of business itself. Thomas Murphy of General Motors drew a lot of heat back in the 1960s when he said that his company was in the business not of making cars but of making money. His cynicism aside, the heat was only partially justified. The business of General Motors was, and is, making money; selling cars is just the way they do it.

A less cynical fix on this idea was given by the dean of management studies, Peter Drucker, in *The Practice of Management*. While businesses need to make a profit to stay viable, Drucker says, the purpose of business is really more subtle than that. The core purpose is to provide value to your customers. When you do that successfully, you make a profit, and in fact doing it is what entitles you to that profit. Or, as Johnson & Johnson's CEO James Burke said in a speech to the Ad Council some years ago, "I have long harbored the belief that the most successful corporations in this country ... were driven by a simple moral imperative: to serve the public in the broadest possible sense better than their competition."

The bottom line? The core work of any viable business is sustained generation of revenue, achieved through the sales that satisfy its customers' expectations. Products or services are simply means to that end.

When you understand sales in this way, it becomes obvious why we refer to our individual programs as inseparable pieces of a "sales operating system." Why we insist that everything from production and R&D to follow-up calls must also be understood as parts of that seamless fabric. Why Becton Dickinson's Mike Johnson says that the basic challenge in converting to a process-oriented sales system is educating everyone that "What we do is selling." And why KLA's vice president Mike McCarver observers, "Today the whole company sells. The salespeople orchestrate."

You don't have to be an industrial or high-tech giant to pull this off. One of the best examples of "full organizational commitment" that we've ever heard about comes from a small Midwest firm that manufactures musical instruments. Its major market is high school band departments, and even though it has only half the resources of the major instrument makers, it has maintained a healthy share of this market for several years because everybody in the company is committed to securing that revenue.

The company's commitment may first become visible out in the field at the beginning of each year, when its four-person sales force talks to band directors to determine the specific needs of students. But it's reinforced in a hundred "non-sales" ways, as everybody in the company works overtime for the customers' satisfaction. It's reinforced when a student breaks a valve spring on Thursday afternoon and the repair department has it back to her for Friday night's game. It's reinforced when a band director calls for pricing information and the receptionist asks him how that new trumpet model is working out.

It was really reinforced last year, when one band director was having trouble locating the sheet music for an obscure march. The president of the instruments company hired a search service, tracked it down, and sent fifty copies, free of charge, to the astonished director. The company didn't make a cent on that deal—in fact, it cost a couple of hundred dollars—but after the director opened up that package, TNT couldn't have gotten him to switch to another supplier. It was a perfect example of everybody selling—and knowing why.

Second, sales must be seen as a process, not a series of events. It's not something that starts and stops, like the sales cycle for a particular piece of business. Rather, it's the ongoing management of account revenue, before, during, and after individual transactions.

This second point reinforces the first one. If selling is what we do, then we do it all the time. Not just when a sales representative goes out on a sales call, but when marketing sends out mailers and when technicians refine production specs and when receptionists answer the phone. A process-oriented company is pointed toward the reduction of fragmentation, toward the development of a customer-driven selling culture.

Finally, satisfying customers' needs must be seen as a full-time job. This final principle refines and expands on the second one. If selling is what we do, and if we do it all the time, then it stands to reason that we connect with our customers on a regular, frequent basis—and that we do not stint on resources in addressing their needs. At customer-focused companies, this means that full-time account teams dedicate themselves every day, exclusively, to the ongoing work of steadying and growing the revenue stream. It means that key customers are contacted on a regular basis not only by field people but by sales managers and other executives in the sales organization. It means, ultimately, that process selling depends on two types of integration: the integration of the sales group's own operational complexities, and the integration of the buying and selling organizations, so that they move beyond transactions to create alliances.

DOING IT RIGHT: CLIENT EXAMPLES

We indicated the potential power of alliances in Chapter 7, when we described the "cross-company reengineering" that has developed between manufacturers as part of a broader trend toward single-sourcing. We could also mention the example of General Electric, which stations its own technicians in customers' plants, both to head off operational glitches and, in Catherine Romano's words, to "alert the sales force to market opportunities as they develop." Or the example of our pharmaceuticals client Syncor, whose sales representatives conduct some sales calls in concert with representatives from Du Pont, which manufacturers the pharmaceuticals they sell.

Some of the most sophisticated examples of the alliance model come from three of our other clients, the "imaging" leader Eastman Kodak, the data-management firm Sentient Systems, and the semiconductor equipment giant KLA Instruments.

Big Yellow Meets Big Blue. John H. Erbland is vice-president for strategic global accounts at Eastman Kodak. One of the most global, and most strategic, of Kodak accounts is IBM, and the two companies' relationship, as John explains it, is a highly complex weave of different factors.

"It is not a simple customer-to-vendor arrangement," says John. "They buy a lot from us, but they also sell us a lot, so we're really a bit like international trading partners. In addition to that, like trading partners, we also compete for the same business in some areas. Last but certainly not least, we're engaged in various joint development ventures, mutually developing and mutually marketing new technology. And all of this happens not in a vacuum, but dynamically—with a hundred things going on at once.

"One area where cooperation has really paid off has been in mutual targeting of specific market segments. Take the home computer sector as an example. There's a growing desire for more sophisticated graphics, as part of software expansion and the rise of the Internet. IBM is on top of the computing and transmission aspects of this marketing opportunity, and Kodak brings the expertise in imaging. By working together, we can develop customer solutions that will be more attractive, and that will bring us both greater returns, than anything that either of us could have put on the boards by ourselves.

"In some cases," says John, "we might go straight to co-branding. In others, one of us might serve as an equipment manufacturer or OEM.

There are different scenarios, but they're linked by an underlying premise and strategy. By pooling our resources, we can improve both our products and our penetration."

Sentient and Cooperative Development. Are buy-sell partnerships as much an emerging reality as the business press indicates? When we asked Sentient's Vice President for Healthcare Joel French that question, we got an unequivocal yes. "In our business," Joel says, "things are changing so fast that vendors who can't keep up are quickly squeezed out. If you want to be among the remaining players, you've got to work cooperatively with your customers to develop solutions. This is so critical to the way we do business that, on occasion, we even work jointly with customers and competitors.

"We don't know what's coming in the future, what our customers will need, and it's to our benefit to find out in advance, even if that means sacrificing some competitive advantage. We'll go to the customer along with other vendors and say, 'Can you help us develop a list of the five or ten products you're going to need most in the next decade?' Then we'll pool our resources to come up with appropriate solutions.

"The downside here is that nonselected vendors can be squeezed out, but for the rest of us it's a very productive development. We're willing to trade off the advantage of some features and benefits to get increased security and the ease of a managed relationship. It works great for customers, too, because we can custom-develop solutions for them that might otherwise have been cost-prohibitive, or have cost us heavily in terms of market research. The whole idea is based on sharing the risk. It's very logical. Our best customers are willing to absorb some of our risk, and in return we're more willing to do business with them."

A High-Tech Buyer-Seller Alliance. KLA Instruments sales VP Mike McCarver, a big fan of the idea of "whole-company selling," articulated the model extensively in a recent conversation. In Strategic Selling, we speak of multidecision transaction scenarios as complex sales. In Mike's view, the current trend toward partnerships, or alliances, is a natural outgrowth of what he calls the "ultracomplex sale."

"Over the past ten years, we've gone from something like $80 million to an annual rate of $800 million in bookings. One of our large U.S.-based customers in Texas has grown from less than $20 million just three years ago to $100 million per year now. Growth like that generates tremendous complexity—much greater than it was even ten or fifteen years ago. As companies get bigger and products get more sophisticated, there's a strong move toward centralization, and that makes selling to corporations all the more complicated. The real challenge of selling today is weighted toward big-ticket opportunities. That means focused account teams like those we have for our major worldwide customers. It means account managers dealing with the same account the same way all around the world. And it means, more and more, the building of alliances.

"This is a major change, and it scares a lot of companies. The old thinking says, 'Don't rely on a single source; you're bound to get screwed.' That's the past, though. High-tech firms like ours are involved at the leading edge, but the change toward partnering is inevitable. Soon, all types of industries will be following this new pattern.

"The large Texas customer, for example, is way beyond being afraid of single-sourcing. We are so wired in to each other's way of doing business and long-term needs that a mutual trust and a level of responsibility have developed between the two companies. They understand that the leverage for them is in influencing our product development strategies to best fit their needs, not in wringing out the last few percentage points of price discounts. This is something that is understood at all levels in both companies. We both nurture the relationship at the highest levels.

"This is how big-ticket selling works today. You've got to do it, just to keep up. If you don't, you're going to get zapped by those who do. Alliances aren't the future. They're the wave of the present."

THE BOTTOM LINE: RELIABILITY

If Mike is right—and we are convinced that he is—it's because alliances provide an advantage that no amount of competitive price-bickering can ever provide: the reasonable expectation of secure account revenue and, even beyond that, of business relations that are not subject (or at least less fitfully subject) to market whims.

"The single most important trend in procurement today," write Mark Blessington and Bill O'Connell, "is the rapid shrinking of the supplier base"—a shrinkage of 8 percent on average in the beginning of this decade. Even where this trend does not reach the logical end result of single-sourcing, it dramatically reduces the number of real players in the supplier base, usually by about half within a few years. Naturally, this means that competition for the remaining slots is intense, but—as we emphasized in our discussion of the Buy-Sell Hierarchy—this need not be an open door to the low-bidding nightmare.

Companies who are able to add value for cost-conscious purchasers may enjoy a significant opportunity in "strategic supplier partnering." An example cited by Blessington and O'Connell confirms the importance of teamwork as a general principle, while underlining the value of "cross-company reengineering."

> Wal-Mart expects some of its suppliers to put permanent sales and service teams in place. Procter & Gamble, for example, has an 80-person team in Bentonville, Arkansas, where Wal-Mart is based. Wal-Mart expects its vendors to be marketing partners—to do marketing research for Wal-Mart and give presentations on how best to sell their products through Wal-Mart. Wal-Mart's information system gives suppliers updates on sales by product and store every 90 minutes.

Summarizing the lessons here, Blessington and O'Connell emphasize a distinction between the old "competitive-coercive model" of selling that "pits buyers and suppliers against each other" and the new "cooperative-collaborative model," where the focus is on "the total cost of the purchase and on mutually advantageous relations."

This latter model, we believe, is the wave of the present. It follows the Win-Win design we have been recommending for years, and it offers a revolutionary perspective on today's constant shakeouts. In retarding account erosion, it may be the best friend you have.

MANAGERS' CHECKLIST 6: RETAINING ACCOUNTS

Winning an account and holding on to it are not the same thing. In the words of one account manager, "Retention is everything." To ensure that your people are attending effectively to this critical process element, ask the following questions:

1. *When was the last time we closed a significant piece of business with this customer? Have we followed up on that sale? Do we have solid evidence that all the Buying Influences in the customer's organization are fully satisfied with our solution?*

2. *If any of the Buying Influences is less than fully satisfied, what steps have we taken, or should we take, to remedy the situation?*

3. *Where are we currently positioned with this customer on the Buy-Sell Hierarchy?*

4. *What specific extra value have we brought the customer? What makes us confident that the customer understands the value?*

5. *What evidence do we have that we are helping this customer to run his or her business better? Are we partners, or just one of a list of possible suppliers? How do we know that this customer sees us as a business partner?*

10

DOES ANYBODY HAVE A TWENTY-FIVE-HOUR DAY?

"You know how many hours a week salespeople spend in actual selling–I mean in direct engagement, talking with customers? I've asked hundreds of people that question. On average, the answer is six. We've got to use that time effectively."
–Brian Polowniak
Sales Consultant
Miller Heiman

"The hurrieder I go, the behinder I get."
–Pennsylvania Dutch saying

I F   Y O U   C O U L D   H A V E   A L L   T H A T   Y O U   W A N T E D   O F any single thing, what would it be?

We ask this question periodically of our program participants. Once in a great while, we get coyly conventional answers like "money" or "sex." Nine times out of ten, though, the answer is the same. If you're involved in sales, whether you're out in the field or behind a manager's desk, the one thing you want more of is *time*.

Given selling today, this is predictable. Caught in a squeeze between shrinking staffs and expanding territories and responsibilities, sales organizations are in the challenging but uncomfortable position of having to do more with less—and having to do it, usually, in record time, before an astute competitor beats them to the punch. No wonder one harried branch manager we know suggests jokingly that people who survive selling careers these days ought to be rewarded not with gold watches but with "red-eye Rumpelstiltskin" pins. "For consistently spinning straw into gold," she smiles. "And for doing it on the midnight flight from Grand Rapids."

This problem, of course, is not peculiar to salespeople. Everybody today could probably use more time. Business professionals, attorneys, nurses, night watchmen—whatever you do for a living, the chances are good that you wouldn't turn up your nose at a few extra hours, or be uninterested in a method that could help you make more of your time. For that reason, the method we lay out in this chapter has a very broad, perhaps even universal, application. We discuss it in the context of sales because sales is our business, and because we believe in the truth of Robert Louis Stevenson's observation: Everybody, in the long run, "lives by selling *something*." Whether that something is labor, or a skill, or a professional service, to deliver it effectively while keeping your head above water you've got to come to grips with the time-crunch problem.

That problem affects selling professionals in a variety of areas, but its exhausting effects are felt most acutely in two of them.

In the first of these, the "macro" area of territory development, sales teams must decide daily which leads are worth following, and whether any lead is worth chasing down into the hills of Montana. Here the question hinges on the deployment of limited resources, and that question is continually complicated by a jet-era paradox: the fact that so-called "instant access" to Bora-Bora has actually increased the time that sellers are in the air—and therefore, by definition, not with their customers. As one of our sales consultants, Brian Polowniak, puts it, "Our average sales call used to cost maybe $400 or $500. It's twice or three times that now. So, you've got to be asking yourself every day, Do I really need to get on a plane for this one? Do I need to give up another whole day of my time?"

In the second area, the "micro" area of personal time management, the territory manager's problem is simultaneously miniaturized and multiplied, as every field rep wrestles with his or her own private "hurrieder and behinder" demon—facing all that that implies in terms of personal anxiety over productivity and quotas. Here, too, the root cause is having to do more with less. Jim may be the most accomplished, hardest-working salesman in the Northeast, but if he's got sixty accounts to call on between Pittsfield and Pittsburgh—and sixty is on the low end of today's average territory size—then the sales tool he could use best is a twenty-five-hour day.

We admit that, at Miller Heiman, our prototype for a twenty-five-hour day is sitting on the same rickety shelf as our crystal ball for "reading the customer's mind" and our handbook "Fail-Sale Closes." What we *have* perfected is a field-tested tool for time and territory management that can help make your actual selling time—those precious six hours a week—more productive, whether you're qualifying leads, making follow-up calls, or approaching the close.

We call this management tool the *Sales Funnel.* It's pictured in the diagram on the following page. As we tell our clients, and as we prove every quarter in our own business, the Sales Funnel optimizes your selling time by helping you perform the following five tasks more efficiently:

- *Sort your sales objectives into four different stages of the selling process, depending on how close they are to becoming actual orders.*
- *Resequence your priorities for working the opportunities at each stage, so that you avoid the deadly "boom and bust" cycle that plagues most salespeople.*
- *Allocate your time appropriately, so that you don't end up smothering some customers with attention while neglecting others.*
- *Track the pace and regularity of each sales objective, as it evolves from an untested lead to a finished order.*
- *Forecast your future income on a systematic basis, rather than relying on traditional "pie in the sky" guesswork.*

In this chapter, we'll explain, with examples, how the Sales Funnel helps you facilitate these five tasks. We'll begin by clarifying our preference for this particular metaphor.

SALES FUNNEL

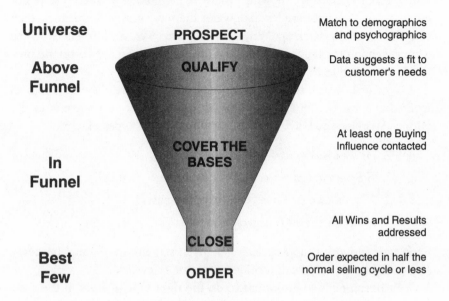

Universe	PROSPECT	Match to demographics and psychographics
Above Funnel	QUALIFY	Data suggests a fit to customer's needs
In Funnel	COVER THE BASES	At least one Buying Influence contacted
Best Few	CLOSE / ORDER	All Wins and Results addressed / Order expected in half the normal selling cycle or less

DRIFT, FLOW, AND "WORKING THE FUNNEL"

In tracking sales objectives from start to finish, many companies use the metaphor of a "pipeline" or "flow" to visualize prospects entering the sales cycle at one end and emerging at the other end, perhaps months or years later, as finished orders. Our own metaphor, the Sales Funnel, is similarly optimistic. But there are significant differences between pipelines and funnels, and we consciously chose the latter for specific reasons.

First, as you can see from the diagram, a funnel is wider at the top than it is at the bottom. As obvious as that may be, it points to an analogy with selling that, in our experience, is often overlooked. Entering the funnel is easier than coming out the other end. The "pipeline" metaphor can give salespeople the false impression that all prospects eventually turn into orders. By using the Sales Funnel instead, we are continually reminded that some prospects never make it this far. They get "stuck" in the funnel, or the funnel "leaks." We speak more about these scenarios in Chapter 13, when we discuss some of the more common "problem funnels," and how regular review can help you address them. Here we stress only the distance–in time and labor–between even your best leads and your finished orders.

Second, precisely because of this distance, sales objectives cannot be allowed merely to "drift down" the Funnel toward the close. They won't.

The Funnel functions less like a snapshot of where you are than like a constantly running filmstrip, showing where you're going—or where you're not going. Sales objectives are less like water than like gravel. Sometimes, they clog the Funnel or back up. When this happens, you need to check to see what's creating the blockage and stir it up. As we say in our corporate programs, you need to *work the Funnel.*

Third, as the diagram also indicates, there are different types of work that must be done, depending on where a sales objective is in the Funnel. Working the Funnel means attending to four types of work:

1. *At the Universe stage, you* prospect.
2. *When an objective moves Above the Funnel, you* qualify.
3. *When it's In the Funnel, you* cover the bases.
4. *When it's in Best Few, you* close.

Each type of work is appropriate to a given stage of the Funnel process—and would be entirely inappropriate at the other levels.

Because it's so important to do the right type of work at the right time, it's critical to know, for any given sales objective, when it's time to move a piece of potential business from one level of the Funnel to the next—and to be able to identify when you are stuck, when you are unable to move the sales process forward. Knowing that isn't a matter of instinct, because the idea of instinct, for even the most experienced salespeople, is an invitation to guesswork and wishful thinking. It's a matter of identifying when specific *conditions* have been met to justify your saying that an objective has progressed toward the close. In the following discussion, we spell out those conditions.

THE FIRST TASK: SORTING

Let's begin at the beginning, at the stage before you have even started to move things down the Funnel—the stage when you're still flipping through leads to see which of those midnight flights, if any, you want to get on.

If you could get on all twenty flights, this first, early stage wouldn't be a problem. But you can't. The fact is that there is simply far more business out there than you can possibly handle. In managing time, you have to begin with that ostensibly happy dilemma. The dilemma is illustrated well in a famous parable that is attributed to the medieval philosopher Jean Buridan.

Of Numbers, Odds, and Jackasses

Buridan described the predicament of a hungry jackass tethered in a field between two piles of hay. There is plenty of food to satisfy the animal's needs, but every time he moves toward one of the piles, he changes his mind and backs away toward the other. Eventually, surrounded by food, he starves to death–becoming philosophy's most famous victim of "fatal misattraction."

Starving to death while you're surrounded by plenty. This paradox, we believe, is painfully relevant to selling. Like Buridan's jackass, too many of us undermine our own chances for survival, not by ignoring the opportunities that are within our reach but by being unable to decide among good alternatives. That's the first real dilemma of territory or account management: we're overwhelmed, not underwhelmed, by the choices.

There are differences, of course, between the jackass's indecision and that of the average salesperson, and the dissimilarities are just as instructive as the likenesses. For one thing, no sales professional today has the luxury of a simple either-or choice. Our "piles of hay" are hundreds of alternatives. For another thing, we are never "stuck in the middle," unable to decide which of two customers to call on. On the contrary, in a given week, we may call on dozens of customers, sampling one opportunity after the other, in a continual process of pecking at the territorial banquet. In addition, within each large account, we may be attending to dozens of different tasks at the same time. Large, complex accounts are like territories themselves, in that they constantly stretch our resources among competing alternatives.

But the outcome in terms of sales "nourishment" is often the same. Spread too thin to cover all opportunities effectively, we end up pecking and running, like yuppie grazers, trusting in the power of numbers to help us make our quotas, but always racing, always just a little behind.

In the conventional approach to selling, this nightmare is considered acceptable for two related reasons. One is the "positive thinking" philosophy which says, in effect, that the harder you work, the better off you will be. We've already told you what we think of that Horatio Alger nostrum. The other is the seemingly more pragmatic notion that success in sales follows a law of averages, and that selling therefore is basically a numbers game.

You've heard a hundred variants on this idea. The broader your customer base, the better your chances. The higher your sales call average, the bigger your take. The more doors you get your foot into, the bigger your commissions. It's the approach that the "supersalesman" Joe Girard, whose enthusiasm is as conventional as it is infectious, calls "filling the seats on the Ferris wheel." The "method" couldn't be simpler: Follow up every lead, no matter how pitiful it may look, because you never know when a buzzard might magically become a bluebird. After all, even a blind lead is better than no lead at all.

Girard himself is so committed to this "more is better" approach that he gives his stamp of approval to what must be the lamest of all methods of generating leads–cold phone calls. "If you have a few dead minutes or an unfilled hour," he writes, "you can afford the hard physical labor of making half a dozen phone calls to get nothing, and maybe just one that gives you a live lead. All that effort may turn out to be a little more valuable than scratching your nose or listening to a bad joke." Furthermore, he concludes, "even this least productive way of getting business–cold calls from the phone book–is better than doing nothing."

Impeccable logic. We couldn't agree more. Except that, where we come from, "unfilled hours" are only slightly less scarce than benevolent buzzards, while the options open to the enterprising professional salesperson are a lot broader than scratching your nose, listening to a bad joke, and doing nothing.

The numbers game sounds like a logical approach, in other words, but when you look at it closely, and especially when you compare it with a more systematic approach to territory and account management, it turns out to be the logic of the no-system gambler. Since we live in Nevada, we're very familiar with gamblers of this type. Step off a plane at Reno–Lake Tahoe airport any day of the week and you'll pass a dozen people plugging quarters into the slot machines in the terminal, minute after minute and sometimes hour after hour, on the theory that the more you play, the more you'll get paid.

The fact is that, when you chum for opportunities in this haphazard manner, your odds of coming out ahead are slim to none. Maybe that's fine when it comes to gambling–plenty of people we know gamble for fun and are willing to incur some degree of loss for the pleasure of the pastime. But if you treat your business as a pastime, you're going to be in trouble. In business today, it makes no more sense to treat all leads as if they were alike than it does to generate those leads by throwing darts at a phone book.

As we told *Sales and Marketing Management* magazine in an interview in 1994, "Often the percentage of viable sales opportunities to 'junk' in territories is way out of line. The cure is simple: Clean out the territory so that all that is left are accounts where there is some clear indication that there is a possible order." This principle works even better when you apply it *before* you clutter up your territory with lousy leads. Today, the first step in getting your sales territories under control is to make some difficult choices between the available piles of hay, and to concentrate only on those that can actually provide you with nourishment.

A friend of ours who's not in sales once asked us, with a puzzled expression, "How can Janet possibly cover all of the Midwest herself?" His evident impression was that Janet's Midwest "territory" meant every stretch of sidewalk, every storefront, everybody with a pulse, between St. Joseph, Missouri, and the Rocky Mountains. We explained that in sales, "territory" describes not geography but accounts, and that Janet's potential customer base was thus considerably smaller than the population of the Midwest.

Our friend's mistake was understandable, given his non-sales background. What's less understandable is that many salespeople make a similar error, failing to draw a distinction between potential and real prospects—and failing to draw it well before they start working leads. The common result is territories that are both crowded and unprofitable. The cure, we maintain, is as simple as it is unconventional. Begin your sales cycle by thinning out your potential customer Universe.

We've already introduced the tool that you need to do that.

Thinning the Universe: Ideal Customer Revisited

When we introduced the concept of Ideal Customer in Chapter 6, we emphasized its value as a sorting tool for getting you to Win-Win–that is, for helping you zero in on those customers who would most likely want to form mutually beneficial partnerships with you, rather than play competitive games that were designed to make you lose. We'll reiterate that general point here, and amplify it by giving an example of how using an Ideal Customer profile can further focus your attention on the best opportunities by measuring prospects not just against specific "demographic" characteristics (which most companies are already using) but also against the "values and attitudes" criteria that we refer to as *psychographics*. The example comes from Elizabeth Ngonzi, the Micros Systems sales executive whose insights on customer Concept we related in Chapter 5.

To Elizabeth, the most obvious advantage of the Ideal Customer profile is that its utility as a sorting device saves her time. "A real prospect isn't just a warm body," Elizabeth says. "It's important to qualify–actually, to prequalify–every prospect. Otherwise, you're going to be wasting a tremendous amount of time on so-called business that never has a chance of coming through. Measuring every prospect against your Ideal Customer profile really helps you to maximize your limited time.

"At Micros, for example, we sell sophisticated ordering systems at a high sticker price–we're known as the Cadillac of the industry. Our customers have to be comfortable with that image, technologically astute enough not to be intimidated by our capability, and solvent enough to be able to play at our level. When I measure prospects against my Ideal Customer profile, I keep all that in mind. If somebody's really technophobic, if he just doesn't feel comfortable with computerized systems, I'm going to have an uphill battle from the beginning; I'd much rather be talking to prospects who *like* computers. If somebody's not creditworthy, even if he can come up with the equipment down payment, he may have a problem down the line with installment or service fees. For us, a customer like that may not be worth pursuing.

"Also, of course, a real prospect has to *need* our systems. At the very least, he has to be in the market for an upgrade or replacement of his current system. That's part of my Ideal Customer profile too. I made a call last year on a Boston nightspot that was using one of our competitor's register systems. It had only been in place a couple of months, and the owner was obviously content with how it was working. Sure, there were some technical areas where we could have improved things for him, but after talking with him for half an hour, the bottom line was he just wasn't dissatisfied. Not enough to make it worth my time trying to win him over.

" 'Lack of need' signals me loud and clear: this prospect doesn't pass my Ideal Customer criteria. Not now, anyway. Maybe in another three months, his system will crash and I'll get a call that he's desperate for our help. But right now, he's a prospect without need. So he just isn't qualified. And I'm not about to spend time with unqualified prospects."

As Elizabeth's example illustrates, thinning out the field is the first painful step you have to take in managing your precious selling time more effectively. In doing this, your Ideal Customer profile serves as the basic guideline to help you determine which leads you should select to work on out of your virtually infinite Universe of possible opportunities. When this is done well, it involves psychographic as well as demographic checks.

What about the second step? Should every lead that fits your Ideal Customer profile automatically move down into the Above the Funnel position? No. We mentioned that in order to move a sales objective down the Funnel, you must first confirm that it has met certain conditions. The Ideal Customer profile constitutes only the first of these conditions. Before you can legitimately move a sales objective into Above the Funnel, you need to be sure it meets a second condition.

Above the Funnel: Anybody Got a Match?

The condition for moving a potential piece of business from your Universe into Above the Funnel is that you have at least one piece of information suggesting a match between your products or services and a customer's needs. The information could be something as tentative as a news story indicating that the customer has a problem, or as concrete as a request for a proposal. But something has to indicate that you can fill a current or upcoming need.

And that means "need" as perceived by the customer himself or herself—not as filtered through your own eagerness to make a sale. Recall our discussion in Chapter 2 about why customers buy: they buy to fulfill an expectation of results, to close a gap between their current reality and where they want to be. If a prospect doesn't have such an expectation—if there's no "discrepancy gap"—then it hardly matters how close to the Ideal Customer profile the prospect is. You'll be wasting your time trying to plug up a hole that's already filled. In Elizabeth Ngonzi's terms, a sales objective should be "prequalified" before you move it from Universe to Above the Funnel. Information about a possible match is what provides you with that prequalification.

Qualification proper is what happens next, and that's the type of work you do Above the Funnel. By "qualification" here we mean verification. The work you do on a piece of business that is Above the Funnel is to verify that the suggestion of a match is in fact accurate. You do that by talking to the various Buying Influences in the account.

In the Funnel: Are All the Bases Covered?

The condition for moving a sales objective into the next level, In the Funnel, is that you have contacted at least one Buying Influence for the sale and have spoken to him or her about Growth or Trouble issues. In traditional selling terms, this is a form of "qualifying the prospect," but you will notice that our definition of qualifying is more precise, and more demanding, than the usual one. It's not just, "This customer could use our product." That's an Above the Funnel question—a prequalifying question. The In the Funnel requirement is, "We have determined, from personal contact with a key player, that we could provide a solution to a Growth or Trouble issue." We don't acknowledge a sales objective to be truly In the Funnel, in other words, until we have concrete evidence of the customer's interest and need.

Once you've made that determination, of course, the level and type of work change dramatically. If you are convinced that you can address a

Buying Influence's Growth or Trouble concerns, then the qualification process is effectively over, and you move to *covering the bases* with this initial contact as well as with all the other Buying Influences. This means, for example:

- *Determining the concrete business Results that each Buying Influence wants from your proposal.*
- *Determining how each person will Win if you deliver those Results.*
- *Making sure that each person understands your company's commitment to a Win-Win outcome.*
- *Ensuring, as the sales process evolves, that the Buying Influences are playing Win-Win with you—that is, that they are meeting your commitment with an equivalent commitment of their own.*
- *Making it clear, to every Buying Influence, how you are providing a Concept solution, not just a commodity.*

Best Few: Are We (Almost) There Yet?

To move a sales objective from In the Funnel to the final, pre-close level, Best Few, you need to meet not one but two conditions. First, you need to be confident that you have addressed the Wins and Results of all the known Buying Influences for the sale. Second, you need to be convinced that the sale will close—that is, that you'll have the order in hand—in less than half the time of your normal selling cycle. The first condition is straightforward enough. The second is less so, because selling cycles vary considerably, even on an individual salesperson's work calendar.

When we speak about a normal selling cycle, we mean your average—the average time it takes you to move a piece of business from "unqualified lead" to "order in hand." In determining this average, you can take a tip from gymnastics scoring: average everything but the highest and lowest number. If one greased lightning sale took a month and your worst, grind-me-into-the-dust scenario took a year, ignore those anomalies and average the rest. You don't have to be too meticulous about this. Our point is not to provide perfect calibrations, but to give you an accurate feel for when a sales objective is really in the closing, "about to go to order" stage.

When you're at this point in the process, the work you do should change from covering the bases—you've already done that at the In the Funnel stage—to "end of cycle" tasks like getting final confirmation and order signing. If you find that a sales objective you've placed in Best Few is still requiring you to double-check your customer's Win-Results, then maybe you've moved that piece of business down to Best Few prematurely.

We stress this point because it's not an uncommon tracking error for a salesperson to move a potential order down too early—and subsequently to lose the business to an alert competitor. Our rule about "half your normal selling cycle" provides a check against relaxing your guard too early, and thus increases your chances of turning every Best Few objective into an order.

THE SECOND TASK:
RESEQUENCING TO FIX THE "BOOM AND BUST" CYCLE

The second task that the Sales Funnel helps you perform more effectively is the appropriate sequencing of the four types of selling work.

We don't mean the sequence that you adopt on each individual sales objective. When they're working on an individual sales objective, most sales professionals begin by sorting through leads. Then they prospect. Next they qualify. Then they cover the bases, and finally they close. This is both logical and natural. To bring an individual deal from start to finish, this is pretty much the sequence that you have to follow.

So far, so good. Here's the problem. When it comes to managing multiple opportunities—that is, account territories or opportunities in a large account rather than individual sales objectives—we prioritize our tasks into a weekly (or daily) work pattern that feels natural and logical, but actually isn't. Here's the pattern we're talking about.

- *First, we work on business that will help us close orders. That is, we start each week by focusing on our Best Few objectives.*
- *Second, we cover the bases on those pending deals that are most likely to move to orders next.*
- *Finally (and very reluctantly), we look for new business.*

Unless you developed your workweek patterns on another planet, this is almost certainly the sequence you follow. Why? Because it's comfortable. It's reassuring. It's ego-gratifying. It allows us to focus our attention on our Wins and upcoming Wins, while forgetting (at least temporarily) about the dirty business of prospecting.

We don't think "dirty business" is too strong a term. The prospecting phase is filled with uncertainty and rejection, and we have yet to meet a salesperson who approaches it with glee. In fact, we know of only two kinds of salespeople: those who say they hate prospecting, and those who lie and say they love it. When it comes to going after new business, most of us are like the kid with a plate full of brussels sprouts. He knows that he's got to eat them eventually, but he doesn't mind waiting.

The problem with following this comfortable trajectory is that it leads, with absolute predictability, to the boom-and-bust revenue cycle that most of us know all too well. When you consistently put off the despised work of prospecting and qualifying, you set yourself up for "dry funnels" down the line, for a very simple reason. Unless you *regularly* spend time at the "top" of your Funnel, sorting the Universe and qualifying your prospects, the potential business up there will stay there forever. The best match in the world to your Ideal Customer profile will not drop magically into your sales cycle all by itself. Thus, the more time you focus exclusively on immediate business, and the more you ignore the long-term business, the more certain it is that a dynamite quarter will be followed by one that's tinder-dry.

What do you do about this problem? The solution is painfully simple: you *resequence*. Instead of backing up the Funnel until you hit Death Valley, you follow an unnatural, uncomfortable working sequence that is designed to eliminate the boom-and-bust pattern. You still begin each week or each day by working on your Best Few objectives. But, once you've started your cycle by working on those gratifying closing tasks, you break with tradition and jump to the *top* of the funnel: you prospect or qualify *next*. Or, to quote an adage that we use in Strategic Selling, "Every time you close something, prospect or qualify something else."

The terminology is from selling, but the point is universal. Anyone who has to juggle competing responsibilities can make more of his or her time by following this resequencing rule. Here are two examples from people who don't consider themselves salespeople.

The first is a friend who writes articles for technical magazines. He loves the writing, and he loves getting the acceptance checks, but he hates—absolutely hates—his version of prospecting, which is sending out query letters about possible new articles. But every time he gets a check, he writes one of those letters. "I've come to accept it as a necessary evil," he told us once, "because I've learned from painful experience that if I don't do it, it's going to be a long dry summer between acceptances."

The second example is a carpenter we know in California. Rob does exquisite cabinetwork as well as basic, heavy-duty work in framing and roofing. Like the writer, he has his preferences. Until recently, when he was working on a one-of-a-kind, museum-quality cabinet ensemble, he would actually turn down framing and roofing jobs—until he started to see that, every time he did so, when he finished the cabinets he would have nothing else to do for two weeks. That wreaked havoc with his cash flow until he adapted our resquencing rule. Now, every time he accepts a cabinet job, he spends the next day hunting up future roofing customers. The result? "I still don't like roof work," he says, "but at least we eat steady."

"Every time you close something, prospect or qualify something else." A generalized variation of that rule might go like this: "Every time you finish a task that you love, make the next thing you do one of your necessary evils." It's as ridiculously simple as it sounds. And it works.

TASKS INVOLVING TIME, MOTION, AND MONEY

So far we've stressed the two most obvious tasks that regular use of the Sales Funnel can help you do better: sort your multiple opportunities in a realistic fashion, and sequence your work to avoid the bitter blips of revenue cycles. But, as we mentioned, the Funnel is also a useful tool in terms of allocating time, tracking account activity, and forecasting revenue. That is, it helps you clarify your understanding—again, with realism as the watchword—of time, motion, and money.

Third Task: Allocating Time

Although the sequence we recommend that you use to order your work should remain the same over time, your allocation of time to the different types of work may vary considerably, depending on how many of your sales objectives are about to close, how many unqualified prospects you have, and so on. As a framework for clarifying where your objectives are in the sales cycle, the Sales Funnel helps you allocate your time most efficiently.

Because the Sales Funnel is a dynamic, not a static, tool, there's no "best" division among the four types of selling work. Each Funnel provides a snapshot of how you should best be dividing your work at that moment. As pieces of business move toward closing, the clustering of Above the Funnel or Best Few objectives will change. The Funnel helps you visualize that change more easily—so that you can adjust your "type of work" schedule to reflect the new alignment.

Fourth Task: Tracking Activity

By the same logic, the Funnel can also help you visualize how quickly, or how sluggishly, a given piece of business is moving from lead to close. Not only can this help you determine where you need to increase your efforts to "unstick" or ease the process. It can also help you establish parameters for managing new business opportunities with accounts that you have tracked down your Funnel before. And this can help you correlate your company's normal selling cycle with the buying organization's typical purchasing patterns.

Say you've sold the Rollins Group five times before, and you've tracked each sale, month by month, down your Sales Funnel. As sale number 6 approaches, you can use those previous Funnels to map out a likely course, observing how rapidly the Rollins people have made decisions in the past, anticipating where in the selling cycle you are most likely to encounter difficulties, and planning what specific actions you might have to take to keep number 6 on a schedule that is appropriate for both your companies.

At Miller Heiman, we conduct *Funnel Reviews* with our sales staff every sixty days. We'll give you an example in Chapter 13. Here the basic point is that tracking sales opportunities, if it is to provide you with helpful information, has to follow a reliable and consistent format—one whose data your sales management may compare from month to month, or from quarter to quarter. The Sales Funnel provides that reliable and consistent format.

Fifth Task: Forecasting Revenue

Just as it brings logic into tracking current business, the Sales Funnel can also bring logic into predicting future income. By comparing individual sales reps' Funnels over time, and by assessing the activity in accounts with multiple opportunities, managers can increase their understanding of "close ratio probabilities," and thus generate forecasting stats that go way beyond guesswork. In addition, as many of our clients have pointed out to us, a multidivision company can generate national sales projections by extrapolating from the projected figures of branch, regional, and individual Funnels.

In most companies, revenue forecasting is some combination of "pie in the sky"—wish fulfillment—and the "add 12 percent" method of extrapolating future income from last year's figures. In our opinion, neither of these methods is appreciably more reliable than reading tea leaves. The Sales Funnel, because it allows you to extrapolate from real figures and real current account activity, can serve as an infinitely more reliable forecasting tool.

DOING IT RIGHT: CLIENT ADAPTATIONS

How does this all work out in practice? As with any other tool or process, the Sales Funnel is used most effectively when it is not simply adopted, but adapted to the particular needs and trends of a given company. Many of the sales organizations that have learned Sales Funnel management from us do just that. We'll end this chapter on time and territory management by giving a few examples.

Sentient's Goldmine. Sentient Systems, Inc., delivers data- and information-management systems to corporate clients. Sales at the healthcare division are under the watchful eye of vice president Joel French. According to Joel, Sentient's adoption of the Sales Funnel process was a natural extension of a process that was already in place, the company's customized version of Elan Software's customer database application, Goldmine.

"Goldmine helps us keep track of both prospective and past business with our clients," Joel says. "We cover dozens of Veterans Administration hospitals alone, for example, and we rely on Goldmine to tell us what we've sold each one in the past, what federal regulations we've got to keep on top of, and so on. It's been a key management tool for us, and the Sales Funnel makes it even more useful. Integrating the two systems has made it much easier for us to see where each customer fits overall, and where our business is going with each one."

A "How Close to the Close?" Percentage System. At Massachusetts-based Datex-Engstrom, Inc., which sells medical equipment, the sales team uses a percentage system to sort and track opportunities as they move down the Funnel. "Management requires a Funnel on every monthly report," says Datex-Engstrom sales representative Tina Aiken. "In the top part of the Funnel—what Miller Heiman calls Above the Funnel—we put sales that have a 25 percent chance of closing within a month. In the middle section, In the Funnel, sales have a 50 percent chance. At the bottom, in Best Few, go sales with a 75 percent chance.

"But you can't just guess. There are regular management checks on these estimates. To give a piece of business a 25 percent ranking, you've got to have evidence that the account is at least in the market for replacing its equipment. And you've got to have established contact with at least one Buying Influence. If you're identifying something as 50 percent likely, you've got to show that you've already contacted all the Buyers and that at least one of them *inside* the operating room—these would be our User Buyers—has given us a positive evaluation.

"As for Best Few, you can't put something in the 75 percent category until the Economic Buyer has been contacted and the budget has been approved. And this can change. One of my colleagues had a piece of business in the Best Few segment recently and had to move it out–back up the Funnel–because the client went through a reorganization and the budget power changed."

Tina's comments reiterate what we constantly say about the Funnel. Since it's a dynamic, not a static, tool, it sometimes leaks, backs up, or both. When that happens, you roll the videocam again. Reset, reframe, and reallocate how you're spending your selling time.

Seven Steps to a Design Win. At VLSI Technology, adaptation takes a somewhat different turn, because sales management at this computer chip company has deliberately subdivided our four basic stages. As the former vice president of sales, Charlie Parr, explains it, this adaptation grew from the recognition that the Miller Heiman process approach could be simply and effectively merged with VLSI Technology's current operations.

"Strategic Selling," he told us, "described the direction that we were already moving in, and the one we wanted all our new people to get behind, but to find it all mapped out in an orderly way ... that was a revelation. We just looked at each other and said 'That's it!' " The resulting adaptation was especially useful, Charlie points out, in modifying the company's tracking of sales opportunities–or, as VLSI Technology prefers to call them, Design Win opportunities.

"Working on the Sales Funnel segment of the program," Charlie says, "forced us to break down very clearly the steps that we typically go through from a first contact with a prospect to the close of a Design Win. In the Universe segment of the Funnel, we didn't have to adapt anything, because what we do there is exactly what Miller Heiman recommends–search for companies that fit an Ideal Customer profile. That makes sense to us, because our sales cycle is very long and our design investments are substantial, so we want reasonable assurance that we're making those investments where they will pan out. We ensure that by looking for three criteria.

"One, our customers have to be market leaders in a segment that we've targeted. Two, their preferred design methodology should match ours; we're most comfortable working in cell-based methodologies, so it's best for us that our customers see value in that approach. Three, they've got to be willing to work toward partnerships with us. The firms that throw a spec sheet on the table and say, 'Follow this'–they're not for us. We prefer to work with people who respect our intellectual property and are willing to work collaboratively for the most suitable designs.

"When we got down beyond these three criteria and actually started working business through the selling cycle, we found that we needed to subdivide the process beyond the Miller Heiman model, and in doing so we came up with seven steps.

"In Above the Funnel, we break the process down into two steps. Step 1 is to identify an opportunity, a potential Design Win. This means that one of our salespeople has become aware of a design project that might fit well with our capabilities and where the prospect involved is a match to our Ideal Customer criteria. In step 2, we qualify the opportunity: to move to this step, the fit has to be confirmed, and we have to have identified at least one Buying Influence.

"We also divide the In the Funnel portion into two steps. At step 3, we complete a needs assessment. That means we contact all the Buying Influences, get detailed project requirements, and determine the customer's own skill level; this last determination is important for us because it gives us an early sense of how well we're going to be able to collaborate technically—what we'll have to do ourselves, where we'll need to guide their design people, and so on. Step 4 is the presentation of an actual proposal, the submission of a VLSI solution.

"The Best Few segment of the Funnel we break down into three steps. Step 5 is for us to submit a binding offer, with whatever detail, references, and backup documentation the customer requires. At step 6, we get either an oral or a written commitment from the customer that they are going ahead with our Design Win solution. And at step 7, the actual close, the Design Win is booked."

A FINAL WORD: REGULATING THE IRREGULAR

Few things are more seemingly irregular than sales activity. Whether you're looking at the fluctuating needs of once reliable customers, the forays into your market of "out of the blue" competitors, or the roller-coaster effect of Wall Street business cycles, the world of selling seems virtually governed by the ungovernable, while the idea of bringing any predictability into this revenue-rattling chaos seems a pipe dream on the order of peace in the Balkans or a balanced budget.

As we've tried to indicate in this chapter, however, a significant amount of this chaos is self-generated, and it can be reduced by a more rigorous approach to time management. The Sales Funnel is a valuable tool in

206 ■ SEVEN DEADLY SCENES

providing that rigor, but of course it is only as valuable as the people who employ it. Like everything else we've proposed in this book, Funnel management is a vehicle whose ultimate effectiveness only begins with application, and grows with reapplication. It can, and does, turn reliable leads into orders. But it will do that only if you turn it on—and if you do so, reporting period after reporting period, with regularity.

In Part III of this book, we emphasize regularity, both as a general principle for implementing process and as a necessary element in making the Sales Funnel operational. Because of this emphasis, we are ending this chapter unconventionally, without the Manager's Checklist you have come to expect. The Sales Funnel, in our estimation, is so central to the effective management of the sales process that we have expanded its checklist into an entire chapter. You'll encounter it later, under the title "Review."

PART THREE

THE SALES PROCESS
AS
AN OPERATING SYSTEM:
THE THREE Rs
OF IMPLEMENTATION

11

BEYOND
TRAINING
EVENTS

As promising as reengineering sounds, its success ... depends upon that old management theory bugaboo, top management commitment.
–William Keenan Jr.
"If I Had a Hammer"

It is not a training program. It is an organizational culture change, an ongoing process that requires years to achieve excellence.
–Robert F. Lee
Vice President, Sales and Marketing
Foxboro Canada

S HOLLY AND BETH'S RECOLLECTIONS IN Chapter 9 indicate, most Miller Heiman clients are pleasantly surprised to find that we follow up with them after they take our programs, to determine how effectively those programs are being implemented. There is a positive and a negative way of viewing this reaction. On the positive side, it means we are doing something right—that we have identified, and are trying to address, the postprogram problem of improving the sales process in practice, not just in theory.

On the negative side, it signals us that there *is* a problem. Our participants don't just glide back blissfully to their desks and start putting the process to work on a day-to-day basis. Some do, some don't, and some are prevented from doing so by company environments where management is simply not committed to the essential cultural change.

Beth and Holly hear complaints about this scenario all the time. For every client who says his or her company's executives are gung-ho behind the new process, another one identifies a gap—in communication and practice—between the people in the field and the managers who are reviewing their productivity. The following are typical of the comments that our client-support staff hears:

> *"The processes are great, but it's easy to fall back into business as usual, especially when you're not being told that you're required to change."*
>
> *"It's like anything else new—there's a transition period. Until you do it for a while, and it becomes habit, it takes time. A lot of us don't feel that we have that time."*
>
> *"If you're in the field, you're going to use this stuff, because it works. But management isn't as close to it. If management actively reinforced it, things would go even better."*
>
> *"They say that they're going to reward us for customers' satisfaction, but when push comes to shove, it's still the numbers that count."*

Aside from frustration, the common thread in these observations is inertia or, to coin a term, a corporate brand of *revertia*, a tendency for things to revert to the tried (if not true) practices as long as the people in charge don't mandate change. Because organizational cultures change from the top down, it's not only reasonable but predictable that no matter how fired-up and radicalized a new idea makes your sales team, without the "old buga-boo" of senior commitment, they will soon revert to doing business as usual.

If you or your people have ever experienced any "sales training," you're probably already familiar with the revertia syndrome. You shuffle off for two days to Seminar Junction, where a guru in pinstripes whacks you with a twenty-pound notebook. You trade war stories, feign astonishment at the guru's wizardry, and go home with a briefcase full of buzzwords that you'll never use again. Once you're back at your desk, you put the note-book in your "training events (completed)" pile, try out the new jargon on your colleagues for a couple of days, and by the end of the month are back to your usual routine.

The training event has become just that—an event. Not a spring-board to revitalized action, but a piece of the past.

THE REVERTIA SYNDROME: WHY IT HAPPENS

For years we thought we understood why this happened. It happened be-cause the quality of sales training out there was so poor that it practically invited participants to forget what they had "learned." As sluggish and dis-organized as most companies' sales routines were, they were still more pro-ductive than the gimmickry that was trying to replace them. No wonder revertia set it: the "improvements" weren't improvements.

This explanation, however, ceased to satisfy us when we discov-ered that our programs, too, were often victims of revertia. As good as our sales lessons were, they weren't always "taking."

Why? Why did some of our clients—even our most enthusiastic ones—pay us handsomely to revitalize their companies' sales efforts, and then fail to implement the processes that would get them results? After all, we joked a little grimly, it cost no more to book a program that was fully supported than one that company management allowed to die on the vine. Why pay top dollar for a meal and then not eat it?

About two years ago, we wrote sales managers at several of our most valued client companies, soliciting their help in understanding and solving this problem. A particularly insightful response came from Bob Lee, vice president of sales and marketing at Foxboro Canada. Bob identified several factors of resistance that get in the way of managerial commitment. We believe that five of these factors deserve special attention: (1) fear of change, (2) "trainophobia," (3) the "not my job" syndrome, (4) skepticism, and (5) the executive time crunch.

Factor 1: Fear of Change

Given sales professionals' traditional reputation as aggressive go-getters, fear might seem an unlikely factor in their behavior. Bob Lee feels, however, that it's a central factor—and, comparing what he says with our experience, we think he's on the money.

Most prospective buyers feel a certain anxiety when they are considering change, and the Buying Influences for your customers aren't immune. Like everybody else, they have a healthy fear of the unknown. And like Hamlet, they sometimes respond to that natural anxiety by opting to bear the ills they already have rather than "fly to others that we know not of." The result? Like Hamlet's plans, the sales process splutters, victim to apprehension and irresolution.

"In every company I've worked in," Bob explains, "the adoption of any new process becomes very political. When you're trying to put in a sales process that is truly revolutionary, if you haven't introduced it yourself, you can see it as a threat. A manager sees the possibilities, but also the risks in terms of rocking the boat and dislocation. Besides, it isn't his idea, so it often becomes hard for him to get on the team. If a sales manager commits to the new process and it fails, he's in trouble. On the other hand, what if it succeeds so well that it puts him out of a job?

"People are very fearful of committing to a whole new culture that begins as the result of a two-day course. Whatever happens, it could work out badly for them, personally. Personal Wins and Loses are always a factor. You're taking a major risk by getting on board, but you're also at risk if you hesitate and it leaves you behind. For many people, it seems as if there's no way to Win."

What Bob is describing here is particularly common when the people who have to get on board are trainers themselves. At Miller Heiman, because of our commitment to ongoing process rather than "fix-it" modules, we never describe ourselves as "sales trainers." But we deal all the time with people who describe themselves that way, and often this brings us face to face with the "not invented here" syndrome. Many people in corporate "training departments" are understandably suspicious of a company whose business is based on rebuilding, not just repainting, the sales function.

There are, to be sure, dramatic exceptions to this pattern. We've worked with some truly innovative and brilliant training professionals, people who have been indispensable to the implementation of our processes. Tony Cueva, for example, who is manager of national accounts for the payroll- and human-resources services company Ceridian, was part of the training department when we met him; Ceridian's success with our principles could not have happened without him. At Hallmark Canada, another excellent training executive, Leeanne Lehr, has been equally indispensable to the adoption of our processes. And there are many other examples among our clients–trainers, for example, who are assigned to a division or area charged with becoming "process experts" available to branch managers and salespeople.

Sadly, though, most training departments are charged not with developing this type of expertise but with determining "needs analyses" and then coming up with events to "fill" the need. Although they're often involved in purchasing decisions, they're seldom responsible for implementing what they've bought. This leaves them feeling, understandably, out of the loop.

We try, consistently, to involve client "trainers" in our work–to show them how a revitalized process can help them Win too. But, as we admitted in Chapter 4, on Buying Influences, there seems to be an unfortunate natural antagonism between process-oriented "revolutionaries" and members of the training function. Working to overcome the fear trainers naturally feel, therefore, is part of the challenge process specialists face.

Factor 2: "Trainophobia"

If trainers distrust sales consultants because of what they might do, others denounce the training function for what it can't (or won't) do. In Bob Lee's words, "There is a significant contingent of people at the management level that simply don't believe you can teach anybody to sell. You hear it all the time among salespeople: 'Selling is intuitive,' 'You've got to have the personality for it,' or 'Either you know how to do it or you don't.' Managers with this attitude are generally resistant to all sales development programs."

Listen to the grumbling that starts bubbling up in the sales force when management announces an upcoming sales seminar, and you can probably attest that Bob's insight here is on target. Among managers and field reps alike, the old seat-of-the-pants approach to selling is still very much a factor in professionals' self-image. To older professionals especially, and to those who respect their example, you learn to sell by selling, not by attending a program. And every minute that you spend away from the trenches is a minute that costs you in customer contact–and money.

Moreover, this aversion to "training" has an interesting corollary– an equally passionate aversion to pre-call planning and to any honest critique of the call once it's over. Account analysis, thinking things through before and after the call, writing down questions to be asked and actions to be considered—all of this, to a traditional cast of mind, is a drain on the salesperson's "real" time, which should be spent in the field. Jackie Smith, a top sales representative for Air-Shields, which sells neonatal incubators and monitors, has been successful largely because he recognizes the value of such analysis. But, as he admits, he's almost an anomaly. In most situations, Jackie says, "Doing paperwork is against the sales rep's idea of time well spent."

Salespeople with attitudes like that—and there are thousands of them—make analytic programs like ours an extremely hard sell. And they make their own internal implementation even harder.

Factor 3: "That's Not My Job"

A third factor in poor implementation is the conviction on the part of both line and senior management that putting a process in place is not their responsibility. This follows from the "trainophobia" syndrome. In probably the majority of companies, line managers view sales training the way they view any other kind of training: as a staff function, not a selling function. Senior managers, at the same time, tend to view their responsibility for sales training as that of a distant supervisor with budgetary discretion. Their thinking seems to be "I bought it and I paid for it—now *you* make it work."

In both cases, management is dropping the ball. If there's one critical lesson we've learned in watching companies try to put the process in place, it's that no process will succeed without management support. Paying for a process is only the beginning. If that's the only commitment you're willing to make, you're wasting your money. The same point goes for the involvement of line sales managers. As valuable as good trainers can be to the adoption of a process, if the folks on the line are not involved, it will not fly.

Factor 4: Skepticism

A fourth factor is skepticism on the part of good field people who have been told that a revolution is on, but don't see the evidence. This is a natural and reasonable response where management's commitment is vague, and where the signals from executive levels are imprecise or contradictory. "It's difficult," says Bob Lee, "to convince sales professionals that they really are being judged on how they utilize the process. They expect that the new way of doing things is just another fad, and they're waiting for management to turn around and say, "Get out there and sell!""

What's really difficult, Bob points out, is making the transition from "only the numbers count" to "assessment on the process." "People have to understand that although the numbers are important, they are also being scrutinized on how well they implement the process–because management understands that sticking to the process is ultimately the surest way to guarantee the numbers. Some salespeople will implement it enthusiastically, some will do so reluctantly and with reservations, and some won't change at all. Those who won't change have to realize that they cannot remain as salespeople in the new organization–and that this is a real commitment on the part of senior management."

Of course that message won't come through if the commitment isn't there. When that's the case, people sense it–and you're back to square one.

Factor 5: The Time Crunch

Implementing an integrated sales process means changing a culture, and nobody ever said that was easy. Call it inertia, the disorientation generated by change, or simply laziness. Whatever you call it, the fact is plain. Many managers are not prepared to expend the time and effort that implementing a new process often takes. This is often true of sales managers themselves, and almost always true of senior executives.

There's a bitter irony here, as managers hire sales consultants like us to work the kinks out of their revenue flow, but then refuse to commit the very resources–including the most important resource, their own time– that can turn our recommendations into reality. It's a higher-level version of the sales rep's reluctance to plan, and in firms where the attitude is endemic, it can scuttle all your work.

Granted, reengineering is a lot of work. That's true whether you're fixing a snag on an assembly line, a mess in accounting, or sales. But once you've committed resources and personnel to the effort, it's almost worse than doing nothing to pull halfway back. And that's exactly what happens, time and again.

Usually it's verbally justified with one of two excuses: either the managers who should be on board are "too busy elsewhere," or they don't see the "sales function" as part of their job. Both of these excuses, while understandable, betray a common error: the arrogant notion that sales is a peripheral function, and that valuable managerial time should be spent on "business" matters.

We explained in Chapter 1 why the disintegration that follows this attitude can do irreparable harm to your revenue flow and your business. In a sense this entire book is a corrective to that notion. But it's important to acknowledge, once again, how common the notion is. In fact, it's far more likely to be true than not true in your organization–even if you're recognized as an industry leader. If allowed to go unchallenged, it can eventually "de-engineer" all the good that you've done.

A story that appears in our 1991 book on large accounts makes the point with brutal lucidity. It bears repeating here as an instance of the "time crunch" excuse, which so often causes executives to clobber their own companies by acting as if they have no interest in, or stomach for, selling.

> Several years ago, when Australia's national airline, Qantas, was debating where to order $500 million worth of new planes, Boeing's chief executive officer flew to Canberra to meet personally with Australian authorities–including the country's prime minister. When his counterpart at the competition was asked to do the same, he responded, "That's what I have salespeople for." Box score after this episode: Boeing $500 million, competition zero.

The lesson is clear. In global arenas, the blue suits must get involved. That in itself won't guarantee you solid business, because it's only one element of a companywide process approach. But it is essential. If you're in the driver's seat at a company and you're too busy to sell, check to see if you're still in business at all.

Here's the real irony. Managers say continually that they don't have time, and this is exactly what many field people also say: they don't have time to do a Situation Analysis, to update a Funnel. But those who make the time consistently discover that selling through the process is a phenomenal timesaver. The investment in process streamlines all selling activities, so that the companies who commit to front-loading it are more efficient in the end. And the time that is ultimately saved is money in the bank.

A Sixth Factor: From the *What* to the *How*

To Bob Lee's excellent assessment of these fearsome five factors, we would add one more. The most fervent commitment in the world won't get the process implemented unless the people in charge know, in detail, what to tell the sales force. It's not enough to abstractly "stand behind" them. As a manager, you've got to be able to specify the *how*–to direct and shape that complex mass of behaviors through which the goal of a solid sales process is achieved. Such shaping doesn't come with the territory of knowing how to sell. Everybody we know has a teeth-gritting story about a supersalesperson who gets promoted to manager and immediately turns into Bozo the Clown.

Selling and Coaching are two related but distinct operations. Most managers, whatever their commitment, don't Coach well. They want to re-inforce the process, to implement the program. But they don't know the steps to follow to make this happen. They understand what must happen, but not how to get there.

It's *not* a matter of rah-rah examples and inspiration. That's the most common error that inexperienced managers make: they think they can fire up the troops by yelling "Let's go get 'em!"–like the classically ob-noxious branch manager in the play and movie *Glengarry Glen Ross*, who uses a blend of intimidation and grandiosity to insult his reps into "putting the close" on their customers. That may work in some businesses, but not in ours. If you want to change your salespeople's behavior, you've got to show them how.

Our field representative Sam Manfer, commenting on his experi-ences teaching Strategic Selling, notes that this is not an automatic process. Referring to the Situation Analysis forms that program participants use to assess and improve their account positions, Sam notes, "You always run into some people who won't use them that way. Or start to and then fall back into old habits. A few months after the program, and they're using the forms as reporting tools–something to hand in to a manager, saying 'Here's what the account looks like' rather than 'Here's what we need to do to con-solidate our position.'

"What a manager needs to say, when he gets that kind of report, is 'Okay, where do we go from here? What's the next step? How can we work together to get rid of that Red Flag, to capitalize on this opportunity, to get some better Coaching about that Buying Influence ...' Unless you pin it down like that, the analyses become just another piece of paperwork, something to pacify the manager. And the process that you've worked for will never take off."

As Sam correctly observes, reinforcement is concrete. Generalities won't do. You've got to focus specifically on those selling behaviors that are improving your revenue stream, you've got to model them in your own work, and you've got to find ways to make them second nature to every member of your selling team.

Fran Tarkenton, who led the Minnesota Vikings to three Super Bowls in the 1970s, now consults with major corporations on productivity problems. In his 1986 book *How to Motivate People*, he agrees that behavior change must focus on the specific; better productivity, he advises, begins not with that old inspirational chestnut, a better "attitude," but with a "Pin-pointing technique" that helps you to "focus your motivation." "A guy could have steam coming out of his ears and hit the left defensive tackle like a freight engine," he writes, "but it wouldn't do us any good if his target was supposed to have been the middle linebacker. A Pinpointed objective would be . . . to block the right person."

In recalling his team's tough road to its second Super Bowl, Tarkenton emphasizes the importance of "isolating the ingredients of winning" (like blocking the right person), and then putting them into practice, over and over, until you succeed as a team in "making them second nature."

> There's an awful lot of data in a football game, and it can get lost in the shuffle unless you break it down into its components. . . . Putting our strategy together was like putting an airplane model together. We didn't throw 150 pieces in a box together, shake it, and say "Let's go get 'em." We sorted everything out, labeled the pieces, put it together step by step—and came up with a championship offense.

Our approach to managing the sales process is similar to Tarkenton's. We also think it's important to isolate the ingredients, to break it down into components, to sort things out. Much of what we've discussed in previous chapters gives you practical advice for following such a game plan. In this final section we take the same tack with regard to implementation.

The chapters that follow include tips on pinpointing the *how*–tips that are derived from our Managers Coaching program. It was designed to ensure that our clients got regular, concrete support from their sales and senior management—and to ensure that this support had measurable effects on sales behavior.

In previous chapters we outlined, step by step, what you need to know to give your company's revenue management a Super Bowl caliber. In this final part of the book, we both summarize what we've said and give it a managerial, or a Coaching, perspective, by discussing, just as concretely, what managers can do to ensure that the sales process actually transforms their businesses—that it actually delivers the benefits we know it can provide.

Putting the sales process in place involves three elements—factors that we call the *three Rs of implementation*: (1) reinforcement, (2) review, and (3) reward. They all proceed from the top, from the senior management level. They all respond to the manager's need to show how. And they all help to integrate sales into bottom-line strategies, making *process* the driver of your company's operating system.

12

REINFORCEMENT: "FULL ORGANIZATIONAL COMMITMENT" REVISITED

"Good management consists in getting average people to do the work of superior people."
–John D. Rockefeller

"If you want the process to stick, your people have to review and internalize, review and internalize, over and over. It takes time, but it's the only way to get from 'This is interesting' to 'This is important.' "
–Larry Smith
Vice President, International Sales
Harris Corporation Communications Sector

WE'VE JUST DESCRIBED SOME OF THE COMMON factors that tend to move things, even in the best selling organizations, backward toward a nonproductive "business as usual" syndrome. In this chapter we provide some guidelines for correcting this tendency, as well as a method that sales managers in our client companies have consistently found effective in reinforcing process so that it becomes a daily reality.

Some reinforcement, we should say at the outset, can be handled on a very informal, ad hoc level, by publicly recognizing individuals who use the process well. A few client examples:

Hallmark Canada At Hallmark Canada, where our Conceptual Selling process has been put into place under the direction of the imaginative Leeanne Lehr, there's an ongoing contest to reaffirm the sales force's understanding of process elements. Once a week, at varying intervals, the sales manager uses the company voice-mail system to pose a question relating to Conceptual Selling, one that can be answered quickly only by a representative who is actively implementing it in his or her work. The first person to submit the right answer wins a prize.

Vangard Technology Vanguard is running a somewhat different contest. Here, when a salesperson does a full Situation Analysis on a sales objective and that objective closes, his or her name goes into a pool for a biweekly drawing. Two times a month, someone pockets $500.

Ceridian At Ceridian, management keeps salespeople on their toes by offering occasional bonuses–$100 for the salesperson and an extra $50 for his or her manager–for the most effective use of Situation Analysis. Judges award the bonuses on the basis of how "thorough and creative" the salesperson has been in "finding innovative solutions for customers."

We could cite many other client examples of such ad hoc reinforcement, and we've used similar incentives at Miller Heiman. Contests, games, public recognition, notices in company newsletters, free dinners, memos of thanks–all such forms of reinforcement are inexpensive to maintain, and they keep the importance of following the process constantly evident.

To ensure that your salespeople have fully internalized that importance, however, you also need to address their use of the process individually, and on a systematic rather than ad hoc basis. To put it another way, you have to coach them, regularly, on how effectively they are implementing the principles you require.

Today's best sales managers are both players and coaches for their teams. Much of what we say in this chapter will be addressed to managers who are ready to take on that dual role, but who need some "coach's coaching" to get them started. This is the situation of roughly 90 percent of our client managers, and it's probably the same for 90 percent of our readers. Being a good coach is not the same thing as being a good player, and the best salespeople in the world, once they move into management, almost always need assistance in learning coaching tasks. We developed our Managers' Coaching Program specifically to teach them these new tasks, and this chapter introduces that program's highlights.

MANAGERS' COACHING: BASIC ASSUMPTIONS

At the opening of our Managers' Coaching programs, we ask participants to accept a few commonsense assumptions about management, about coaching, and about people. These assumptions are the bedrock of the sales coaching process. If they don't seem commonsense to you, you severely limit your chances of changing your people's behavior.

Assumption 1: Most People Want to Do a Good Job

Yes, every organization has people who don't care, and yours probably has its share. In addition, most salespeople haven't exactly been shortchanged when it comes to ego, and that too can be an impediment to improved performance. As our own Beth Rutherford comments about the people she calls in our follow-up process, "Some people won't adjust their thinking no matter how bad things are. Once in a while you get someone who's just in denial."

These hard cases aside, however, 99 percent of the people we meet in business are committed, on one level or another, to their own excellence and improvement. Whether this commitment is motivated by some "quality" gene that is yet to be isolated or by a need for the approval of others, it seems to be a nearly universal human characteristic. This means that, in attempting to convert a sales staff to a solid sales process, one major hurdle is virtually asking to be overcome. Given half a chance, people want to do things more effectively. They want to improve.

Assumption 2: People Can't Coach Themselves

Again, this is true of probably 99 percent of the people in the world. Granted, there are some odd duck geniuses—people like Michelango or Thomas Edison—who can take the bit in their teeth without any guidance and produce the Sistine Chapel or a marketable light bulb. The rest of us need somebody else to assess our abilities, to provide an objective, nuanced view of how we could improve. This is true of even the most accomplished performers, including performers like Luciano Pavarotti, Michael Jordan, or Meryl Streep. Everybody needs outside, objective feedback in order to improve performance. If you're managing a sales force, it's your task to provide that feedback. If you don't do it, the performance will not change.

Assumption 3: You Can't Coach What You Don't Know Yourself

You know the old saw, "Those who can, do; those who can't, teach." Obviously concocted by someone who never met a real teacher. A real teacher, like a real coach, knows the subject at hand more intimately than the students do. It's true that in certain "subjects"—sports is the prime example—the coach may not be physically able to perform the required tasks with the same facility as those he or she is teaching. Nonetheless, the coach understands the logic and the process of performance better than anyone else. That's why he or she is the coach. So to be a winning coach— to excel at any kind of teaching—you have to begin by feeling comfortable with the subject. If that subject is the sales process, you must be able to apply it as well as your sales force. This means showing as well as telling, and it means modeling.

Assumption 4: You Can't Hold People Responsible for What They Don't Know

This flies in the face of the conventional teacher's wisdom, "Stick it to 'em," which says that an effective test must be difficult and "challenging" to the student. This is true if your goal is to weed out, rank, and put down. But if your goal is to produce more effective students—or a more effective sales force—then your focus should be on teaching people what they don't know, rather than chewing them out for not having already learned it.

This final assumption underlies the particular style of coaching that you have to adopt if what you're really after is changed sales behaviors. In Chapter 11 we mentioned some of the so-called "teaching" styles that we recommend you keep away from–negative styles that undermine what they are trying to achieve. The style that we recommend you adopt–the style that you have to adopt to be successful–stresses the positive rather than the negative, not because the positive approach is "nicer," but because in the long run it gets you better results. In applying this style to our own sales management situations, we have found four interrelated tactics to be of special value.

"ACCENTUATE THE POSITIVE": COACHING TACTICS

Good coaching, like all good teaching, succeeds by reinforcing and supporting the positive, not by condemning or attempting to stop the negative. This is the most difficult part of managing, because it sounds backwards. We have labored so long with a "fix-it" mentality that, like most doctors and mechanics, we take a narrowly technical view of how systems go wrong. We hunt down the source of the problem–the bug in the works–and try to eradicate it. It sounds logical enough, but it's just not efficient. Efficient coaching is, to use a nursing-oriented term, more "holistic." In effect it ignores the "problem" and resets the system. By reinforcing those behaviors that make it run more effectively, it creates an environment where bugs and problem behaviors just can't thrive.

Here are some specific coaching tactics that will help you create that kind of environment.

Coaching Tactic 1: Don't Evaluate—Assess

This follows from our general observation that positive reinforcement accomplishes more than negative, and from our caution in Chapter 8 against acting as a judge, inquisitor, or scolding parent. When you assess, you record and reflect, playing back to the salesperson what you've observed. When you evaluate, you make judgments. There's a time and a place for making judgments, but it's a technique that is prone to overuse, because it gives evaluators a sense of their own superiority. In managing sales professionals, that sense can be more than merely annoying. It can be confrontational and counterproductive, because people who perceive that they are being judged quickly become defensive and unresponsive. The law of limited returns sets in, and evaluation leads to demotivation–exactly the opposite of the effect that you want to achieve.

Unfortunately, many managers are so attached to this confrontational style that they use it 90 percent of the time in talking to their people, reserving the more productive tactic, assessment, for the remaining 10 percent. We think those figures ought to be reversed. And don't worry, if you do this, that the necessary judgment of behavior won't get done. What usually happens, when you assess rather than judge, is that people being assessed make the judgment themselves. Since most people want to do a good job, they'll take your observation as a trigger for self-improvement, rather than resisting it because it's being phrased as an attack.

One technique for keeping this subtle distinction in mind is to phrase your observations in a positive manner—positive grammatically, not just emotionally. It's the subtle but critical difference between saying "Don't forget your keys" and "Remember your keys." Our sales consultant Sharon Williams puts it this way: "People remember the positive observation. When you tell somebody, 'Don't think of a blue rabbit,' guess what he'll think of? That's why it's important to state the desired behavior *as you want it*, not in the form that's already giving you headaches. This has nothing to do with being Mr. Smiley Face or a Pollyanna. It's a matter of describing what you need in the most effective manner."

Coaching Tactic 2: Check Your Reality with That of the Person You're Assessing

This is another tactic that derives from an observational, rather than confrontational, style of management. One excellent way to begin coaching sessions without alienating the people whose behavior you're trying to change is to put the ball in their court, by asking for their observations. "How do you see what happened at today's meeting, Jim?" Or: "What did you observe on our last joint call?" You'll have your own observations about the situation, of course, and if you're like most managers you'll be tempted to come out with them first. Resist the temptation. Letting the person you're coaching give his or her fix on things first brings you two immediate benefits that you should not ignore. It defuses possible defensiveness by letting people know that you value their assessment of the situation. And it invites the introduction of account information that may clash with or contradict yours, or that you may not have considered.

Perhaps you've seen the cartoon of the two railroad crews who have met to join their tracks in the middle of a desert, only to discover that they're about two feet out of line. It happens all the time in business, and it's not very funny. It's especially annoying because it's so easily avoided. If the two crews had been talking to each other all along, they would have discovered the misalignment ten miles back, in plenty of time to adjust it before they actually met (or, in this case, didn't meet). The same thing goes for the interaction between salesperson and manager. If you want results, check the other person's blueprint early and often.

This recommendation really flows from a very basic Miller

Heiman principle: the belief that effective selling is a matter of managing information, and that the more information you have, the better positioned you will be. That includes observations about the account from new or inexperienced or ineffective sales representatives. If you don't listen to their views of what's going on, you're depriving yourself of information that may prove useful, even when—and in some cases especially when—their understanding of the case turns out to be "wrong." You can often learn as much from mistaken views as from on-target views, and failing to check your reality against another person's gets you self-satisfaction at the expense of account understanding. That's like asking to be left in the desert on a track that goes nowhere.

Coaching Tactic 3: Focus on the Difference between the Planned and the Actual

That is, in assessing salespeople's behavior, hold them accountable only for those behaviors that your developing strategy said they would perform. If Ken was supposed to prepare a three-page report for a key User Buyer by March 15, and he doesn't, then *that's* the behavior your coaching session should address. "Our plan was that your report would be ready by the fifteenth, and it wasn't. How did that happen?" Focus on the gap between where your sales team was supposed to be and where it is.

If Ken's failure to prepare the report has broader, more dire consequences, you will be tempted to blame him for all those consequences as well. Unless what he's done has totally wrecked the business, or unless his negligence is part of a larger, continual pattern, our recommendation is that you resist this temptation also. As a sales manager you're in the business of *developing your people*, not just of correcting mistakes. You develop people by positive attention to closing specific gaps. As perversely satisfying as it may be to condemn Ken for everything from the loss of the Cornell account to the latest NASDAQ dive, it's probably not in your company's best interests to do so. Not if you want him to be part of the team you're developing.

Coaching Tactic 4: Focus on One Behavior at a Time

Just as you should focus on one event at a time, it's best, in any given meeting with a member of your staff, to concentrate your coaching attention on individual behaviors. There are two related reasons why this is so. First, from a personal standpoint, if you try to fix all a salesperson's difficulties at once, he or she will decode this as, "You're worthless as a salesperson," and will conclude, "Why should I bother?" This will virtually guarantee that you'll get no results. Second, from a practical standpoint, you can't adjust a person's entire behavior repertoire with a single swipe of your sales manager's magic wand. It's just too big a job.

In Ken's case, chances are that somebody who neglects to deliver a critical report is also experiencing difficulty in other areas. Maybe he hasn't learned yet how to locate User Buyers, or he mistakes inside friends for Coaches, or his listening skills leave something to be desired. You can't fix these problems all at once. The way to address Ken's problems–assuming, of course, that he's worth salvaging–is to adopt what Peters and Waterman call a *chunking* approach. Take one nonproductive behavior as the focus of your March meeting. Check in a month to see that he's made some progress on it. Take another chunk for him to work on in April, and so on.

The same thing goes in assessing positive behaviors. The more concrete and focused your assessment, the more likely it is that you'll get the person to repeat the desired behavior in the future. Saying "Great sales call, Kelly" may be nice for Kelly to hear, but it doesn't help her see what made it great–and she may not be able to replicate her success. If you say, "You got great clarification from that customer about scheduling," it's likely that Kelly will get good scheduling information in the future–that she'll internalize the importance of that task without being asked.

Sharon Williams describes the importance of chunking in this way. "One thing that managing a process does for you is to change you from the kid at Christmas or Hanukkah who wants every toy he sees to a more realistic mode where you realize that you can only get three or four things–and that even those have to be things that you work for, step by step with each person and one at a time. If you want to make applesauce, you start by picking one apple."

SITUATION ANALYSIS: FINE-TUNING THE CHECKLIST

In identifying selling behaviors to reinforce, you can begin with the Managers' Checklist that we presented Chapter 8, in the section on Situation Analysis. The questions there are designed to uncover problems–and attendant problem behaviors–in the most common nightmare scenarios of selling. To help you refine your understanding of the situation review process, we present a supplementary checklist here. It includes ten checkpoints that managers in our client companies identify as especially critical, along with sample questions that you should ask the salesperson responsible for the account, in order to clarify your company's position with regard to your current sales objective.

Notice in all cases that these questions are stated positively, are precise, and are nonconfrontational. In other words, they reflect the principles implicit in our coaching tactics regarding pinpointing, reality checking, and assessment. Their collective goal is not just to isolate the salesperson's "mistakes," but to offer guidance for replacing mistakes with positive behaviors.

You can offer that guidance only if the salesperson meets you halfway, that is, if he or she has done the necessary homework to make a manager's check of position a worthwhile endeavor. Therefore, when this review elicits responses that are overly brief, incomplete, or contradictory, you should become alerted to one very dangerous Red Flag: lack of adequate preparation by the salesperson. If you encounter this situation, you next have to determine whether this failure was the result of simple laziness or lack of interest, or whether it happened because the salesperson didn't know how to follow the process effectively. Given our 99 percent rule, we think you'll usually find that it's lack of knowledge–which gives you an ideal opening for positive reinforcement.

Checkpoint: Concept

Does the salesperson fully understand the customer's Concept? To determine whether or not the salesperson grasps the customer's "solution image," ask:

- *"What discrepancy is this customer trying to overcome?"*
- *"Would you describe, from the customer's perspective, what the end result they want is going to look like?"*

Checkpoint: Our Sales Objective

Does the salesperson have a well-defined picture of the proposal or sales objective we're currently trying to accomplish? To determine his or her understanding of our immediate objective, ask:

- *"Would you clarify for me exactly how much of which product or service we're trying to sell this customer, and by what date?"*
- *"What's the reason you selected this sales objective?"*
- *"What's the evidence that we can achieve it, to specifications and on time?"*

Checkpoint: Buying Influences

Has the salesperson identified and covered all the key decision makers for this sales objective? Ask:

- *"What makes you feel confident that the person you've identified as the Economic Buyer can actually release the funds for this sale?"*
- *"Describe for me how each Buying Influence base has been covered."*
- *"Explain how your Coach meets each of the three Coaching criteria."*
- *"Who else, in your wildest flight of fancy, could possibly have an impact on this sale?"*

Checkpoint: Win-Results

Has the salesperson clearly identified each Buying Influence's Win-Results? To determine whether Wins and Results have been adequately identified—and separated—ask:

- *"Will you explain how our proposal will guarantee each Buying Influence the specific business Results he or she is looking for?"*
- *"What evidence do we have that, once our solution is in place, each of these key players will personally Win?"*

Checkpoint: Receptivity

Has the salesperson accurately identified each Buying Influence's level of receptivity to our current proposal? Ask:

- *"How did you determine that your key players were in Growth, Trouble, Even Keel, or Overconfident?"*
- *"Would you describe the language that each of them uses in speaking about the change that our proposal represents?"*
- *"What resources can we provide to help you leverage your receptive players against your Even Keel or Overconfident ones?"*

Checkpoint: Ideal Customer

Has the salesperson adequately measured this potential customer against our company's Ideal Customer profile? Ask:

- *"For how many of our Ideal Customer characteristics is this customer a good fit?"*

- *(For good fits)* "Could you explain what data enabled you to identify this fit?"

- *(For poor fits)* "In your view, what is our rationale for pursuing business with this customer?"

Checkpoint: Commitment

Is the salesperson getting a level of incremental commitment that justifies our continuing the expense of calls to this customer? To determine level of commitment, ask:

- *"How many times have you called on this customer in the past six months?"*

- *"What's the history of those calls?*

- *What data do we have that we're better positioned now than we were six months ago?"*

- *"What makes you confident that this customer is playing Win-Win with us?*

- *What evidence do we have the customer is carrying his or her share of the burden in moving the buy-sell process forward?"*

Checkpoint: Red Flags

Has the salesperson located all areas of possible trouble and taken steps to overcome them? Ask:

- *"What data made you identify this area as a Red Flag?"*

- *"What makes you confident that you haven't overlooked any other Buying Influence Red Flags?*

- *Remembering Murphy's law, is there anything else that could possibly go wrong?"*

- *"How does your proposed strategy for this objective leverage our strengths to eliminate each Red Flag?"*

Checkpoint: Actions

Has the salesperson generated appropriate actions to consolidate or improve our position? Ask:

- *"For each of these actions, how did you decide who was the person best qualified or best positioned with the customer's organization to perform it?"*

- *"How did you decide upon the appropriate timing?"*
- *"Would you show me how this action capitalizes on a strength or eliminates or minimizes the impact of a Red Flag?"*

Checkpoint: Missing Information

Does the salesperson know what information is still missing and how to get it? Ask:

- *"Are you confident that you've noted all areas of doubtful or incomplete information?"*
- *"For areas of remaining doubt, whom would you recommend we talk to in order to acquire a clearer picture?"*
- *"Whom would you recommend we get to approach that person?"*

MAKING IT OPERATIONAL:
THE INSTITUTIONAL FRAMEWORK

The kind of review we've just described is a microsegment of a broader picture. It's what happens at the line level, person to person, between an individual sales representative and his or her manager. It's indispensable, but it's not enough. In order for the sales process truly to become the engine of a business organization, a number of other things also have to happen. These "other things" are not add-ons. They're essential features of the "full organizational" framework within which, and through which, reinforcement takes place.

What's essential for the sales process to take hold, for reinforcement to turn it from an event into an ongoing reality? What we discover over and over again in talking with our clients is that there are three essential ingredients to success. You need (1) "top-down" driving of the process, (2) the involvement of line sales managers as "trainers," and (3) situation analysis done by team review.

Top-Down Commitment

The first factor is indispensable. "If I could pick only one thing that separates places where the process works well from places where it doesn't," says one of our most experienced sales staff, "it's upper-level commitment. The process has to be driven top down. Bottom-up just won't work."

Bob Pickens, who is manufacturing segment director for our client

BFI, agrees. BFI has been extraordinarily successful in implementing our processes, and Bob, who himself has been critical to that success, attributes it directly to top-down support. "The vocabulary of sales process, the teamwork, the analysis of accounts—all of this is pervasive throughout our company," he says. "It has commitment from the top executive offices down."

That commitment, tellingly, shows not just in "sales" but in all the attendant functions that make sales work. "You can't adopt a process like this piecemeal," Bob says. "Top-down has also got to mean across the board. So, for example, before we allow an ad agency to draft a campaign for us, we require their people to attend a Strategic Selling program. We want to be sure that they understand the concept of Buying Influences, and that they provide us with ads that target those specific individuals."

That is a great example of how "full organizational commitment" can help to integrate sales with ostensibly "non-sales" functions. As Bob indicates, such integration can happen only if its value is perceived, and supported, at senior levels.

Managers as Trainers

The second factor in successfully implementing a sales process is that line sales managers are directly involved in the start-up. We consider this so crucial, in fact, that we can see no reason to deliver our programs to companies unless at least one line manager attends along with his or her people, because we know that turning the two-day event into a process will require those people to understand how the process works. In addition, we provide special training for managers to become "client associates"—authorized to introduce their people directly to our processes. Both practices illustrate our belief that you cannot get the process moving without line managers.

After all, as one of our associates puts it, "Line managers have been through it all before. They can bring their own stories, their own background, to illustrate program principles in a way that makes them relevant to their own people's lives. The participants listen more carefully when that happens, because there's a credibility factor and a personal connection."

One company that does this exceptionally well is Harris Corporation. There Larry Smith, vice president for international sales in the communications sector, has been critical to the implementation process. Larry doesn't minimize the difficulties that can be involved.

"When you're trying to change the way your company sells," Larry explains, "you're working against years of salespeoples' established routines. Those routines may have worked great for a long time, so there's bound to be resistance. When we put in the Miller Heiman process, we wanted to signal people that this wasn't just another rookie program. It was something that everybody could benefit from—even the people who were generating $20 million a year in revenue. So we involved everybody, including those top guns, in the start-up.

"In fact, the first people we put through the processes were the sales leaders from each of our seven divisions. That told them—and it told everybody else—that this was important. The involvement of senior management meant that the necessary resources would be made available. And we made sure that the trainers at the roll-out understood sales as well as information systems. I attended the initial programs myself, and so did our vice president of marketing.

"We didn't let it sit where it was, either," Larry went on. "When we did the first spot-checks to see who was implementing the new process and who wasn't, we discovered about a 50 percent success rate. So we took the next necessary step, rewarding those who were using the process effectively, giving them latitude to make adjustments based on their own agendas, discussing problems with those who might have needed a little more enthusiasm. We continue to do this regularly, about every six months. If you don't do this with a new process, you're just throwing away your money. If you want it to stick, it's got to be constantly retooled."

And those who do the retooling, as Larry's comments show, are not "outside experts" but Harris's own sales professionals. That's simple logic. Who is better positioned to understand the company's selling concerns? Or, in Larry's memorable phrasing, to move things from "This is interesting" to "This is important"?

Team Analysis

The third factor is teamwork. Selling today is not the "sales department." The sales force does not, and cannot, sell alone. To sell effectively, you have to draw upon other company resources, and this means that selling necessarily involves people from all levels and all functional arms of the organization.

Take, for example, another one of our clients, the photographic pioneer Eastman Kodak. Kodak is highly diversified. Best known for its ubiquitous yellow-packaged film, it also sells a wide range of other "imaging" products, including X-ray film, microfilm, digital imaging products, printing plates and films, printers, imaging services, software, and of course cameras. With this kind of diversity, explains Kodak's Vice President for Strategic Global Accounts, John H. Erbland, it can be difficult to keep the total

Kodak value in mind, and management processes that encourage a team approach can therefore be a critical factor in continuing success.

"Globally," says John, "we've got seven distinct business units, each one with its own sales channels, product lines, and end users. On the organization chart, these are all nicely pigeonholed, but the reality of the marketplace isn't that clean-cut. You find product overlap; you find conflict between your different sales channels; you find cases where one business unit is well positioned with a major account, but you have trouble leveraging against it to develop business for another unit. All of this can create confusion, not just internally but among our major customers, who buy from several of our units at the same time. Disney, for example, is an important account for all seven.

"That's why, about three years ago, we started investigating management processes that would bring us more predictable penetration, more consistency. We've been developing cross-selling, seeking better positioning at higher levels by bringing management into the selling process—in general getting our units to cooperate with each other.

"It's no easy task," John admits, "when you have literally dozens of different sales forces, and when there's an ongoing debate between the new 'teamwork' mentality and the old 'turf' mentality. But our results have been very encouraging. In the accounts we've targeted for the more coordinated approach, growth has been probably 4 or 5 percent higher than the overall growth of the company. And because these are our major accounts, that really matters: it's a 5 percent rise in a major portion of our business."

TEAM REVIEW TIMING: RESPONDING TO NEED

We're often asked how often a selling team should perform an account-focused team analysis. When we raised the same question about individual Situation Analyses in Chapter 8, we gave a short answer—"As often as necessary"—suggesting that it was the level of urgency or uncertainty that dictated the need for analysis, not any periodic or otherwise prearranged timetable. That's true for team analyses as well. In our Managers' Coaching programs, we recommend that team analyses be performed whenever—and however frequently—an account objective is in transition or becomes more than usually complex, confused, changed, or competitive. That's a mouthful of fairly abstract benchmarks to contend with, and so we clarify the injunction by providing a list of more specific questions designed to test the account's suitability for team review. Here they are:

- *Does the individual Situation Analysis suggest that the responsible salesperson is confused by its complexity? Are there numerous Red Flags? Do you as a manager perceive contradictions or fuzziness in the recorded data? In short, is the account crying out for a second, collective look?*

- *Does the analysis suggest that the salesperson is having difficulty identifying or getting to the Economic Buyer? If the account owner has not identified an Economic Buyer, or believes that there is more than one for a given sales objective, the situation is also crying out for further analysis.*

- *Does the situation have a high dollar potential? Is there major revenue to be gained from this account, either through the current sales objective or down the line, from business that an improved account position might eventually generate? Does the situation represent an important new customer, an untapped market, or both?*

- *Is your company facing competition for the business? The tougher the competition–whether "internal" or external–the more likely it is that the salesperson could profit from a group review.*

If you can answer yes to even a couple of these questions, you may have identified a good candidate for team analysis. But in making your final selection or selections, you need to go a little further. This first set of questions focuses on the account itself. A capable manager also examines the people involved to ensure that the mix is right for a team analysis. When team analyses are done properly, with the requisite level of group attentiveness and reinforcement, the potential value is tremendous and multidimensional. Not only does the salesperson in charge of the account profit from positive feedback, but others in the group–who may have had, or in the future will have, similar problems–are given the opportunity to learn from his or her situation. But this collective, synergistic effect won't fall into your lap. You have to design it.

Thus we recommend that, in selecting Situation Analyses for group review, managers also ask these further questions:

- *Is the situation under analysis either exemplary enough to serve as a model for other situations, or unusual enough to generate novel perspectives? In other words, does the opportunity for learning something practical and important from this account merit devoting the team's time to studying it in detail?*

- *Is the situation one in which the account team can make a real contribution to the solution? The contribution could take the form of insights, resources, or both. However, a chance to elicit the team members' "moral support" is not sufficient reason to select an account.*
- *Can the person in charge of the account–the "owner" of the individual Situation Analysis–profit from the input of the group? Some salespeople react extremely well to a group critique. Others, though, become instantly and fiercely defensive–and a defensive salesperson is a poor candidate for team review.*

So the bottom line returns to need. This means that you may perform a whole series of Situation Analyses–and team reviews–between the prospecting and closing stages for a given sales objective.

But this doesn't hold for the broader element of territory analysis. To track your actions and develop strategies for a broad range of accounts, you need to look at those accounts on a regular basis. Individual review must be responsive to individual need. Territory review must be a periodic process. We explain that process in some detail in Chapter 13.

13

REVIEW:
"THE FUNNEL MASTER SPEAKS"

"When it's regularly reviewed, the Sales Funnel has as much power as a Situation Analysis. Of course, to make it work you've got to change the data whenever anything changes in an account, and Funnel review is a way of making sure you do that. It keeps you honest. It's not just a made-up report to make your manager feel good. If you update it daily, whenever your manager wants a progress check, it's like Prego sauce: it's already in there."
–Robert L. Miller
Sales Consultant
Miller Heiman

"Sometimes it's not so much what your managers say as the mere fact that they're keeping on top of things, that they're giving you regular feedback, not just spot-checking. A lot of the value is simple communication."
–Sam Manfer
Sales Consultant
Miller Heiman

IN CHAPTER 10 WE INTRODUCED A TOOL
called the Sales Funnel for managing time and territory, and we explained
how it helps us and our clients allocate their selling time effectively, track
account activity, and forecast results. In this chapter we revisit that concept
from a sales manager's perspective, showing how periodic review of your
people's individual Sales Funnels can not only provide them with useful
feedback but bring order and predictability into revenue forecasting.

The key word here is *regular*. We've recommended that you review
the status of your people's accounts through a full Situation Analysis only
when circumstances indicate that it's called for: when they're having trouble with a Buying Influence, for example, or when the dollar value is high.
That's a good rule of thumb for working with individual sales objectives,
because analyzing all your selling objectives on a regular basis, whatever
their circumstances, just isn't practical. If your salespeople did that, they'd
have no time left for selling. If you as a manager tried to do it, you'd have
no time left for managing.

When you're considering territories, however—when you're trying
to get a fix on your salespeople's total selling pictures—the rule of thumb
has to change. Even the smallest territory contains too many separate
pieces, too many sites of possible miscalculation, for you to reserve such
overviews for the moments when you see trouble coming. If you wait for
trouble to tell you that it's time for a big-picture overview, it's probably already too late to rescue the situation. Indeed, a principal benefit of doing
periodic overviews is that they alert the sales team to potential trouble before it gets out of hand.

SCHEDULING REVIEWS: HOW OFTEN?

How often should you perform Sales Funnel reviews? It depends on two related elements: the *quantity* of business and the *rate of change* in your individual field people's account activity.

If, like most of our clients, your people have dozens of sales objectives at any one time, it generally makes sense to schedule Sales Funnel review sessions more frequently than if they were working on a smaller
number of objectives. Similarly, if you're in a business where the typical
sales cycle moves quickly and involves numerous rapid changes, then it

makes sense to review activity more often than if the cycle were slower and more predictable.

At Miller Heiman, we require Funnel reviews every sixty days, because experience has indicated that enough things have usually changed in that period to warrant some management involvement in the reassessment of strategies. That's really the determining factor in deciding how frequently to do Funnel reviews: Have enough changes occurred in this person's accounts to require rethinking our position with his or her customers—and drafting new actions to make sure that our position remains secure? If your typical sales cycle is two years, you may not need a sixty-day review; maybe a quarterly; or a 120-day, review would be enough. On the other hand, if your typical sale is riddled with minute complications, the possibility of change will be greater, and you may want to call for reviews on a tighter time schedule.

In Chapter 10 we mentioned VLSI Technology as a client company that has adapted the Sales Funnel very effectively to its own selling cycle. One element of that adaptation has been to considerably tighten the schedule of Funnel review. VLSI Technology's typical sales objective, or Design Win, is so complicated that one salesperson can manage only three or four pending opportunities at a time. In that kind of situation, as former Vice President of Sales Charlie Parr pointed out to us, even though the sales cycle is extremely long, it makes sense to require frequent reviews.

"It takes an incredible amount of time and bandwidth to do this right," says Charlie, "and our strategy is to focus intensely on a few good probabilities rather than spread ourselves thin on a thousand unlikely possibilities. But you've really got to keep on top of those few. So we require Funnel updates every two weeks. Maybe nothing much has happened in that time, but you won't know for sure unless you look."

The bottom line is that big-picture reviews must be keyed to the likelihood of change. Whenever there are significant changes in the Funnel—for example, when a lot of business is moving down from In the Funnel to Best Few; or all the tasks that the salesperson was supposed to have completed since your last review have been completed—then it may be time to take another look at account activity. You have to anticipate this, of course, and also adapt the scheduling to individual cases: extra Funnel reviews may be required if a given representative is new or is having special difficulties. But even when there aren't any snags (this happens only in Utopia), regular review is essential. The key idea isn't necessarily the time between reviews, but the fact that they are done on a consistent basis—and that everybody in the field expects them to be done on schedule.

"THE FUNNEL MASTER SPEAKS": A ONE-ACT REPLAY

What actually happens in a typical Funnel review? By way of response, and in lieu of the Sales Funnel checklist that you didn't get in Chapter 10, we present here an insider's look at a typical Miller Heiman review—one of the sessions that we require of our field force every sixty days. The conversation that follows is not a verbatim record. It's a composite of Funnel reviews that we've conducted with dozens of our salespeople over the years. We'll preserve their confidentiality by not giving their names, and by referring to all of them collectively with the pseudonym "Sal."

The person at corporate who conducts the reviews we refer to, somewhat whimsically, as the Funnel Master. Often this role is taken by our key account supervisor, Tom Martin. Whenever possible, however—and always when there's truly critical business at stake—a second Funnel Master role is played by Diane Sanchez, as CEO of the company and "salesperson in chief"; in fact, Diane makes it a point to be personally involved in at least every other Funnel Review for each salesperson. That's a significant investment of her time, but as at any sales-driven company, it's worth it. In the following replay, therefore, the three speakers are Tom, Diane, and Sal.

You need to know that, before the review begins, Sal has already mailed or faxed a Sales Funnel form to our Reno headquarters. We ask that this be done one or two weeks before the scheduled review, so that Tom and Diane will have time to look it over carefully; to compare it with Sal's previous Funnels (kept on file in our headquarters and also available on E-mail); and to prepare their observations, suggestions, and questions to prompt discussion.

Let's assume that Sal has supplied the Funnel Masters with the Funnel report that is reproduced on the following page. (Actual Funnel reports, for our company, are often longer, covering an average of twenty or thirty sales opportunities). It provides a succinct overview of each developing sales opportunity by identifying the prospect or customer, the process or processes which we believe will best meet that customer's needs, the estimated date by which Sal expects us to deliver the process ("run the program"), and relevant comments on the status of the sale. You'll note that Sal gives estimated dates only for sales objectives in Best Few and In the Funnel. Business that is still in Universe or Above the Funnel is generally too far away from the order to make such estimates reliable.

The review can take place in person or over the phone. However that is managed, the review aims to fulfill two major objectives: (1) to classify everyone's understanding of the *potential* in this salesperson's territory,

SAL'S FUNNEL

	Prospect /Client	Process	Est. Date	Comments/Actions
Best Few				
	Alpha	SS	2/98	Order in. Booked for 3/98
	Beta	LAMP	3/98	Widmer block. Client support info sent?
	Gamma	CS (x2)	2/98	Pending Taylor's sign-off
	Delta	SS	4/98 (?)	Met G. Wills. Need Barnes input
Universe				
	Theta			PC World cover story
	Kappa	SS		Sigma merger. Tim Myers potential new VP
	Lambda			LeMotta: UB/TB. Who is EB?
Above				
	Omicron	SS		Met J. Locker 2/12. Budget issues.
	Sigma	SS/CS		Schedule meeting w/Mary Beck
	Iota	LAMP		Pending Kappa acquis. Where does Mulligan go?
In				
	Tau	LAMP	Summer 98	Red Flag: implementation
	Upsilon	SS	6/98	Need showcase story
	Omega	SS	9/98	Untapped divisional potential

and (2) to develop concrete *actions* that both the salesperson and the corporate office can perform to move pieces of business toward the close.

Tom begins this particular review by reinforcing Sal's latest sales success.

TOM: I see that the Alpha sale has gone to order. Congratulations. That was an incredibly complicated deal, and it's been great to see how well you've kept on top of all the pieces.

SAL: Thanks. It's good to have that finally under wraps. By the way, they'd like to run the program in the last week of March if possible. Any problems with that?

TOM: None I can see. We'll get you confirmation by the end of this week. Is there any other Best Few business that's gone to order?

SAL: Yes. The Gamma Group's two Conceptual Selling programs. They're booked, and they're supposed to be taught on February twenty-sixth and twenty-seventh.

DIANE: What do you mean by "supposed to?" Is there anything that might put that off?

SAL: Not really. Rick Taylor has to give his signature, and I'm expecting that by next Monday.

TOM: Is he the Economic Buyer?

SAL: Yes. He's waffled in the past because he's got an old connection with another consultant, but my Coach, Jane Curran, says he's now a strong supporter. I talked to him two weeks ago myself, and it's clear that the other consultant isn't giving them the productivity they want—and that we can deliver. So I don't anticipate any problems.

DIANE: Is there any way they could still not pick us?

SAL: Very doubtful, but I could get Jane to talk with him once more before Monday. Just to be sure.

TOM: Good. Let us know if she turns up any surprises. Any other new orders?

SAL: No. I'm getting close with the Beta people. There's one sticky Technical Buyer who is going to slow the process down for a bit, but the situation is manageable.

TOM: The sticky Technical Buyer—is that Widmer?

SAL: Right. Kelly Widmer. She's head of development for all their training, and she's nervous because she sees us as a threat. But there's a big Win here for her, when I get her to see it.

DIANE: What is it?

SAL: They've been looking for better follow-up, more quality assurance, in their training. Dick Chen, the new president, has made bang for the buck a priority, and for this sale he's the Economic Buyer. Since we can give them that, booking us will have Kelly come out looking like a genius. I've already spoken to Tom about this. We were going to send them a packet of testimonials stressing our client support. . . .

TOM: On the way. It was mailed last Friday. But I'll double-check.

DIANE: OK, so if she can bring that literature to the Economic Buyer, you think she'll see the Win for herself?

SAL: Right. And that's why I'm having her cover the Economic Buyer base. Kelly's support is going to be pivotal in implementation, and we want to secure it up front.

DIANE: Tom, if the testimonial packet wasn't in the Friday mailing, let's add that magazine piece with the quote about our callback process. From Moira Quinlan at Zentax?

TOM: I'm pretty sure it was included; but, again, I'll double-check. Any other last-minute hurdles on this one, Sal?

SAL: No.

DIANE: Any other actions you need from Reno?

SAL: No.

TOM: All right. Let's look at Delta. When are you going to be seeing George Wills again?

SAL: We've got a meeting scheduled for later this month. The twenty-fourth, I think . . . no, the twenty-sixth. He's the sales manager for the Buffalo branch, and it's a joint meeting with Harriet Gorowski, whom he reports to.

DIANE: Is she the Economic Buyer?

SAL: No. George can sign off on this one himself, but there's a good chance of future business with other branches in her division, and I wanted to get her involved early.

DIANE: Good idea. Do you need anything from us to make that connection more solid? And is George the right person to position you at the level? Is he your best bet for learning more about their organizational concerns?

SAL: At this point, yes. But I'll know better after the meeting with Gorowski.

TOM: Jerry Quaid knew her when they were at Creighton Industries together. You want me to have him give you a call?

SAL: Yes. It would be good to get that ball rolling early. There's a potential for very solid, across-the-board implementation if she becomes a strong supporter.

TOM: Okay. Expect a call from him. If there's nothing else in Best Few, let's move to Universe. Theta is new to me. Where did that lead come from?

SAL: They're start-up firm, small but on the move. I read a cover story in a computer magazine about their expansion plans and sent them a query.

DIANE: How small? Is there enough critical mass there for it to be a good fit for us?

SAL: I'm not sure yet. I have yet to meet a Buying Influence—that's why it's still in Universe—so I don't know if they've got the number of salespeople we'd like, or the psychographics. But they sounded very hungry, so I figured it was worth investigating.

DIANE: All right. But let's see if we can do it without your getting on a plane. Tom, would you run a database check for Sal on them? See if there's more in the press than one article, maybe get the names of some key executives. Then you can start with the phone and go from there. And Sal, have you thought about their possible interest in Conceptual Selling too?

SAL: Sure. As soon as I make an initial call, I'll check into that, and into the chances of a combined program.

DIANE: Another good option. You were supposed to have received brochures on the new combined program.

SAL: Got them last week.

TOM: All right. Next is Kappa.

SAL: I'm looking at their consumer products division, but they're in the process of considering a friendly offer from Sigma, so there's going to be a delay on this one until the new organization chart gets drawn up.

TOM: Who are your contacts so far?

SAL: I've gotten some preliminary Coaching from Tim Myers, who's a branch manager I've known for ten years. A great contact if the deal goes through, because he'd be on tap for a VP slot. But, as I say, it's still too early. If Tim doesn't survive the shake-up, I don't want to have wasted all that time.

DIANE: Is there anyone else you know who could Coach you about the Sigma offer?

SAL: Gerry Mulligan at Sigma itself. But a done deal still wouldn't tell me what's going to happen to Tim. So I think the key here right now is watchful waiting.

TOM: All right. The last one in Universe is Lambda. They're in peripherals?

SAL: Right. And that one has actually moved down. I met with Cheryl LaMotta last week. She's a systems manager, but their systems people are very much involved in the sales process, so she'd probably be playing both a User and a Technical Buyer role. I confirmed her interest in a pilot Conceptual Selling program and am in the process of trying to confirm the Economic Buyer.

TOM: Is she in a position to give you Coaching on that?

SAL: I'm not sure she's that committed yet to our getting this order. She's more of an information giver at this point.

DIANE: When do you meet with her again?

SAL: Sometime next month. I've got to get back with her to confirm a date.

DIANE: So she doesn't sound incredibly committed at this point. She wouldn't commit to a second meeting?

SAL: She'll be out of the country for the next three weeks.

TOM: Can you spend that time looking for Coaching somewhere else? Do we know anybody else at Lambda who could help us clarify what results they've been looking for?

DIANE: Mickey Paris has worked with them for years. Tom, let's arrange for him to give Sal a call. Or they can hook up at the sales meeting in a month.

TOM: I'll have Nancy set that up. Any preference for you, Sal?

SAL: Whatever's easier for him.

TOM: Okay. So I'm moving Lambda down into Above the Funnel and noting that our action is to put you in touch with Mickey no later than next month's meeting. Next in Above the Funnel is Omicron. You met with Jason Locke about their interest in Strategic Selling. How did that go?

SAL: Reasonably well. We're well positioned with upper management and Jason definitely wants to introduce process into their account planning, but they've had some cost overruns this quarter, and they're rethinking budgets.

DIANE: What cost overruns?

SAL: A huge advertising campaign that didn't pan out. It's made them a little gun-shy about the whole prospecting process.

TOM: Sounds as though they could use some work on developing an Ideal Customer profile.

DIANE: Exactly where we might bring them the most value. Can you use that to position us, Sal?

SAL: You mean our potential as a cost saver?

DIANE: Yes. What we're offering them isn't another budget outlay, it's a way to reduce the funds they might otherwise throw away on unprofitable business.

SAL: I'll make that case to Jason.

TOM: When's your next meeting with him?

SAL: End of March. Can I get client comments about this issue before then?

TOM: I'll get Lucy to check the client database. If you get a packet of material by March 15, will that be time enough?

SAL: Yes.

TOM: All right. Next in Above the Funnel is Sigma. You say they're about to acquire Kappa. What effect is that likely to have on our direct business with them?

SAL: Same as with Kappa itself, except that I'm very well positioned at Sigma, even with the sales VP. That's Mulligan. You know him, Diane, from that conference a few years ago.

DIANE: Yes. Very straightforward, no-nonsense guy. Would it be helpful if we made a joint call on him?

SAL: I think I'm well covered with him already, but if the merger moves him up in the organization, it probably would be a good idea. Can I tell you after our next meeting?

DIANE: Sure, I'll be in Hong Kong in August, though. When do you see him next?

SAL: Before he leaves for London in June. I'll give you a confirmed date before the next Funnel review.

TOM: All right, I'll make that note. Next in Above the Funnel is Iota. They weren't even in your Universe at the last review. Where did they come from?

SAL: It's a small business, still family-owned, and they still make decisions without a lot of going back and forth. They've got a sales force of only fifty or sixty, so they're marginal in terms of our demographics, but psychographically they're perfect. I've already met their two sales VPs and the old man himself, Jimmy Iota, and they're all incredibly enthusiastic about developing their people. So it's a small gem that I think is worth pursuing.

TOM: Go for it. What's your next action?

SAL: I've arranged to meet with Mary Beck, their head of accounting–she'd be a key Technical Buyer.

DIANE: And when do you expect to do that, Sal?

SAL: The third of next month.

TOM: Okay. Anything else in Above the Funnel?

SAL: That's it.

TOM: Okay, for In the Funnel, we begin with Tau. You've noted that one Red Flag is their concern about implementation. What's that about?

SAL: I'm talking with Rollin Kulthau about that. He's 99 percent sure, he says, but he's very concerned that they could make a major budget commitment and then find that their people end up not utilizing the process. They've been burned in the past with training that didn't take, and he's wary about having that happen again.

DIANE: What's his responsibility?

SAL: His title is director of sales, and he holds an awful lot of budgetary power.

DIANE: Is he the Economic Buyer?

SAL: Yes.

DIANE: In that case, his wariness looks like a real advantage for us. Does he know how committed we are as a company to implementation? I mean, that's certainly one of our unique strengths— the fact that we don't "train" people; we help them implement a process.

SAL: I've made that point, but I'm not sure it's sunk in—or that he believes it. He reports to the sales VP, Catherine Cantwell, and her commitment seems shakier than his. Even though she doesn't officially have to sign off on it, maybe Rollin's afraid that without her support, the thing wouldn't fly.

DIANE: He's probably right, too. Have you met Cantwell?

SAL: Briefly. She's a bit distant. Doesn't get too involved in the nitty-gritty of selling.

TOM: Sounds like she's the problem, not Kulthau.

SAL: I think that's right. Maybe I need to cover that base better before we can move on. Or maybe you should cover that base, Diane. Cantwell is very bottom-line, very interested in profitability. Maybe an executive call would be in order, to stress our views on implementation, to show both of them how we can help them make the process work.

DIANE: That's a good idea, and for another reason, too. If Cantwell's not on board with this, it's not going to work anyway. She needs to understand before they book a program that her involvement is essential. In fact, she should attend the program.

SAL: I should make that point to Kulthau.

DIANE: Absolutely. And we'll both make it to her. You can call Karen to schedule a joint call. I'll need to see a Situation Analysis and a call plan before we go in, but definitely we need Cantwell in the picture from the start.

SAL: All right, good, this is making things a lot clearer.

TOM: Next is Upsilon. It's been stuck at In the Funnel for the past two reviews, and last time your proposed action was to meet with Janice Fogarty. I don't see that noted here. What happened?

SAL: Acts of God. She got caught in that midwestern flooding, and her house practically floated to New Orleans. We've rescheduled it for later this month—the twentieth. It was a blessing in disguise, actually, because she'll be bringing Chandler, the executive vice president, with her now. He's the Economic Buyer, very enthusiastic, but I know that only secondhand, since she's been covering him for me. Meeting him directly ought to move this thing into Best Few.

TOM: Good. Have we sent you everything you need for that meeting?

SAL: One thing that might help is a showcase story from one of our other financial management clients. Can we use our work with an accounting firm as leverage here?

TOM: We'll get you a packet on that.

DIANE: There are some great quotes in the database about our improving the profitability of the Fairview Group.

SAL: Am I authorized to show them?

TOM: Not a problem. We've already received the releases for our use, so they're available to us. Anything more on Upsilon?

SAL: No, I'm in good shape with the other Buying Influences. As I say, it should be in Best Few at the next Funnel review.

TOM: Good. Last is Omega.

SAL: No problems here either, except for their incredibly slow buying process. That's why I haven't moved them into Best Few. All the bases are covered well, but it's just one of those snail-like places where every signature takes two months.

TOM: Anything we can do to hurry it up?

SAL: No. I've got incredibly good Coaching there, and everybody agrees that pushing their process will just push it off the track. One thing we could do is a mailing to some of their other divisions. I've got a list of division managers I'll send you. There's a lot of potential we haven't tapped here, and this might be a good time to start opening things out.

DIANE: Do we need a customized mailer?

SAL: It wouldn't hurt to personalize it. They're very concerned about competition, in all their divisions, so we might highlight the way we're covering that point now, in the revised version of Strategic Selling.

TOM: We'll get a draft ready for you to look at, Sal, and we'll look forward to getting the list. Can you fax it today?

SAL: As soon as we hang up.

TOM: Anything new for In the Funnel, or is that it?

SAL: That's it.

TOM: Anything you need to add, Diane?

DIANE: No, that's it. Thanks for all your hard work, Sal. Is there anything else we need to send you before we talk again?

SAL: No, I'm all set. I'll fax the list right away, and talk to you both again in a couple of months.

FIVE PROBLEM FUNNELS

Sal's Funnel, while not without its minor problems, displays one characteristic that the Funnel Masters at Miller Heiman always try to encourage: balance. Since the Funnel is a dynamic instrument, you can't expect—nor should you want—perfect equity among its four basic stages. But, other things being equal, Funnels that show a reasonable balance of activity among the four stages are going to be easier to manage than those that do not. The ideal is to keep working the four parts of the Funnel with such regularity that the "flow" from first contact to order is naturally maintained. When you don't do that, you encounter "problem Funnels" like the following.

Champagne Funnel

Champagne Funnels are a result of insufficient qualifying. The salesperson reacts indiscriminately to each and every prospect, and fails to sort the good ones down into Above the Funnel. This is a common syndrome among new or inexperienced salespeople, but it also occurs when salespeople fail to resequence, find themselves at a loss for incoming leads, and then overcompensate by taking anything they can find, no matter how unlikely, as a "lead."

CHAMPAGNE FUNNEL

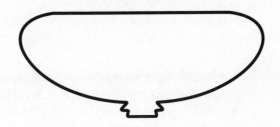

The first piece of Coaching we would give such a person is to qualify early and often by attending more closely to the Ideal Customer profile, utilizing it as a tool for discriminating and winnowing. Next, we'd urge the person to select one or two of the best-qualified leads each week and devote some time to moving each one into Above the Funnel—that is, to contacting at least one Buying Influence and speaking to him or her about Growth or Trouble.

Clogged Funnel

Whereas the champagne Funnel is too "swollen" at the top, the clogged Funnel is too swollen in the middle. This configuration arises when the salesperson has moved numerous sales objectives into positions Above the Funnel and In the Funnel, but is uncertain about the closing activities required to move them down into Best Few. Perhaps such salespeople haven't fully understood the customer's decision-making process, or perhaps one or more resistant Buying Influences are impeding progress. For whatever reason, we call a Funnel clogged, or backed up, when there seems to be an invisible border between In the Funnel and Best Few.

The real problem with a clogged Funnel is that the activities re-

CLOGGED FUNNEL

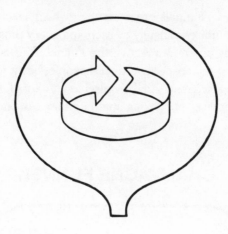

quired to cross that border are the most time-consuming ones in the sales cycle, and when you're focused intently, if unsuccessfully, on attending to them, it leaves you very little time to do anything else. That's why, when we're faced with a clogged Funnel, we Coach the salesperson to get assistance from the rest of the selling team. We ask him or her—as we've asked Sal in this example—what corporate can do to help break the logjam. Often, if salespeople in this situation don't hand some of the selling and support work off to others, they end up following the path shown in the diagram—an endless circle of frustration and diminishing returns.

Ping-Pong Funnel

This third scenario is a variation on the second one—at least, the outcome is roughly the same in both. When salespeople lack a clear understanding of their individual sales objectives, when they jump from one thing to another with little or no design, we say that they are presenting a Ping-Pong Funnel. The Ping-Pong Funnel looks more "active" than the clogged Funnel, but its activity isn't moving the sales process forward.

When we encounter a Ping-Pong Funnel, we Coach the salesperson to focus on one thing at a time or, to use the terminology we stress in our Strategic Selling process, to distinguish clearly between different *Single Sales Objectives*. A Single Sales Objective describes how much of a given product or service you expect to sell a specific customer by a specific date. By definition it's precise, concrete—and very focused. By doing Situation Analyses on their Single Sales Objectives, salespeople frequently discover that they have been confusing two or more separate sales, and that their

PING-PONG FUNNEL

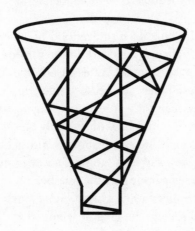

jumping around is an index of that confusion. They also discover, as our client-support staffer Holly Jenkins indicated in Chapter 9, that breaking things down into more readily manageable "chunks" can bring them double the business in half the time.

Whistle Funnel

This situation is the opposite of the Ping-Pong Funnel. In the whistle scenario, salespeople are so narrowly focused that they are unable to work on more than one objective at a time. We call it the whistle Funnel

WHISTLE FUNNEL

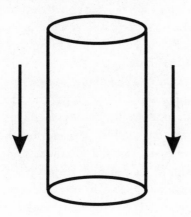

because that's these salespeople's ostensible ideal–to have each sale "whistle" through the Funnel from lead to order, before they can turn their attention to another lead.

In a sense this might be understood as *every* salesperson's ideal: what could be better than a rapid-fire journey from start to finish? The trouble, though, is that the Funnel in this case is underfilled. Usually, when we encounter whistle Funnels, it's because salespeople have qualified only those leads that they feel are a sure thing. Maybe the majority of those leads do close quickly. But in concentrating only on the easy, quick-to-close business, these salespeople are sacrificing a world of opportunities that demand more work. Eventually that "no risk" strategy makes the Funnel dry up–as real opportunities whistle *past* the salesperson to the competition.

Often, salespeople with a whistle Funnel are merely following the logic of conventional selling: the goal of selling, they think, is to close this order, now. That's why, in Coaching such a person, we reiterate a basic belief: We're in this business to achieve long-term returns from reliable accounts. We're aware that following this philosophy takes more time and deliberation than going, over and over, for the quick-buck close. But it's something we value, and we hope that you do too.

Teardrop Funnel

Finally, another example of a "swollen" Funnel–this one with a majority of objectives stuck at the Best Few stage. Like the whistle Funnel,

TEARDROP FUNNEL

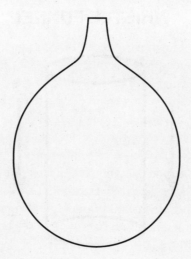

this looks like an attractive situation, but it actually displays a couple of dangerous possibilities.

First, the person with so much closing work to do can easily fall into a kind of mini Ping-Pong effect, jumping from one potential killer commission to the other, without giving any of them the serious, concentrated work they deserve. Second, when you're focusing all your energies on closing matters, you're bound to neglect the other parts of the Funnel—especially the part that is furthest from the close, that is, qualifying.

Our Coaching here is to reiterate the maxim that we gave in Chapter 10: Whenever you close or do some closing work, go to the top of the Funnel and prospect or qualify. Not only is this necessary to prevent the boom-and-bust cycle, but it is also the most effective time for you to qualify. You're more likely to qualify effectively when you're on a high, and nothing makes a salesperson higher than bringing an order to close.

The Coaching for these five Funnels varies considerably, but the underlying message—the underlying goal—is the same. To achieve consistent success in Sales Funnel management, you have to give regular attention to all four kinds of selling work. To do that, you must allocate your time in a balanced fashion.

BENEFITS OF FUNNEL REVIEW

What are the benefits of periodic, required Funnel review? There are many, but we'd emphasize particularly the value of five, the first two fairly obvious and the next three more subtle: (1) clarification, (2) communication, (3) perspective, (4) forecasting, and (5) teamwork.

Clarification

This is also known as verification, checking, or feedback. It is the most obviously helpful aspect of regular review, for managers and sales representatives alike. Having a process in place that enables managers to ask clarifying questions of the field person decreases the likelihood that important information will be missed, or that the salesperson will substitute wishful thinking for clearheaded analysis of an account's true position. Using a review session for clarification also reinforces the value of team selling: here, for instance, it turned Sal, Tom, and Diane into a mini-team devoted to realistic strategizing and realistic tracking of a sales objective's progress. As one of our field people is fond of putting it, "Funnel review dispels the fog of your own best intentions. It helps you to see how near you *really* are to the close." Or, in Bob Miller's pointed phrase, it "keeps you honest."

Communication

This is a "softer" benefit, but it's no less valuable. Sam Manfer alludes to it when he says that the Funnel Master's just being there, showing an active interest, brings a value to the process that transcends the data discussed. A Funnel review is an opportunity not just for managers to oversee and guide, but for people out on the line to air their grievances, to tell war stories, to establish the personal rapport with the people who are tracking their progress that is indispensable for companies where the development of people really matters. Of course, as we stressed in Chapter 12, this can happen only when managers are strongly committed to *positive* reinforcement.

Perspective

We mean the kind of perspective that comes only when someone takes the broadest possible view of a sales force's accounts. One of the things that we discover again and again in doing Funnel reviews is the hitherto hidden interactions between accounts, as well as between individual pieces of business in the same large account–the overlapping players and interlocking themes uniting sales objectives that, to the person focusing exclusively on closing one of them, might seem invisible. In this case, you can see how Sal might utilize the expertise of Mickey Paris and the Miller Heiman experience with Fairview to position himself more effectively in "unrelated" opportunities. Sometimes salespeople see these connections themselves, but not always, and good managerial review helps to bring them to the surface.

Forecasting

To a manager, this is perhaps the most satisfying benefit of all. By doing regular Funnel reviews, and by comparing individual reviews with each other, managers can attain a level of precision in revenue forecasting that would be unthinkable if they relied on conventional methods, such as the "add 12 percent" method we described in Chapter 10. To anyone concerned with organizational growth and survival, having the constantly refined database of regular Funnel review allows for better planning both of sales and of the resource allocation that, increasingly, is required to support the sales effort.

Teamwork

Finally, and perhaps most importantly, regular Funnel review helps the sales representative maintain active, productive contact with other members of the organizational selling team, ensuring that he or she receives promptly and effectively any support that is needed to move the sales process forward. You'll notice how many times in this brief conversation Diane and Tom ask for confirmation that Sal's work is being adequately supported by the "home office." That's not just courtesy. It's pragmatics. Since we believe so strongly in the value of team selling, we insist that asking "What can we do?" on a regular basis is an indispensable element of the sales process.

This is also a way of reinforcing our conviction that Funnel reviews, like all managers' Coaching, must be both positive and action-oriented. The "positive" aspect of this description goes without saying, and it explains why Funnel reviews at companies like ours are 180 degrees away from the conventional territory review, in which salespeople are called on the carpet and denounced for their shortcomings. Because we believe that most people want to do a good job, we know that, if our salespeople–or others on our staff–commit to some action and fail to perform it, there must be a good reason why. Funnel reviews help us to identify those reasons and work together toward overcoming them in the future.

As for the actions themselves–these are really the pragmatic point of the exercise. After each Funnel review, Tom prepares a detailed checklist of each action, individual or corporate, that has been agreed to during the review. We use this list as a benchmark at the next review, to determine the progress of events, to reassess the salesperson's positions with regard to his or her various sales objectives, and to suggest whatever reallocation of time might be needed to maintain Funnel "balance." If the positions haven't improved as anticipated, we know we need to find out why, and to reframe our actions so that, by the next review, they do improve. When it's utilized in this positive and action-oriented way, Funnel review is as powerful a management tool as Situation Analysis itself. Used properly, it serves as the self-correcting driver of the entire sales process.

14

REWARD: "GOOD-BYE, KEMO SABE"?

"Even the most sacrosanct aspect of a life in sales–commission-based pay–is under siege. Many companies have not determined how their sales reps should be compensated, but they are beginning to realize that commission-based pay contradicts the partnership concept companies are working so hard to foster."
–Catherine Romano
"Death of a Salesman"

"Corporate is very responsive to information from the field, and it's also committed to standing behind a sales process that looks beyond the numbers to customer relationships. But at the end of the day, the figures still have to be there."
–Brad Teed
System Engineer
Documentum

THROUGHOUT THIS BOOK WE HAVE ACKNOWLedged the value of teamwork, and we have praised two types of teamwork in particular. On the one hand, we have stressed how important it has become for selling organizations to adopt a team approach in engaging with and satisfying their customers' needs: we fully endorse the current trend toward "full organizational commitment" to revenue generation. On the other hand, we have shown how much can be gained, for buyer and seller alike, by the move toward alliances, or partnerships, which function in a very real sense like intercompany teams. On both counts the Miller Heiman philosophy is clear: the best, and most consistent, results are achieved by organizations where the spoken or unspoken watchword is, "Work together."

In keeping with the team approach, many firms today are experimenting with compensation schemes that are as revolutionary as anything we've mentioned so far, and that seek to make teamwork a functioning fiscal reality by subverting the sacred cow of sales commissions. "The No. 1 trend in sales compensation," the compensation specialist Craig Ulrich told *Business Week*'s Christopher Power a few years ago, "is building customer satisfaction into pay plans." This trend has not been nearly as widely endorsed, or as unambiguously applauded, as the trend toward senior management's involvement in selling and training, but the signs are there, and you can't deny that this radical retooling of the reward system is a growing, if nettlesome, feature of the sales revolution.

In this chapter, we look at the way in which a growing cadre of businesses, including several of our clients, are approaching this controversial element of sales reengineering.

THE TREND OBSERVED: TWO STRANDS OF CHANGE

It's important to observe at the outset how closely the movement away from commission-based pay reflects both types of teamwork we have just described—and also how intimately those two types of teamwork are now related. If you search the business literature today for stories of the "anticommission" trend, you will find two entwined strands of change being mentioned over and over:

> 1. *More and more, sales professionals are being rewarded for achievements that precede, and also go beyond, getting the order. Industry surveys rou-*

*tinely report moving sales compensation away from 100 percent com-
missions and toward guaranteed salaries, away from pay based on orders to pay based on overall profitability and the building of customer
relationships.*

2. *Just as increasingly, non-sales people are being rewarded for the contributions that they make to the overall sales effort–and to the customer
satisfaction that it enhances.*

Taken together, these two developments may herald the rise of exactly the
"customer-oriented selling culture" that we described in the early chapters
of this book, and that increasingly is closing the divide between sales and
non-sales functions.

The first strand here sounds pretty radical. Guaranteed salaries?
Compensation based on building satisfaction? For anyone who came up in
the sales game believing in the Lone Ranger ideal, such notions may seem
both fuzzy-headed and subversive. Yet, if you've been following the argument of this book–particularly our insistence that it is developing relationships, not nailing down orders, that makes for success in sales–then you
will appreciate that these ideas illustrate the logic of the future.

What about the second strand? What about the equally radical notion that people in marketing or customer service or delivery might get rewards based on the success of the total selling effort?

According to the Hewitt Associates 1996 report "Hot Topics in
Sales Compensation," the radical nature of this idea hasn't prevented it
from being adopted by a large and growing number of American companies. The Hewitt research group interviewed over 200 sales organizations,
including 19,000 nonsupervisory sales personnel and nearly 3,000 sales
managers. Forty-six percent of the companies surveyed used some sort of
team selling, with most teams concentrating on some combination of traditional selling, sales and marketing, and customer service. In nearly half of
these companies, "team-based incentive pay" was a working reality.

What was that pay based on? In terms of the mix of sales and non-
sales–and of the potential conflict between the two–this was the most interesting finding of the Hewitt study. The companies that used team-based
incentive pay relied on a variety of performance measures to determine
compensation, including account profitability, customer service measures
like on-time delivery, and customers' satisfaction as determined by surveys.
But by far the most popular measure was account sales volume.

For teams that were industry-focused, 78 percent used this
measure. It was also used by 85 percent of geography-based teams, and by

a whopping 94 percent of customer-based teams. That means that, among companies that use team-based compensation, the overwhelming majority reward their non-sales team members for the volume from orders that the sales force is out there closing. You could hardly find a more dramatic example of the belief that revenue generation is a multifunction responsibility.

IN THE REAL WORLD: SOME SUCCESS STORIES

Research reports and statistics are all well and good, but how is the compensation part of the revolution working out in the real world? We'll acknowledge up front that it hasn't all been roses, and that many firms—indeed, a majority—still resist this idea as too drastic a break with tradition. But there are also lots of success stories about this new, post–Lone Ranger trend in compensation.

McFarland. Let's begin with our client McFarland Office Products and Business Interiors, whose vice president for sales and business development, Dave Laabs, spoke eloquently about the customer's Concept in Chapter 2. McFarland made the shift to team-based compensation a few years ago, and in Dave's view, the experiment has been a rousing success.

"Traditionally," he told us recently, "our sales force made a draw plus commission, or just straight commission, while support staff made a salary plus bonuses. We found that, with this system, our non-salespeople were experiencing a lot of resentment. We had told them that they were a necessary part of the overall customer effort, but then, when that effort went well, only the reps were rewarded. People were starting to ask a legitimate question: Why should salespeople make more money than we do when they're doing just one part of the work?

"So we had to shift our thinking. We had to recognize that, like everybody else today, we were in the customer service business—the products we sold were simply a means to that end, and everybody who helped to meet that end ought to be rewarded. If we were serious that we wanted to delight the customer, then everyone who contributed to that delight should get part of the benefits. If we said that we valued the input of all team members, then we should get serious about it, and reward the team, not just the guy who wrote the order.

"That's where we've moved now. We have teams within the company, like small business units, that include one or two sales reps each, plus members from non-sales areas—everything from clerical to marketing and design. The teams have team goals, and compensation is keyed to people's contribution to meeting them."

Does it work? Are there positive benefits to this team-based scheme? Dave says that the benefits have been quickly apparent.

"For one thing, the resentment is gone, and that's great for morale. But there's also a kind of synergy—an unexpected plus. Since people have been working in teams, they understand better that their personal self-interest is linked to the achievement of collective goals. So they've come to appreciate the advantages of working together. You see people filling in when others are absent, or learning to compromise and trade off in doing joint assignments. There's less compartmentalization, more fluidity. It's like each team has its own purpose and direction, and its members see the wisdom of keeping it moving on track. They get more done, and more quickly, than they ever did before."

Powersoft. Bruce Thomann is a technical advisor at this client company. As is the case in many software firms, technicians pretty much have to get involved in customer contact, to explain sophisticated programs prior to a sale, to troubleshoot once a system is in place, and to consult with clients on issues of service and upgrading. As Bruce sees things—and as Powersoft encourages its technical advisors to see things—this makes him much more than a backup or assistant to the sales force. "We're all in the same game," he says, "and what we do is really an extension of the sales force's work. We naturally work in teams, and we have required team meetings every Monday morning."

As for compensation, Bruce and his fellow technical advisors draw a salary, but they also receive incentive bonuses based on sales. As a result, they think of themselves consciously as sales-oriented, and when their customer contacts relay problems to which Powersoft might provide a solution, they're eager to pass on those leads to the "actual" salespeople. In fact, as Bruce acknowledges, "most of our consulting precedes the sale, so we're in on the selling part from the first point of contact. My personal interests are quite technical, so I'm probably going to go next into production. But for most TAs, the natural next step is into sales."

IBM. A couple of years ago, the computer giant made two revolutionary changes in its traditional, commission-based payment plan. First, it switched from straight revenue to profitability as a basic measure of a salesperson's value to the company: 60 percent of sales commission is now based on that measure. Second, the company began to base the remaining 40 percent on customers' satisfaction: managers try, in Catherine Romano's words, to determine "if customers are happy and if sales reps have helped client companies achieve their business objectives." You'll recognize the similarity here to what we've been saying about long-term business relationships, and about how they are solidified by helping the customers run their own businesses better. It's still a little early to tell how well the IBM mix has panned out, and Romano acknowledges the "experts who believe that a 40 percent tie-in is too high." But the new mix is still a strong index of the direction in which many firms are beginning to move.

Saturn. Since its plant in Spring Hill, Tennessee, opened several years ago, this automobile company has become a minor legend in American business in terms of employee relations and customer satisfaction. Stressing integrity toward the customer and mutual trust among workers, the company has fostered an esprit de corps that is virtually unique in the automotive industry. This leads to such priceless benefits as strong word-of-mouth advertising and a customer-satisfaction rating that squeezes in right under those of Lexus and Infiniti.

A little-known aspect of this success story is that a revamped compensation scheme has helped to make dealer-based salespeople just as loyal to the Saturn game plan as the folks who rivet on the panels down at Spring Hill. Ron Marhofer owns a Saturn dealership in Akron, Ohio, as well as outlets selling Ford, General Motors, and Japanese models. As David Woodruff reported in a *Business Week* cover story, the company's recommendation that dealers switch from straight commissions to a mix of salary and customer-satisfaction bonuses has led to an unplanned boon for people like Marhofer. Not only has the scheme blunted the lot salespeople's traditional zeal to "make quota by any means necessary." It has helped to cut down dramatically on traditionally "nomadic" salespeople's wanderlust. As Woodruff puts it, "Marhofer says only two of fourteen salespeople have left since he opened his Saturn outlet a year and a half ago, compared with 100 percent annual turnover at his non-Saturn stores."

THIRD R OR THIRD RAIL?
PROBLEMS WITH REVAMPING THE REWARD SYSTEM

Results like these are impressive, but where do they point? Is the so-called "number one trend in sales compensation today" actually the wave of the future, or only the latest business-literature panacea for the ills of an increasingly restless and demotivated work force?

There are certainly fundamental problems–and detractors. Even the Hewitt Associates report, which stresses the growing popularity of sales incentive plans based on customer satisfaction and quality of service, admits that, as of 1996, only 17 percent of the companies surveyed were utilizing such plans. In general these firms seem to prefer introducing such thinking more gradually, by making these measures part of individual performance reviews first: 64 percent of the firms surveyed were taking this route.

Catherine Romano's report for *Management Review* isolates several factors that may account for the slow uptake. First is the sheer complexity–administrative, financial, psychological–of putting such a change into place, and the attendant difficulty of knowing just how to redesign it. "Muddling through the choices," Romano writes, companies are asking whether incentives should be tied to "product mixes, new accounts, the size of contract, individual sales, the number of clients, customer-survey results, or team goals."

Second is resistance on the part of sales personnel who feel that team-based incentive programs will threaten their superstar Lone Ranger status. "Some star performers may be resentful," Romano writes, "because they believe their compensation is being held down by others on the team." That's putting it mildly. As any sales manager knows, the heaviest hitters are often the worst team players, because they resent the loss of independence (and feared loss of income) that team play entails.

A third difficulty is resistance coming from the other direction–from salaried employees who see pay based on customers' satisfaction or quality of service as a potential threat to their financial security. Salespeople are used to having some of their pay "at risk"–that is, having some of it based on revenue results–but the same is not traditionally true for non-sales workers.

Finally, there's the old difficulty of providing an accurate assessment of "customer satisfaction." It can be judged roughly by such measures as follow-up surveys, timeliness of shipments, and account retention, but all such measures are in a sense inferential: they're educated guesses rather than hard figures.

As least one professional who is directly involved in rethinking sales compensation packages believes that the difficulty of measurement is a formidable hurdle. William Ghormley heads the Polaroid Corporation's customer fulfillment team. An advocate of straight salaries for salespeople, he says that "satisfaction" is just too watery a concept to base rewards on. As he told Catherine Romano, "It's not an American thing. There is no metric for that yet, and if you don't have clearly defined metrics, you're going to drive teams crazy instead of driving them to do better."

There's no doubt that there are serious hurdles to be overcome before team-based or satisfaction-based pay becomes a business norm. As Brad Teed's comment at the beginning of this chapter suggests, companies that are very forward-looking in their attitude to process can be more traditional when it comes to writing out paychecks. In addition, even where pay schemes are being restructured to accommodate team selling, serious hitches remain. Citing the same attitude and measurement problems as Romano, Blessington and O'Connell describe numerous instances where a company's good intentions have foundered on the shoals of "unintended consequences." Consider only a few of their recent horror stories:

The Juggler's Dilemma. A financial services company, newly committed to rewarding activities rather than just numbers, implemented an employee review plan that incorporated no fewer than fifteen performance measures. This ran the risk, Blessington and O'Connell say conservatively, of "confusing and misdirecting the employees." In trying to juggle all those measures at the same time, the employees were in danger of dropping them all. On top of that, when the company tried to winnow the list down to a manageable handful, it ran up against a classic dilemma of compensation: "Should the firm pay for financial results or the nonfinancial results that might lead to strong financial performance?" There was a world of miscalculation waiting in that "might."

How Much Is That in Units? An insurance company tried to get its salespeople to concentrate more on profitability by shifting their basic reward measure from units sold to revenue signed. They failed to take into account the mental gymnastics this required from people who had plenty of practice in converting units into dollars, but "had not been trained to think in dollars" per se. "The result was an overly complex pay plan which described how the firm made money but not how its sales staff could make money."

You Want Me to Share What? To promote a collaborative team approach to selling, a furniture company set up a "split credit" system, where individual remuneration would be based on individual contribution to the team effort. Rather than increasing teamwork, the system produced exactly the opposite result. "Most salespeople tried to close their deals alone to get all the sales credit and to avoid contentious negotiations with other salespeople."

MAKING IT WORK: SOME DRASTIC LESSONS

Stories like this make it painfully clear that implementing a more "progressive" or balanced reward system is never simply a matter of writing it down on paper. Resistance to a complex transition can throw roadblocks in the way of even the best-intentioned plans. Because this is so, companies considering reengineering their reward system would do well to attend to the lessons of those who have tried and failed. Of the many lessons that Blessington and O'Connell identify, we would point to four as most significant—as significant as they are organizationally drastic.

Lesson 1: Aim for a Win-Win Balance

As we've stressed throughout the book, effective selling today means balancing the needs of your own organization with those of your customer—in an atmosphere of mutuality that we've been calling "Win-Win." That's a benchmark for redesigning performance measures too. Managers don't always get what they want, it has often been said; they get what they reward. If that's true, then you should aim to reward your people for providing your customers value without sacrificing the profitability that their accounts help you to achieve.

Lesson 2: Take It One Step at a Time

That is, go slowly and work on implementing one revamped performance measure at a time. This lesson is consistent with what we said in Chapters 11 and 12 about pinpointing behavior and addressing one negative behavior at a time. Asking your people to change their entire tool kit overnight is inviting what we've just called the juggler's dilemma. According to Blessington and O'Connell, the best protection against the risks of hasty adoption is to "test the new performance measures without connecting them to pay for at least six months. Report the new measure, but continue to base pay on the old measure." This is an excellent way to accustom people to a new paradigm in a nonthreatening and temporarily risk-free environment.

Lesson 3: Take Teamwork Seriously

This means that if you've adopted a team-based compensation scheme, have enough faith in it to reward team members as team members, not as superstars and slugs who happen to be wearing the same uniform. In the most drastic application of this principle, you reward everybody equally. Blessington and O'Connell make a sensible defense of this option, arguing that the inevitable "freeloaders" on a high-performance team constitute "a sales management problem, not a sales compensation issue," and should be dealt with accordingly, as individuals who need either to improve or to leave the company. In one automotive company that adopted this type of "100 percent team plan," the sales force "consistently secured the highest market share and the best margins in their category."

That doesn't, of course, solve the opposite problem: how to reward the ultraindependent superstars. Because these people exist–and because you certainly don't want to discourage their performance–it's doubtful that "equal pay for all" is a practical or even a desirable compensation system. Different company members have different levels of responsibility, after all, which are routinely–and rightly–recognized in their compensation. Similarly, even in a team-based sales system, some incentives should be kept in place to keep the high achievers performing at stellar level.

Lesson 4: Detach Performance from Pay

This may sound like a step backward, but in practice it's a step forward. It reflects the experience of those especially committed companies that "put teeth in their performance reviews by adopting probation systems." That is, they make adherence to the new approach–whether it's based on teamwork, customers' satisfaction, or a combination of the two–a condition not of higher pay but of continued employment. The idea is drastic but logical. If you consider a Win-Win focus on the customer an essential ingredient in your company's success, then the appropriate response to employees who don't share that philosophy isn't to reduce their pay. It's to replace them with people who do share your thinking, people who can foster the productivity that you require.

Drastic? Absolutely. But for anyone who makes a living in sales, these are drastic times.

QUO VADIMUS? WHERE ARE WE GOING?

As we rumble toward the end of the twentieth century, and as selling becomes increasingly challenging and complex, plans that aim to reengineer the compensation process may prove to be the most difficult challenge of all. For all the reasons that we've stated–to say nothing of plain old-fashioned inertia–the payout patterns at even the most innovative companies are still largely a matter of an ancient formula: The more orders you close, the closer you'll be to that Porsche.

This is as true at our clients' companies as in the business world generally, and we're still working out what this picture may portend. When we were interviewed by Catherine Romano in 1994, we said that, in spite of the "new" compensation push, it was still the "person making the sale," in most American companies, who was receiving the lion's share of compensation. This, we said, was "where sales hasn't caught up." It hasn't changed that much in the past few years. As far as the "third R" of implementing the sales process goes, we're still working out the design bugs, still in the preplanning stage.

But in the view of several valued clients, this is bound to change–not because of any concerted effort to promote change but because the internal logic of sales process moves companies in this direction. "We still pay salespeople on individual results," says KLA Instruments' vice president of corporate sales, Mike McCarver, "and our whole compensation package is still very product-related. But it's going to change. As alliances become more important, it's not the order any more. We've got to look at the team efforts; the team results, that keep those alliances alive. And that means longer-term compensation schemes, a different mix of rewards. It's inevitable. It's where it's going."

Becton Dickinson Infusion Therapy's vice president of customer alliances, Michael Johnson, makes a related point, tying the compensation of the future to customers' satisfaction. "If you believe in Win-Win," Mike told us, "it doesn't necessarily mean putting more of your product in place. It might mean, ironically, helping your customers to reduce the utilization of your products. Because that helps both your businesses in the long run.

"And this means that we've got to realign our incentives. We've started doing that already. Our people don't get paid just for closing the business. One-third of our representatives' compensation is based on total customer satisfaction–and that's based on the customer, not us, doing the performance rating. If our goal is to convert competitive customers into Becton Dickinson customers, this isn't optional. We've got to be thinking like this, if we want those long-term partnerships."

We'll give a final word to Tony Cueva, Ceridian's manager of national accounts. Like all executives who have to consider both the short-term goals and the long-term health of their organizations, Tony is aware that reengineering a compensation scheme–like reengineering any other feature of the sales process–is constantly threatened by the "make the numbers" philosophy, which has been the watchword, and the bane, of selling since its inception. In discussing that philosophy, he raises a critical question not just about compensation but about the long-term fundamental impact of the selling revolution.

"Wouldn't it be nice," he asks rhetorically, "if you could just stop the clock and say let's not worry about the financials? But of course you can't, and even though that's obvious–even though you know you can't run a company without looking at the monthly and quarterly figures–it's also obvious that the financials can get in the way. They can stop you from focusing on the customer in the way you say you want to.

"Everybody *wants* to focus on the customer first. But with downsizing and budget cuts, sometimes that becomes almost impossible. We struggle with this all the time. We're aware–painfully aware–that the financials can take you away from Win-Win. This can drive you away from your customers and your employees, because you're focused so much on making the numbers for your stockholders. That's a central question when you're making these process changes. Who is your customer, really? Is your customer the customer, or is your real customer the stockholders?

"Executives, for the most part, are conditioned to lean toward the stockholders. That's inevitable. The company's got to survive, got to grow. But it's a serious problem if you believe in the value of people, if you believe that long-term survival means helping people grow. That's why it's a struggle. There aren't easy answers. But we believe that if you want to stay in business for the long run, you'd better be willing to go on asking the questions."

THE BOTTOM-LINE PARADOX

As you go on asking the questions, what about the bottom line? If you fiddle with the time-honored quota system, if you start introducing radical concepts like team ownership and team reward, aren't you going to lose the numbers you need? Is it really possible to compensate people for following a process without destroying the profit?

Let's be clear. We've never said that you don't need the numbers. The most progressively managed business in the world still needs to stay in the black, in order to go on delivering value to its customers. That's a central premise of this whole book. We agree with Peter Drucker that you're entitled to profit only if you give value to your customers. But whether or not you're entitled to it, profit is still the pulse that shows you're alive.

We differ from most business analysts, then, not in the honor we pay to the profit principle. We're proud of our 300 percent growth rate over the past decade, and we intend to keep it moving in the same direction. We differ in our understanding of how you get those figures–how you turn the requirement of quotas into the benefit of growth.

The conventional wisdom says that quotas are a stick–one without which your sales force will not perform. You've got to give incentives in the form of "stretch" quotas, because unless the sales force makes the numbers, quarter after quarter, your partnerships and alliances with customers are just so much cotton candy. The facts speak plain, as painful as the "progressives" might find them: if you want the numbers, then you've got to reward on the numbers.

True or not, we say this puts the cart before the horse. At Miller

Heiman, and at many of our most successful client companies, there's an irony at work that we call the *bottom-line paradox*. If you concentrate only on the numbers, maybe you'll get them—and maybe not. But it's almost certain that you won't get anything else. If you're assiduously numbers-driven, you won't get customer loyalty, employee loyalty, or the teamwork that you need to make it in today's frenzied sales world. On the other hand—and here's the paradox—if you concentrate on developing the processes that sustain long-term relationships, you'll be able to get those relationships, and the numbers besides.

The reason goes back to an issue that was posed earlier in this chapter. Should a judicious firm pay directly for financial results, or pay for nonfinancial results that might lead to financial results? To a degree, the paradox gets you around that issue, because if you ask the leaders of the companies we've been profiling here, it's very clearly the nonfinancial results—the subtle changes in culture, the attention to process—that underwrites every upturn on the balance sheets.

John H. Erbland, Eastman Kodak's vice president for strategic global accounts, put a nice spin on this point in a recent conversation. Acknowledging the difficulty of selling a "touchy-feely" concept like process to ledger-conscious management, he notes that you have to go beyond financial results to test your strategy. "Looking at leading indicators is equally important so you can more accurately predict financial outcome.

"In measuring success, we concentrate, reasonably enough, on hard figures—revenue growth and profitability. The irony is that these things are lagging indicators. In the cultural debate that's going on inside many companies, it's often tough to see that they come out of much 'softer' processes. What generates the numbers, really, is better customer relationships, better penetration of your revenue sources, better positioning at the top levels of major accounts. If you want better financials, you also need to actively measure and improve nonfinancial data."

Our clients confirm this frequently, and with hard figures. In Chapter 12, John himself mentioned Kodak's experience in this regard: a 4 to 5 percent boost in the major account growth rate after the company's introduction of sales process principles. Another client, a financial services firm, reported that its success rate on key proposals nearly doubled (from less than 30 percent to 54 percent) after it began to implement our process approach. And Marriott Corporation, after being coached by us, boosted its share of convention business so dramatically that it realized a 600 percent rise in key revenue.

These success stories indicate something that we've also proven in our own business: if you weave attention to your customers into the very fabric of your business—if you make process not just *how* you do things, but *what* you do—then the numbers that the quota hounds worry about will follow naturally.

They'll have to. When you organize your entire business around satisfying your customers, not only do you give them value, and thus satisfaction, but the word gets around, both inside and outside your organization, and you begin to attract to your business the enlightened self-interest that the best business analysts, from Adam Smith to Peter Drucker, have always told us is the force on which a free market thrives.

There's a wonderful line in *Citizen Kane* that relates to "going for the numbers." "It's not hard to make a lot of money," Kane's old colleague Mr. Bernstein tells the reporter, "if all you want to do is to make a lot of money." The reason that business is difficult, and challenging, and exciting, is that it involves a great deal more than making money. It involves, as a practical minimum, the satisfaction of needs, mutual commitment, and the development of satisfying professional relationships. To us, in fact, that is what business is about. The money that comes as a consequence is just a validating symbol. It's only one of many Results that allow us to Win.

Is it either better relationships or better numbers? Fortunately, no. By implementing a solid sales process, you *can* have it both ways.

G L O S S A R Y

Above the Funnel Second (from the top) level of the Sales Funnel; potential orders move to this level when you have at least one piece of information suggesting a match between a customer's needs and your solution (*see also* Funnel).

Action Commitment *See* Best Action Commitment, Commitment, *and* Minimum Acceptable Action.

Basic Issues Underlying, unspoken difficulties a buyer may have with you, your company, or your proposal.

Best Action Commitment Highest level of commitment you can reasonably expect a Buying Influence to make as a result of a sales call; this should be specific, measurable, and given a timeline.

Best Few Bottom of the Sales Funnel, and its narrowest part; this is the pre-close level (*see also* Funnel).

Bottom-line paradox Concept that if you concentrate on the numbers, you'll get (at best) only numbers; but if you concentrate on long-term relationships, you'll get not only those relationships but the numbers as well.

Business Results *See* Results.

Buyer Response Modes Types of receptivity that a Buying Influence can exhibit at any given time: (1) Growth, (2) Trouble, (3) Even Keel, (4) Overconfident (*see* Buying Influence, Discrepancy, *and specific modes*).

Buyer's Remorse Buyers' uncomfortable feeling of having been had; likely outcome of pushing a sale through over a customer's valid objections.

Buyer's Revenge Potential outcome when a salesperson leaves a Buying Influence feeling that he or she has lost: the Buyer undermines your chances for future business.

Buying Influence; Buyer Key person who influences a buying decision in one of three ways: funding (*see* Economic Buyer), performance assessment (*see* User Buyer), or screening (*see* Technical Buyer). A fourth kind of Buying Influence provides Coaching (*see* Coach). Buying Influences are identified by the roles they play—the functions they perform—for a given sales objective.

Buy-Sell Hierarchy Five-level concept of how the customer perceives the seller; consisting (from bottom up) of (1) commodity selling, (2) selling quality, (3) differentiating through service, (4) growing the customer's business, and (5) addressing the customer's organizational issues.

Champagne Funnel Problem Sales Funnel that results from insufficient qualifying; the salesperson reacts indiscriminately to all prospects, failing to sort the good ones down into Above the Funnel. A champagne Funnel is swollen at the top.

Clogged Funnel Problem Sales Funnel that is swollen in the middle, or backed up; the salesperson has moved many objectives into Above the Funnel and In the Funnel but seems unable to move them down into Best Few.

Coach A Buying Influence whose role is to provide you with data that will improve your company's position for a given sales objectives. By definition, the Coach's purpose is to help you make the sale.

Cognition; cognitive thinking First step in rational decision making; cognition involves understanding the situation (*see also* Convergence *and* Divergence).

Commitment Third of three tests (*see also* Discrepancy *and* Ideal Customer profile) for minimizing the number of sales calls while maximizing their effectiveness; the commitment test involves determining a customer's willingness to act and securing some level of solid agreement to take action on each sales call (*see also* Best Action Commitment *and* Minimum Acceptable Action).

Commodity selling Bottom of the Buy-Sell Hierarchy; at this level the customer sees no clear distinction between competing products (*see also* Buy-Sell Hierarchy).

Complex Sale A sale in which more than one person is involved in the buying decision.

Concept; customer's Concept Expectation or expectations on which a decision to buy is based; what customers believe a product or service will do for them. The Concept is inside the customer's head: it is a mental picture of what he or she expects to accomplish.

Convergence; convergent thinking Third step in rational decision making; convergence involves choosing the best alternative (*see also* Cognition *and* Divergence).

Credibility In terms of Coaching (*see* Coach), this has two components: the seller's credibility with the Coach, and the Coach's credibility with the buying organization.

Discrepancy First of three tests for minimizing the number of sales calls while maximizing their effectiveness; the discrepancy test assesses the customer's level of receptivity by checking for the presence of some essential perceived gap between where he or she is and wants to be (*see also* Commitment, Ideal Customer profile, *and* Buyer Response Modes).

Disintegration Separation of sales and management into different spheres.

Divergence; divergent thinking Second step in rational decision making; divergence involves considering alternatives (*see also* Cognition *and* Convergence).

Economic Buyer, Economic Buying Influence For a given sales objective, the person who controls the funding—that is, gives final approval for, or vetoes, the budgetary expense.

Even Keel Mode One of four types of receptivity that Buying Influences can exhibit; a Buyer in Even Keel wants to maintain the status quo and sees no discrepancy or gap between reality and desired results (*see also* Growth, Overconfident, *and* Trouble).

5 percent pattern Typical trend whereby 5 percent of your customers bring in at least 50 percent of your business; 15 or 20 percent of customers account for an additional 25 percent; and a small group beyond that can also bring in potentially significant revenue.

Funnel; Sales Funnel Management tool or metaphor for optimizing selling time by making five tasks more efficient: (1) sorting objectives, (2) resequencing priorities, (3) allocating time, (4) tracking objectives or activities, and (5) forecasting. The Funnel itself consists of four levels. (1) Universe, (2) Above the Funnel, (3) In the Funnel, (4) Best Few (*see also* specific tasks and Funnel stages, and Problem Funnels).

Funnel review Periodic review by the manager of his or her people's individual Sales Funnels, to provide feedback and make revenue forecasting more orderly and predictable.

Golden Silence Technique of pausing for a few seconds at two points in a sales call: after every question you ask a customer (Golden Silence I) and after every response you get (Golden Silence II).

Growth mode One of four types of receptivity that can be exhibited by Buying Influences; a Buyer in Growth wants to do more and better and perceives current reality as less than the result required (*see also* Even Keel, Overconfident, *and* Trouble).

Ideal Customer profile Screening test for prospects and existing customers, consisting of a checklist of characteristics that you and your company have found in the customers you most like doing business with; the Ideal Customer profile is the second of three tests for minimizing the number of sales calls while maximizing their effectiveness (*see also* Discrepancy *and* Commitment).

In the Funnel Third (from the top) level of the Sales Funnel; a potential order moves to this level when you have contacted at least one Buying Influence who is in the Growth mode or the Trouble mode (*see also* Buyer Response Modes *and* Funnel).

Integration; integrated strategy Coordination of sales force and senior management.

Lose Opposite of Win: people Lose when they perceive that their personal self-interest has not been served. A Lose is a situation or outcome in which this has happened (*see also* Win).

Minimum Acceptable Action The least you will settle for as a result of a sales call and still be willing to come back another day; this should be specific, measurable, given a timeline, and realistic.

Overconfident mode One of four types of receptivity that Buying Influences can exhibit; an Overconfident Buyer wants to maintain the status quo and—mistakenly—sees no discrepancy or gap between reality and desired results.

Ping-Pong Funnel Problem Sales Funnel in which the salesperson is jumping from one thing to another without a clear sense of direction or process.

Problem funnels Sales Funnels in which the flow from first contact to order is not being maintained; five problems identified here are: (1) champagne Funnel, (2) clogged Funnel, (3) Ping-Pong Funnel, (4) whistle Funnel, and (5) teardrop Funnel (*see also* Funnel *and specific problem Funnels*).

"Product push" Situation in which salespeople are so mesmerized by their products or services that they fail to understand the customer's need (*see* Concept).

Red Flag Symbol for any area of account strategy or sales call planning where you lack information or are not certain the information you have is accurate; more generally, anything that might threaten your position with a customer.

Resequencing Reordering priorities to avoid a boom-and-bust cycle; this involves beginning with objectives in the Best Few stage of the Sales Funnel and then immediately going to the top of the Funnel to prospect or qualify (*see also* Funnel).

Results; business Results What customers' companies get in a solid sale. Results need to be distinguished from Wins, which individuals get (*see* Win *and* Win-Result).

"Revertia" Tendency for things to revert to old practices if the people in charge don't mandate change.

Sales Funnel *See* Funnel.

Selling As redefined in this book, and as part of managing the sales process: all corporate activities that contribute directly or indirectly to the integrity, growth, and profitability of the company's revenue stream.

Situation Analysis Worksheet technique for understanding your position, developing actions based on your company's strengths, and continually reassessing your sales strategy. It brings together the following: (1) Concept, (2) Buying Influences, (3) Win-Results, (4) Receptivity (Buyer Response Modes), (5) Commitment, and (6) Buy-Sell Hierarchy (*see also specific factors*).

"Slam-dunk selling" Selling that goes against the natural flow of rational decision making by trying to move the customer to a decision before he or she has worked through the earlier parts of the process (*see* Cognition, Convergence, *and* Divergence).

Solution image What your customers see your product or service as achieving for them; the customer's Concept.

Sorting Classifying sales objectives in terms of four phases of the selling process, which correspond to four levels of the Sales Funnel: (1) prospect (Universe level), (2) qualify (Above the Funnel), (3) cover the bases (In the Funnel), (4) close (Best Few), *see also* Funnel.

Team selling Targeting accounts as the responsibility of account teams with members drawn from various departments but having a common focus: an unbroken stream of revenue from customers.

Teardrop Funnel Problem Funnel that is swollen at the Best Few stage: too many objectives are stuck there, and other levels of the Funnel are being neglected.

Technical Buyers; Technical Buying Influences Key people in the customer's buying decision who check and eliminate potential vendors in terms of meeting specifications; people who screen for technicalities.

Three Rs of implementation Three elements involved in putting the sales process into place: reinforcement, review, and reward.

Trouble mode One of four types of receptivity that Buying Influences can exhibit; a Buyer in Trouble wants to improve something that's not working and perceives a gap between current reality and a desired result (*see also* Growth, Even Keel, and Overconfident).

Universe Top of the Sales Funnel, the broadest part; level of the Funnel at which you thin out the field of potential customers (*see* Funnel).

User Buyers; User Buying Influences Performance assessors: key people in the customer's buying decision who evaluate how your product will perform; typically these are the people who will actually be using the product in their work.

Whistle Funnel Problem Sales Funnel that develops when the salesperson is too narrowly focused to work on more than one objective at a time; before turning to another lead, the salesperson seems to want each sale to "whistle" through the Funnel.

Win As this term is defined by Miller Heiman, people Win when they perceive that their personal self-interest has been served; a Win is a situation or outcome in which this has happened. Wins need to be distinguished from Results, or Business Results, which are what companies get (*see* Results).

Win-Result Objective Business Result that brings one or more of your Buying Influences a personal Win (*see* Buying Influence, Result, *and* Win).

Win-Win Mutually beneficial outcome, as contrasted with Win-Lose (you Win, the customer Loses), Lose-Win (customer Wins, you Lose), and Lose-Lose (you both Lose); *see also* Lose.

INDEX

About Miller Heiman Inc.

Miller Heiman Inc., an international sales consulting firm, teaches uniquely effective account development processes – processes that led *Success* magazine to call us "the hottest sales training and consulting group in the country." The Fortune 500 companies and other corporate clients who attend our two-day programmes may choose either our traditional in-house or 'private' sessions or our more recently implemented 'open programmes', held in the UK and across Europe throughout the year. With a growing staff of experienced sales consultants, and a track record of over 150,000 satisfied clients, we currently offer seminars in the following processes: Strategic Selling®, Large Account Management® and Managers Coaching™.

If you'd like to learn more about how these processes can maximise the effectiveness of you and your company's sales and account development efforts, please call or write to us for a further description.

Miller Heiman Inc.
2 Vermont Place
Tongwell
Milton Keynes
MK15 8JA
Tel: 44 (0) 1908 211212

STEPHEN E. HEIMAN has worked in sales and sales development for over thirty years. In the 1970s, as national account salesman for IBM, he increased sales by more than 35 percent and was in the top 5 percent for total sales and percentage quota. He continued his success first at Kepner-Tregoe as Director of Marketing and then at North American Van Lines where, in four years as Executive Vice President, he increased sales and profits by 36 percent. In 1978, he joined Robert B. Miller as coprincipal and partner in the sales development company that became Miller Heiman Inc. Steve retired in 1988 as Miller Heiman's President and CEO; he continues to serve as the company's Chairman of the Board.

DIANE SANCHEZ began her selling career in 1970 as a field sales representative for Savin Business Machines. After three award-winning years, she joined the Scholl Corporation, where, in addition to selling, she developed sales coaching and teaching skills and managed promotional programs in conjunction with the sales force. In 1979, as Vice President of Marketing of the newly formed Miller Heiman, she developed a telemarketing and direct mail system which she implemented both there and, in the 1980s, in her own telemarketing consulting practice. She rejoined Miller Heiman as President and CEO in 1988, when annual company revenues were just over $2 million; in 1997, the ninth year of her presidency, that figure is expected to surpass $20 million.

Steve and Diane recently celebrated their twenty-fifth wedding anniversary. They live in Reno, Nevada, with two spoiled dogs. Their combined family consists of seven grown children and six grandchildren.

TAD TULEJA, Miller Heiman Inc.'s staff writer, has cowritten three previous books based on MHI sales processes: *Strategic Selling, Conceptual Selling,* and *Successful Large Account Management.* Among his nearly thirty other books are a study of business ethics, *Beyond the Bottom Line;* a guide to social rituals, *Curious Customs;* and *The New York Public Library Book of Popular Americana.* From 1987 to 1991 Tad directed the business writing program at the University of Massachusetts. He is completing a Ph.D. in anthropology at the University of Texas at Austin.